Who Speaks for Nature?

STUDIES IN COMPARATIVE ENERGY
AND ENVIRONMENTAL POLITICS

Series editors: Todd A. Eisenstadt, American University,
and Joanna I. Lewis, Georgetown University

A Good Life on a Finite Earth: The Political Economy of Green Growth
Daniel J. Fiorino

*Democracy in the Woods: Environmental Conservation
and Social Justice in India, Tanzania, and Mexico*
Prakash Kashwan

Who Speaks for Nature?

Indigenous Movements, Public Opinion, and the Petro-State in Ecuador

Todd A. Eisenstadt
and
Karleen Jones West

OXFORD
UNIVERSITY PRESS

OXFORD
UNIVERSITY PRESS

Oxford University Press is a department of the University of Oxford. It furthers
the University's objective of excellence in research, scholarship, and education
by publishing worldwide. Oxford is a registered trade mark of Oxford University
Press in the UK and certain other countries.

Published in the United States of America by Oxford University Press
198 Madison Avenue, New York, NY 10016, United States of America.

© Oxford University Press 2019

Library of Congress Cataloging-in-Publication Data
Names: Eisenstadt, Todd A., author. | West, Karleen Jones, author.
Title: Who speaks for nature? : indigenous movements, public opinion, and the
petro-state in Ecuador / Todd A. Eisenstadt and Karleen Jones West.
Description: New York, NY, United States of America : Oxford University
Press, 2019. | Series: Studies in comparative energy and environmental
politics | Includes bibliographical references and index.
Identifiers: LCCN 2018035690 (print) | LCCN 2018051161 (ebook) |
ISBN 9780190908966 (Updf) | ISBN 9780190908973 (Epub) |
ISBN 9780190908959 (hardcover : acid-free paper)
Subjects: LCSH: Environmentalism—Social aspects—Ecuador. | Environmental
protection—Social aspects—Ecuador. | Environmentalism—Ecuador—Public
opinion. | Environmental protection—Ecuador—Public opinion. | Indians of
South America—Ecuador—Attitudes. | Petroleum industry and
trade—Environmental aspects—Ecuador. | Ecuador—Environmental
conditions. | Ecuador—Public opinion.
Classification: LCC GE190.E2 (ebook) | LCC GE190.E2 E55 2019 (print) |
DDC 306.4/509866—dc23
LC record available at https://lccn.loc.gov/2018035690

3 5 7 9 8 6 4 2

Printed by Sheridan Books, Inc., United States of America

CONTENTS

ACKNOWLEDGMENTS

This book represents a new foray for both authors into the study of environmental politics. As democracy became more stable in Latin America, it became apparent that elections would not solve all of the region's challenges to represent marginalized populations. The authors' dissertation-era studies of electoral politics in Mexico (Eisenstadt in the late 1990s) and Ecuador (West in the late 2000s) thus seemed a little less compelling than they had been when democracy was new and held more promise. Meanwhile, the study of environmental impacts of wind farming, dam construction, and oil drilling grew increasingly apparent in Chiapas and Oaxaca, Mexico, where Eisenstadt had undertaken recent fieldwork, and the Amazon region of Ecuador, where West had conducted recent field research. As researchers of development and its frequent inequalities, citizens concerned about inadequacies of international environmental negotiations and national regulations, and parents wanting to advocate for a more just future for our kids and the rest of their generation, we felt we should do something. And as scholars, what we do when we take action is conduct research and write. It may not be the most direct or effective form of mobilization, but it does channel our passion and, if we are lucky, it can help condition and contextualize problems and even propose solutions.

Neither author knew when we met at the Latin American Studies Association Annual Meeting in San Francisco in 2012 that our collaboration would involve drinking the *chicha* in the remote Achuar village of Charapacocha, taking the "toxic tour" of oil spills near Lago Agrio, and summers of travel by canoes, planes, and buses all over Ecuador in 2014 and 2017 with dozens of paper presentations throughout the hemisphere in the intervening years. Completing the book manuscript amid the wide range of personal milestones and transitions faced by both authors was a true challenge, and would not have been possible without the guidance of Mario Melo, distinguished director of the Human Rights Law Clinic of the Catholic University of Ecuador; Nancy Córdova, the vice president of the

Centro de Estudios y Datos (CEDATOS) polling firm; and Mark Thurber, general manager of Walsh Environmental Scientists and Engineers, an environmental consulting firm branch office in Quito. All of them provided extensive
context and contacts and answered our endless questions with patience and
grace. They selflessly shared their knowledge of Ecuadorian politics and made
us feel at home in their fascinating and vibrant country. We cannot thank
them enough. A special thanks also goes to three of Eisenstadt's doctoral
students, all emerging environmental politics experts in their own right.
Daniela Stevens León helped construct tables and bibliographies, assisted
with formatting, and raised good questions, as did Marcela Torres Wong,
whose work on prior consultation in the Andes also opened the authors'
eyes. Ifeoluwa Olawole helped put final touches on the manuscript. Lastly,
Larry Engel accompanied Eisenstadt and West on our summer 2017 research
trip to Ecuador, creating and filming an excellent video with creativity, precision, stamina, and humor. The funds for the video, which is available on
YouTube[1], were generated by an Excellence with Impact Grant from American
University's School of Public Affairs, with thanks to Dean Vicky Wilkins.

Research for this book was funded by National Science Foundation awards
SES-1324158 and SES-1324165. The authors also thank audiences at Amazon
Watch, the American University Government Department Workshop,
the George Washington University Political Science Workshop, the Latin
American Social Sciences Faculty (FLACSO) in Quito, Princeton University,
the University of Stockholm, the State University of New York (SUNY) at
Geneseo, Syracuse University, the United States Agency for International
Development's (USAID) Adaptation Group, The Inter-American Development
Bank, The World Bank, and discussants at presentations at several annual
meetings of the American Political Science Association, the International
Political Science Association, the International Studies Association, the Latin
American Studies Association, and the Midwest Political Science Association.
A preliminary version of chapter 2 appeared as "Environmentalism in a
Climate-Vulnerable State: Rainforests, Oil, and Political Attitudes along
Ecuador's Extractive Frontier," in *Comparative Politics* 49, no. 1 (January
2017): 231–51, and an earlier version of chapter 5 appeared as "Indigenous
Belief Systems, Science, and Resource Extraction: Climate Change Attitudes
in Ecuador and the Global South," in *Global Environmental Politics* 17, no. 1
(February 2017): 40–60.

The authors thank Carla Alberti, Moisés Arce, Santiago Basabe, Carew
Boulding, Ryan Carlin, Matthew Cleary, Ken Conca, Larry Engel, Rafael
Fernández de Castro, Patricia Gualinga, Maria-Therese Gustafsson, Eric

1. Spanish version: https://youtu.be/FIMTsWazqhM; English version: https://youtu.
be/WVFAYHQtYrA

Hershberg, Kathryn Hochstetler, Claudio Holzner, Craig Kauffman, Jie Lu, Tofigh Maboudi, Stephen MacAvoy, Raúl Madrid, Pamela Martin, Carmen Martínez, Shannan Mattiace, Carlos Mazabanda, Mario Melo, Ghazal Nadi, Thea Riofrancos, Barbara dos Santos, Mitchell Seligson, Noah Smith, Daniela Stevens León, Ifeoluwa Olawole, Mark Thurber, Marcela Torres Wong, Guillermo Trejo, Ivette Vallejo, Deborah Yashar, and Elizabeth Zechmeister for invaluable feedback at various stages of the project. The authors take all responsibility for any errors but thank Polibio and Nancy Córdova of the Quito-based Centro de Estudios y Datos (CEDATOS) for executing our survey under challenging conditions. Eisenstadt also thanks Vice Provost for Graduate Studies and Research Jonathan Tubman at American University for a seed grant.

At American University, Eisenstadt thanks department chair Candice Nelson and former department chairs Thomas Merrill and Saul Newman for helping facilitate the work, and Dean Vicky Wilkins for helping the authors get needed time and resources to develop and publicize the research. Meagan Snow, program director for geospatial research support at the American University Library, helped us finalize the maps. Doctoral students Daniela Stevens León and Marcela Torres gave very useful feedback, several classes of graduate students withstood a discussion on the challenges faced in researching this book, and the surprising enthusiasm of a class of undergraduates renewed his energy during the lull toward the end of the project. Eisenstadt also thanks his colleagues in the Faculty Senate leadership—Larry Engel, Andrea Pearson, and Elizabeth Worden— for providing an important professional distraction from analyzing survey results. And Eisenstadt thanks his daughters Natalia and Paola Eisenstadt, for helping him remember why he wants to study issues of long-term impact.

West thanks Kasi Jackson, Melissa Latimer, and the NSF ADVANCE Program at West Virginia University for their support of the project through a Sponsorship Program Grant. At West Virginia University, West thanks the College of Liberal Arts and Sciences for a mini-grant that supported the proposal-writing process for the NSF Award, and department chair Joe Hagan for his support in fostering work-life balance as West pursued her career and managed a growing family. At SUNY Geneseo, West thanks Anne Baldwin in Sponsored Research and Betsy Colón and Traci Phillips at the SUNY Research Foundation for the countless ways that they have helped her manage finances related to the project. West also thanks Jeff Koch, her department chair at Geneseo, for his constant support of her research ambitions, and the Joint Labor-Management Committee of New York State and United University Professionals for the Dr. Nuala

McGann Drescher Leave Award that helped facilitate the completion of this manuscript. During the course of this project, West has watched her son Elliott grow from an infant to a child in elementary school, and has welcomed her daughter Marie Kristine to the world; nothing compares to the sense of accomplishment and pride that her children have brought her. And as they say, it takes a village, and West feels so fortunate to have Kristine and Stephen F. West be a part of hers. Finally, West would like to thank her husband Steve, who always gives her greater perspective, and who not only helped make this project possible, but also made it worth it.

Map 1: Survey Sample by Ecuadorian Province

Map 2: Field Research Sites

CHAPTER 1

⚜

Beyond Multiculturalism

Vulnerability Politics and the Environment in Latin America

In 2008, Ecuador became the first state ever to enshrine rights for nature in its constitution. Nature was accorded inalienable rights in Article 71 and every citizen was granted standing to defend those rights.[1] The problem, of course, is that nature cannot sue those who violate its will, nor even represent what nature's will might be; nor can it defend itself against intrusive incursions, such as by oil and mining companies. This paradox has grown particularly acute in recent years, as a plethora of domestic actors has risen up and claimed to be the legitimate representatives of nature's interests. Indigenous groups in Ecuador's Amazon have joined Andean indigenous peoples in proclaiming themselves the stewards of nature and Ecuador's environment—but they are only one of many actors that claim to speak for nature.

---

1. According the 2009 Constitution (Article 71): "Nature, or *Pacha Mama*, where life is reproduced and occurs, has the right to integral respect for its existence and for the maintenance and regeneration of its life cycles, structure, functions and evolutionary processes. All persons, communities, peoples and nations can call upon public authorities to enforce the rights of nature. To enforce and interpret these rights, the principles set forth in the Constitution shall be observed, as appropriate. The State shall give incentives to natural persons and legal entities and to communities to protect nature and to promote respect for all the elements comprising an ecosystem" (cited from Georgetown University's Political Database of the Americas, http://pdba. georgetown.edu/Constitutions/Ecuador/english08.html).

Oil companies such as Texaco/Chevron have left behind notorious oil spills and caused environmental degradation, but argue that they are the ones who harness Ecuador's resource wealth for the benefit of the people, some of whom still lack basic goods such as access to public health and education. The leftist populist Ecuadorian government of President Rafael Correa (2007–2017), first elected in 2006 with the support of indigenous leaders, initially claimed to seek sustainable development and environmental conservation. Yet over the decade he was in power, Correa largely departed from these positions in practice, instead using "extractive populism" to dramatically improve the provision of public services by allying with the most heinous polluters, Chinese parastatal companies with no transparency and few environmental standards. Correa's successor in 2017, Lenin Moreno, is less oriented toward extractive populism, but his hands are tied by the actions of his predecessor, who sold several years of oil production and mining concessions to Chinese state companies at prices well below those of the market after 2015.

Amid a cacophony of interest group players during Correa's decade of governing, who spoke for nature? This book presents the claims of several interest groups, from the government to indigenous communities to international and domestic oil and mining companies. To do so, in 2014 we designed and implemented perhaps the first nationwide survey in Ecuador focusing on environmental issues, asking Ecuadorian citizens how important the environment is to them. We then complemented our diagnostic survey with scores of interviews from around the country over three years to contextualize the "rights of nature" paradox in Ecuador. We find that rather than assuming the traditional format of environmental conservation versus economic development, the rights of nature take a tripartite framing in Ecuador. The three perspectives represented are: 1) that of vulnerable individuals in peasant, indigenous, and rural communities who seek to live off the land as they always have; 2) the government that, despite strong pro-environment rhetoric, relies on oil revenue to finance public works; and 3) a group of indigenous and other public intellectuals who have argued for the rights of nature as a way of life apart from these other two more conventional positions. This third position, known in the indigenous Kichwa language as *sumak kawsay*, or harmonious living, is drawn from indigenous belief systems and promotes the view that the environment and humanity are inextricably linked. Using both our survey and one-on-one interviews, we illustrate the importance of these three positions to determine who speaks for nature in Ecuador.

Indeed, the question of who speaks for nature is central not only to environmental protection in Ecuador, but also in environmental debates around the world. Governments set the agenda by establishing the legal extent to which the environment will be protected, and thus far, the only other country that has gone so far as to grant nature inalienable rights in the fashion of Ecuador is its ally to the south, Bolivia (Neil 2014). And yet, governments are only one actor among many who claim to defend nature in one form or another. From the Dakota Sioux demonstrating against the construction of an oil pipeline on the Standing Rock Reservation in the United States to the scores of Chinese citizens who have protested against devastating levels of pollution across China (Hoffman and Sullivan 2015), there are countless groups and interests that claim to speak for nature around the world. This book seeks to understand why some groups claim to speak for nature by focusing on how the community-level environmental context—such as the presence of oil and mineral extraction—connects with individual values to result in a variety of dispositions and beliefs regarding environmental protection.

In fact, we find that the subjects of our book, primarily the indigenous communities in the Amazon and their advocates, sometimes do claim to speak for nature —or are attributed this authority by others—and do so to preserve their way of life. Departing from conventional social science arguments that such groups speak for the ethnic groups they represent or for their social groups (peasants, forest-dwellers, etc.), we argue that these groups' positions are shaped by environmental vulnerability, such as whether they can continue to "live off the land" as they have in the past, and whether they live close to oil drilling or mining sites that reduce the economic viability of making a living in other ways. After using analyses of our survey results to demonstrate that vulnerability and extraction matter for environmental attitudes, we then argue that groups might have more success mobilizing on behalf of the environment through geographically based "polycentric rights" rather than through multiculturalism. Multicultural rights are those of indigenous and native groups, such as land and governance autonomy, mostly recognized since the 1990s. "Polycentrism," a term first used in the environmental politics literature by scholars like Ostrom (2010), refers to the process of solving issues via many different fronts. To us, both these terms relate to forms of interest articulation in democratic and semi-authoritarian societies that allow citizens to organize and assemble as interest groups. As we seek to demonstrate, encouraging indigenous groups to organize without the input and participation of non-indigenous fellow-victims of environmental degradation may reduce the effectiveness of interest articulation and, in some cases, divide indigenous groups against each other.

A key contribution of this book is that it offers a methodological bridge for research on environmentalism within the social sciences. One set of past works has considered social movements, and predominantly ethnic social movements, as the primary propagators of environmental change in Latin America (Arce 2014; Brysk 2000; Hochstetler and Keck 2007; Keck and Sikkink 1998; Lucero 2008; Yashar 2005). Another set of past works has emphasized the importance of public opinion in shaping social movements (Boulding 2014; Carlin, Singer, and Zechmeister 2015). This book considers both by conducting an original survey of 1,781 adults in Ecuador in 2014 to learn their positions on a range of environmental issues, and then contextualizing these patterns of information through in-depth interviews with scores of indigenous, environmental, government, academic, and civil society leaders all over Ecuador between 2014 and 2017. We find that some abstract issues—like cosmovision, or indigenous worldviews—affect peoples' attitudes toward the environment, but that concrete experience—such as that of people living in areas where the environment has already been damaged by oil drilling—is a much more important conditioner of attitudes toward the environment. In the process, we help qualify post-materialism, an early theory of environmentalism, which in its original form argued that material well-being made citizens more likely to possess a strong interest in protecting the environment.

The overall objective of this book is to argue that indigenous communities are motivated to protect the environment and defend their own ways of life. While they may have loftier claims than do non-indigenous groups as stewards of the rainforest and protectors of Mother Nature, they are also driven by self-preservation. For many groups, that preservation is found in an environment free from contamination and extractive pollution. In fact, many indigenous individuals—and some groups—support oil drilling and mining projects on their lands, but with environmental safeguards, input into decision-making, and guarantees of benefits for communities. Yet many others do not support oil drilling and mining at all. Our contribution is to demonstrate that these claims are more the result of whether they think extractive projects on their lands will make them better off, rather than the product of innate preferences they have as indigenous people or as peasants.

In the section that follows, we discuss the tenets of post-materialism and their limits in application to Ecuador. We then consider an alternative: vulnerability politics, or that peoples' interest in protecting the environment may instead be conditioned by how directly exposed they are to the fragility of that environment. More broadly, we argue with Lucero (2013) that the advent of multicultural rights for indigenous communities, born of "good intentions" in the 1990s, were more "tokens" that led to "uneven patchwork" recognition (23). Several years ago, Lucero vindicated early national government efforts under Correa (Ecuador) and Morales (Bolivia) to implement real, rather than symbolic, multiculturalism. We claim that, whatever the government's earlier intentions, Ecuador has in fact mostly failed to fortify multiculturalism. National government failures to implement multiculturalism (evidenced in chapters 3 and 6), combined with the failures of indigenous communities themselves to unify in their positions (seen extensively in chapters 3 and 4), open the way for polycentric pluralism as a means that might best represent indigenous and other environmental interests.

The term "polycentrism" arose in the literature on environmental policy and politics (attributed to Ostrom 2010, and others). To Brown and Sovacool (2011, 238), "polycentrism posits that when multiple actors at a variety of scales [from local to global] must compete in overlapping areas, they can often promote innovation as well as cooperation and citizen involvement." To these policy analysts (211, 216), policies need global, central, homogenizing elements, but also local, decentralized, and heterogeneous components. Political scientists might simply view polycentrism as pluralist interest articulation in a porous policy environment, where pluralism, in the Dahl (1961) tradition, is the form of interest articulation where every group is free to state its position and contest policies in the intellectual marketplace. Multiculturalism does grant one group—indigenous citizens with primordial land titles and other historic claims—legal standing at the expense of others. However, we argue that multiculturalism does not always elaborate solutions to intra-group conflict, as evidenced by internal disagreements between the Waorani and Achuar peoples publicly displayed in interviews for this book. In addition, inter-group conflict is also often not diminished when multiculturalism grants indigenous people rights, but without specifying exactly who or how, as evidenced in differences between the Andean and Amazonian indigenous groups (conveyed in chapter 4).

At the broadest level, then, this is a book arguing that multiple groups trying to make their interests known at multiple points in the policymaking process may help conserve the environment better than do indigenous groups who may be granted a monopoly on rights in the form of multiculturalism—particularly when those groups have no specified means of actualizing or implementing these rights. We show, through evidence from our nationwide survey of 1,781 people, that indigenous people may be better advocates for the environment than non-indigenous respondents.

We argue, however, that this is mostly because their day-to-day lives are more vulnerable to environmental shifts and because they have been adversely impacted by oil drilling and mining—not because of their ethnic or linguistic identities. As we explain in chapter 5, where we show that those sympathetic to an indigenous cosmovision are more likely to believe in climate change, indigenous groups are not alone in believing in climate change. Indeed, other "Western" religious groups also hold strong beliefs about climate change, meaning that indigenous peoples are not the only ones who speak for nature. This should come as a relief to the increasing number of environmental activists worldwide who want to incorporate the symbolism and priority indigenous peoples give to environmental issues with the sheer numbers and potential for activism represented by the rest of us.

Contrary to previous perspectives in the literature—which emphasized wealth or essentialized characteristics of indigenous identity as determinants of environmentalism—we frame our argument in terms of vulnerability. That is, we argue that survey respondents' levels of wealth and their ethnic identities do not directly affect their attitudes regarding the environment. Rather, their environmental attitudes are affected by how exposed they feel to environmental changes. This affects the environment-versus-development debate by implying that environmental protection comes first, as people need to feel secure about their livelihoods and lifestyles, and any encroachment on the environment that threatens their livelihoods diminishes their consideration of development as a priority. We consider this tension as we address the question of who speaks for nature. We seek an answer by disaggregating to the level of the individual rather than only studying movements or interest groups in the aggregate, although that is also part of our story. We try to understand the implications for domestic politics in Ecuador as well as elsewhere in Latin America where mineral extraction, and opposition to it, has increased dramatically over the last decade.

More-structural causes—post-material contexts and ascriptive ethnic identities—are less important as causes of the general attitudes highlighted in chapters 2 and 5. These structural factors tend to promote the logic of multicultural group rights expression, which we argue presents a variety of problems for interest articulation surrounding environmental issues. As we demonstrate throughout this book, a position parting from individual interests—such as vulnerability to environmental adversity or oil drilling—is more useful to indigenous communities than one relying on traditional multicultural identities. We argue that indigenous peoples should speak for nature, but as individuals with a cosmovision—or worldview—prioritizing the natural order more than Westerners do, not as primordial groups of people with static views that are frozen in time.

As more countries in Latin America follow Ecuador in pursuing development based on resource extraction, it is crucial to understand the implications these economic models hold for individuals, movements, and the environment. Correa's policy of "extractive populism" depended almost exclusively on funds derived from mineral extraction to literally buy the support of the public through the provision of public works. This variety of "extractive populism" pitted nature directly against the basic needs of humans, and his expectation was that people would always support what most benefits themselves in direct material gains. However, what happens to people who lack basic services, but who also depend upon the environment for survival? What are the ramifications of this model when people realize that the longer-term costs to nature are greater than the shorter-term developmental benefits they may receive? Our project answers these questions, perhaps for the first time. Using both survey data and extensive interviews, we analyze the factors that determine environmentalism in developing countries like Ecuador, where a substantial percentage of the population is both poor and reliant upon nature for survival. We show that the threats to the environment posed by Correa's relentless pursuit of mineral resources far outweighed the promise of development, particularly for those individuals who had already experienced the environmental devastation related to oil drilling and mining. Unlike the expectations of post-materialism and those of traditional ethnic politics arguments, these findings highlight the relevance of a new form of vulnerability—the vulnerability to extraction—that shapes attitudes toward the environment.

REFOCUSING THE DEBATE ON SELF-INTERESTS OF THE DISPOSSESSED AS ENVIRONMENTAL ACTIVISTS

Led by Inglehart (1990, 1995, 1997), many scholars have argued that interest in environmental issues is part of a bundle of post-materialist attitudes held by the left-leaning affluent—individuals whose material needs have been met. Such post-material values celebrated diversity and progressive politics across a range of areas. Inglehart and his colleagues based this theory largely on evidence from Western Europe, where prominent Green Parties emerged beginning in the 1980s. More recently, scholars such as Konisky, Milyo, and Richardson (2008), McCright and Dunlap (2011), and Arbuckle and Konisky (n.d.) have argued that value-related causes, such as ideological and partisan affinities, as well as religious beliefs, influence survey respondents' levels of concern relating to environmental issues like climate change. These studies add further credence to the widely held claim that values shape attitudes on environmental issues.

However, this book updates the post-materialism argument by showing that strong environmental attitudes can occur precisely where Inglehart says they should not, such as in poor rural areas, rather than in affluent urban ones. Understanding environmentalism where non-Western cultural values, individual political struggles, and material vulnerabilities condition attitudes requires considering that concern for the environment may be linked to rational self-interest and political identities, rather than being entirely conditioned by the structural cause of material well-being.

In chapter 2, we analyze data from our nationwide survey in Ecuador and find that respondents do not adapt their concern for the environment in accordance with predictions of post-materialist norms. In fact, this new survey evidence from a developing country indicates that the poor who live off the land—those on the front lines of experiencing environmental degradation as a result of oil and mineral extraction—have even stronger perceptions of the importance of environmental problems. Based on our survey, this book analyzes whether vulnerability theory, as argued by geographers and political ecologists, and political identities may better explain citizen environmental attitudes in the developing world, where affluent citizens are the minority and Green Parties have not taken hold. Our argument is based on the idea that environmental attitudes reflect individuals' self-interest, and specifically, the extent to which environmental degradation affects individual livelihoods or is offset by economic benefits. This chapter offers the core argument from which succeeding chapters part.

We also offer important qualifications to ethnic politics as a significant cause of political behavior. Indigenous belief systems (often referred to as a cosmovision) recognize *pachamama* (Mother Earth) as a living being with which humans have an "indivisible, interdependent, complementary and spiritual relationship" (Conferencia Mundial de los Pueblos sobre el Cambio Climático y los Derechos de la Madre Tierra, CMPCC, 2010, as cited in Shankland and Hansenclever 2011, 81). A primordial or essentialist perspective of indigenous identity thus suggests that indigenous individuals should also value the environment. One possible extrapolation of this view is that, because of their belief systems, indigenous individuals should be more likely to engage in environmental movements compared to non-indigenous individuals facing the same economic and environmental circumstances. While somewhat discredited by scholars who adopt an instrumental view of ethnicity, the essentialist perspective still has adherents among many who study Latin America's multicultural rights movements of the 1990s. The sheer act of "lumping" disparate movements into such an aggregation offers some evidence that this explanation retains important adherents (discussed, for example, in the Burguete, Mattiace, Sorroza Polo, and Danielson chapters of Eisenstadt et al. 2013). We argue that indigenous identity has little to do with environmental mobilization. We follow recent research on identity politics in Latin America, which demonstrates that ethnic identity is less important than other, rational self-interest concerns in determining values related to collective action (see, for example, Arce 2014; Eisenstadt 2006, 2009, 2011; Engle 2010; Trejo 2012).

Multicultural rights tend to be precarious, built, as they are in many locales, upon historical standing. However, primordial land titles and governing structures tend to be very difficult to prove, as communities often do not have colonial-era land titles or *de jure* proof that they were the original inhabitants. In much of Latin America, a move toward titling, surveying, and registering has made gains since the 1990s, although overlapping land claims are still common, and recognition has not been accompanied in most cases by public resources enabling indigenous landowners to fully utilize their holdings, neither for economic production nor for environmental conservation. Perhaps the most notorious *de facto* recognition of the poor state of legal claims and titling is the former Oaxaca, Mexico, law regarding customary in elections. The law said that to merit customary law consideration of elections (rather than the "counted ballots" system in other parts of the country), local citizens had to have exercised customary law traditions "since time immemorial, or at least since three years ago" (Eisenstadt and Ríos 2014, 74). We argue that as a counter to pure multiculturalism, polycentric pluralism may help more activists make more environmental claims across a wider range of policies. The argument starts by seeking with our survey to debunk the premise that there is an innate logic to ethnic and class forms of organization. While that may be true in some issue areas, we show in the pages ahead that in the environmental space, vulnerability is a more important determinant of environmental attitudes than is ethnic identity.

Class-based post-materialism and ethnic politics arguments—both more-structural explanations than the interest-based arguments we will present—have predominated within political science. This means that environmentalism among the poor, and in developing countries such as Ecuador, has been under-theorized. However, the interdisciplinary field of political ecology has begun to formulate potential explanations for environmental concern among impoverished communities. Formerly the purview only of human and political ecologists, vulnerability theory seems ripe for consideration by political scientists as a source of political attitudes. As the inter-relatedness of environmental policy impacts grows and it becomes impossible to separate out precise responsibility for the extinction of river otters from particular domains or the precise origin of harmful chemicals in the water table, people's interests seem increasingly to be driven more by how vulnerable they feel to these environmental trends, than by their ethnic group or class.

Vulnerability, or "the susceptibility to be harmed" (Adger 2006, 268), is particularly relevant to the study of environmentalism in developing areas because for many poor populations, access to clean water, biodiverse forests, and uncontaminated land are not merely issues related to their quality of life. Instead, communities of indigenous or rural agricultural workers rely upon subsistence farming or hunting and gathering, so natural resources form the cornerstone of their livelihoods. Thus, we argue that motivation for environmentalism among the poor stems not from post-materialist concerns for the "rights of other species" or moral concerns for future generations of humans, but rather from "a material interest in the environment as a source and a requirement for livelihood" (Martínez-Alier 2002, 11). More specifically, individuals may be objectively vulnerable to environmental damage because they depend upon the environment for their livelihood, or because they lack basic resources such as water and energy that are particularly threatened by environmental change. Individuals may also perceive vulnerability to such change given the extent to which they depend upon natural resources for their livelihood, or the extent to which they believe themselves and their families to be affected by environmental changes.

What is it about vulnerability that affects peoples' environmental attitudes? We believe that how weak they feel vis-à-vis the whims of nature is what matters most. The oil drilling in Ecuador in the 1970s through the 1990s, which left behind extensive pools of waste and contaminated water throughout Ecuador's northern Amazon region, had the effect of increasing their sense of vulnerability. While international oil drilling standards have improved markedly, the pollution from mining varies greatly depending on the form the mining takes and the mineral extracted. Around the world, mining has generated an increasing number of conflicts, while those from oil drilling have mostly diminished, except in places like Ecuador, where oil spills and poor cleanup in the past have caused great concern. The Environmental Justice Atlas (EJOLT) has documented some 535 mining-related conflicts worldwide between 1937 and 2016, and only 288 oil-related conflicts. However, in Ecuador, oil conflicts have been worse over time. There were 288 oil conflicts documented in the years 1937 to 2016, with 61 in Nigeria, 45 in Colombia, 21 in Peru, and 20 in Ecuador (compared to 16 mining conflicts in Ecuador during that time). Latin American incidents constituted some 53 percent of these natural resource conflicts, but of the Latin American total of 449, 314 were mineral-related and 135 were oil-related (author coding).[2] As with vulnerability, extractivism in developing areas—whether relating to oil drilling or mining—often taps into individuals' self-interest when it comes to environmental concern.

Extractivist efforts can harm the land and water upon which poor, rural, and indigenous communities depend for their livelihoods, but extractivism is also promoted by developing-area governments as a means of economic advancement. Mining and oil contracts often stipulate that a percentage of royalties be redistributed back to local communities in the form of development projects (see Becker 2013b for a discussion of this phenomenon in Ecuador), although this discretionary approach to assigning government funds is not considered transparent or democratic (Mahdavi 2017). Indeed, the increasingly state-dominated extractivist efforts across the Andean region promise to redesign the economic model of these countries, reduce dependency on developed nations for assistance (albeit increasing dependence on purchasers of extractive goods), and create an unprecedented level of development. Not only are extractivist debates divisive, they are also crucial for motivating concern over the environment—or lack thereof. Chapter 2 directly tests post-materialism against vulnerability and resource extraction. In the "Outline of the Book and Our Argument" section, we elaborate the means used in that chapter and throughout the book to test peoples' attitudes toward the environment. But first we elaborate further on how we compiled the survey data forming the basis of many of our claims, and then we discuss conditions in Ecuador and how that country offers excellent opportunities to study the tension between multiculturalism and polycentric pluralism in addressing environmental issues.

SURVEY RESULTS AND THE DEBATE BETWEEN ENVIRONMENTALISM AND DEVELOPMENT

Building on contributions from the social movements literature (for example, Tarrow 1998; Tilly and Tarrow 2006), scholars studying anti-extractivist movements have emphasized grievances that embolden social

---

2. Coded using EJOLT data directly from the website (https://ejatlas.org/).

actors to mobilize collectively (Spronk and Webber 2007; Arellano Yanguas 2010), coalitions that groups forge to oppose extraction (Torres 2016), and the political pre-conditions that groups experience for the emergence of protests (Arce 2014). These studies have often focused on specific cases of anti-extractive resistance and underscored the centrality of coalition-building among diverse sets of actors to the construction of effective anti-extractive movements (De Echave et al. 2009; Latorre et al. 2015). Literature on individual attitudes and motivations, based on survey research, mostly fails to study the aggregation of these attitudes into movements and what they can achieve together as well as apart. The experimental turn in political science seems to be exacerbating this tendency (see, for example, Lagan Teele 2014) as scholars tend to study the views of individuals and how these change with experimental treatments. However, this extreme focus on the role of individuals seems to de-emphasize the gap between the achievements and limitations of actual movements on the ground. The gap is widening between the methodological individualism reflected in the behavioralist literature and the aggregated state-society relations assessed in traditional social movements studies.

True to this broader pattern, most recent work on social movements in Latin America (Arce 2014; Boulding 2014; Inclán 2009; Latorre et al. 2015; Trejo 2012, for example) has focused on coding social movements to understand them. The unit of analysis has, understandably, been the movement itself, as classic social movement theories—political opportunities structures, resource mobilization, and framing—all tell us it should be. However, such studies do not allow us to understand the individual incentives of leaders and followers as much as we would like. Exceptions include Inclán's (2009) and Trejo's (2012) studies of the Zapatista rebellion in Chiapas, Mexico. These scholars have, through analytic narratives and process tracing, followed up on coding of protests to understand and ascribe incentives to individual actors based on important theoretical insights from choice-theoretic perspectives pioneered by Olson (1965) and Hardin (1971). However, they have not systematically looked at individual-level attitudes relating to these movements and participation in them.

Recent work by Boulding (2014) and Madrid (2012) assess the choices made by individual voters considering motivations such as ethnic identities, perceived power of their movements or parties, and resources at their disposal such as knowledge networks. Additionally, a new literature is emerging that assesses individuals' vulnerability to natural disasters (Carlin, Love, and Zechmeister 2014) and crime and political instability (Trejo and Ley 2018) using survey data and electoral results. But those works do not fully develop theories to integrate the individual and group levels of analysis. This book strives to achieve some of that integration, parting from the level of the individual, but also considering group variables of identity, knowledge, and power in the analysis, and using the issue area of the environment. Attitudes toward the environment are crucial to understand from this perspective because while not everyone has views about the big ideas motivating social movements, everyone does have views about conditions where they live.

How can we identify the factors that lead individuals, particularly indigenous individuals, to join together collectively to protect a public good, such as the environment, when all face temptations to free-ride, shirk, or otherwise act opportunistically? Because many indigenous groups whose livelihoods depend on natural resource subsistence do not become activists in the face of environmental threats alone, we argue that the community-level context in which environmental degradation occurs plays a crucial role in activating indigenous environmentalism. In this regard, ecological studies have demonstrated that environmental preservation is fundamental to the livelihoods of indigenous citizens. And studies on the effects of natural disasters on relations between otherwise antagonistic groups, who gain a reprieve from conflict by the prospect of facing a "common enemy," offer insights we can use. Broadly speaking, we seek to show that with regard to attitudes toward environmental protection, self-interest can in fact be normatively good. Individuals who feel particularly vulnerable to environmental degradation—where lands are still free from such pollution—tend to feel more strongly about protecting the environment.

Using survey data, we elaborate our claim that conserving the environment via multicultural rights, largely exercised by indigenous communities, may be less effective—given that most people in extraction-impacted areas have strong environmental attitudes—than a broader and multifaceted "polycentric pluralism" approach. We first make this argument using survey data in combination with ethnographic case studies.

Our nationwide survey was conducted in Ecuador between March and June 2014 after several focus groups and trial questionnaires were administered throughout different parts of the country in January 2014. The survey yielded 1,781 respondents based on some 2,550 solicitations of responses administered in three separate strata: about 1,200 to the urban Ecuador population usually polled (some 300 each in Quito, Guayaquil, Cuenca, and Manta/Portoviejo); some 600 to rural dwellers in rural areas of the nation's central Andean indigenous region provinces (some 150 each in Azuay, Pichincha, Imbabura, and Tunguragua); and some 750 in provinces located in the Amazon region (approximately 150 each in Napo, Sucumbios, Orellana, Zamora Chinchipe, and Pastaza). While not all of these surveys were executed and of those executed, there was a non-response rate of about 26 percent, this sample still assured us of coverage of most of the nation's poor, rural, and indigenous communities and, among each of the three samples, ensured a 2.33 percent margin of error at a 95 percent confidence interval. (See appendix B for a more thorough description of our sampling technique.)

The national probability sample design was of voting-age population (over sixteen years old), with a total size (n) of 1,781 persons. Data were collected via face-to-face interviews conducted in Spanish as well as in other languages, as the final dataset included a booster sample of 640 indigenous people, representing the following groups: Kichwa (Sierra), Shuar, Achuar, Andoa, Chibuleos, Salasacas, Cachas/Coltas, and Otavalos. The survey was implemented by the Ecuadorian company CEDATOS, which included on its interviewer team monolingual as well as bilingual and trilingual speakers (Spanish and other indigenous languages). The confidence level expected for the entire national sample is 95 percent (Z .95 = 1.965) with a margin of error of +/- 2.33 percent, assuming a 50/50 ratio (P = 0.50, Q = 1-P) for the dichotomous variables, in the worst of cases. While we use the data to construct individual-based arguments, we also consider the role of individuals in constructing movements. We outline the argument in the next section.

OUTLINE OF THE BOOK AND OUR ARGUMENT

The use of this nationally representative survey, with an oversample of indigenous communities both in the Andean and Amazon regions of Ecuador, helps us attain findings not available through more traditional social movement studies. While most social movements, and especially ethnic social movements, understandably frame environmental issues in black and white, we discern nuances. In chapter 2, we show that the environment-development dichotomy in Ecuador is more of a trichotomy (with *sumak kawsay* occupying an important role in many peoples' environmental positions), and we show through empirical experience that vulnerability (measured as whether they live with environmental fragility, and also as how close they live to sites of resource extraction) may contribute more to the enthusiasm of respondents in supporting the environment than abstract issues like indigeneity or post-materialism. In other words, beyond the parameters of what coding social movements or interviewing leaders would tell us, we find that people who live in areas on Ecuador's extractive frontiers already drilled for oil are much less likely to prioritize the environment over development, whereas those in areas where oil is debated and who expect extraction to provide them with benefits are more likely to prioritize the environment over development. This finding has implications for environmentalism and also defines how polycentric pluralism is relevant for determining interest expression when it comes to the environment. Extending this argument that individual political interests overrule structural identities based on ethnicities or social values, we argue in chapter 3 that mobilization against extraction has emerged because Ecuador's government exploits institutional mechanisms meant to protect the environment to pursue extractive populism and maintain power. Populism, modeled after personalistic leaders like Juan Domingo Perón of Argentina, is generally taken by Ascher (1984) and others to mean putting short-term interests (such as re-election and the provision of patronage and other goods) ahead of long-term interests (like balancing budgets and cleaning the environment after extractive projects generate revenue).

A tension that pervaded the Correa administration and that of other populist leaders like Morales is that they sought both to "speak for nature" as leftist and pro-indigenous leaders, but while needing to finance social programs through extractive royalties. Hence, these leaders would rhetorically and symbolically support environmental causes (such as through Correa's pledge, later abandoned, to stop drilling for oil on the biodiverse Yasuní National Park), but while consistently approving and facilitating extractive projects. In chapter 3, we show that the mechanism of free, prior, and informed consent (FPIC, also referred to as *consulta previa*, prior consultation, CP), which was designed to protect indigenous communities from unwanted extraction by requiring their explicit permission for extractive activities, has become a political tool of the Ecuadorian government. As such, the factors that influence public support for prior consultation are largely political, and individuals who hope to protect the environment are less supportive of the process. Prior consultation is neither explicitly individual nor explicitly collective, and thus we consider it both as an individual practice and analyze survey findings, as well as an interest group process, for which we evaluate group decisions relating to prior consultation (and the absence of such consultation).

In chapter 4, we similarly situate into collective contexts individual-level preferences relating to peoples' willingness to mobilize in opposition to extraction. We first assess individual survey responses regarding practical determinations—like level of extraction in a given area and citizens' perceived vulnerability to environmental degradation and change. Then we evaluate political activity by mobilized groups, particularly indigenous groups, addressing their internal divisions and efforts by the state to weaken opposition and win extraction.

After chapters 2 through 4 on the internal dynamics of indigenous movements and the environment, we seek in chapter 5 to compare indigenous attitudes to those of other groups, and in chapter 6 to look comparatively at how indigenous and non-indigenous groups view relations with the "outside world" (here the international community). We find in chapter 5 that adherence to indigenous cosmovisions—as opposed to other more conventional Western Christian belief systems—and experience with extraction are the most powerful predictors of belief in climate change, while post-materialist values and ascriptive ethnic identities have no impact. Chapter 6 further illustrates the strategies used by Correa to foster extractive populism, focusing this time on his domestic and international policies toward environmental protection and climate change and finding that in this case, while post-materialism continues to be irrelevant, factors that are important include the respondents' physical location on the extractive frontier and political variables, like party affiliation.

The conclusion, chapter 7, broadens out the discussion, striving to reconcile environmentalism as studied via survey responses with environmentalism as studied via social movements. We conclude that these two approaches may seem to yield different results to the question of who speaks for nature. However, we argue, subject to further research, that movement leaders' abstract and symbolic appeals may help improve bargaining positions to attain the concrete objectives that individuals actually care about most. More broadly, we conclude with a summation of extensive evidence presented, that indigenous communities and other victims of some of extractivism's excesses are best served by polycentric pluralist interest articulation, where individual interests can aggregate into a range of articulations, rather than multiculturalism, where the interests represented are primordial, predictable, and static.

Another main finding of this book, simply stated, is that abstract post-materialist concerns about the environment are not the most salient for most citizens. We show in chapter 2 that concern for the environment is driven by peoples' sense of vulnerability, and further demonstrate in successive chapters that such concrete manifestations of self-interest predominate when addressing concrete issues like whether prior consultations on extractivism should be required (chapter 3) or whether drilling will take place on indigenous lands (chapter 4). However, in chapter 5 we explore causes of beliefs in climate change, and do find, contrary to earlier chapters, that while economic post-materialism is not relevant, whether respondents possess an indigenous cosmovision does positively affect whether they believe in climate change. In chapter 6 we revert back from abstract to more-concrete questions, but with an international dimension, to demonstrate that in this sphere too, concrete expressions of self-interest, such as vulnerability, trump more abstract values. Our conclusion in chapter 7 suggests policy implications from this finding, arguing that multicultural rights should be expressed by sector rather than by ascriptive identity. If vulnerable rural dwellers all have a place to express their views, such views might be taken more seriously than if only indigenous people get rights to negotiate extractivist entry to their lands, based on their ancestral land claims. While multicultural rights helped historically disenfranchised indigenous peoples weather the shrinkage of state services and defense of rights during the neo-liberal 1990s, these rights may not have served them as well as polycentric pluralism could serve them during the twenty-first century.

In the section that follows we consider the rise of social movements in Ecuador, in the context of multicultural rights, and how these rights have not been respected in practical terms. While economic and structural arguments—including the more primordial arguments on ethnicity—have perhaps explained pro-environment attitudes in affluent, developed countries, these arguments are less adequate in poorer developing nations like Ecuador, especially those where many citizens' attitudes are shaped more by feeling vulnerable to ecosystem change. We also test ethnic identity as a cause of environmental attitudes and do find, as discussed in chapter 5, that while ascriptive identity is not important, an indigenous cosmovision (defined as a Kichwa view of the fluidity of relations between humans and nature) does make respondents much more likely to believe strongly in climate change. This book parts from the premise that acceptance of this cosmovision perspective by the Ecuadorian state—at least in rhetorical terms—as expressed in the granting of rights to nature in 2008 was a landmark moment for environmental protection, despite its failure to fully implement these provisions. We elaborate on this effort by the government of Ecuador to improve its reputation in chapter 6.

Of course, we cannot literally discern who gets to speak for nature, but we do inventory the groups making this claim. We find that, rather than the usual dichotomy between environmentalism and economic development, so prevalent in much of the literature, Ecuadorians have sought also to develop a "third way" known as *sumak kawsay*. This is economic development on a smaller scale, directed by indigenous cosmovisions or indigenous worldviews shaped by their culture and history that are more sensitive to the relationship between humans and nature. However, as oil prices dropped, social spending has diminished, and the governing regime has found its credibility increasingly challenged.[3] During Correa's administration, the central government responded to mounting public pressures by resorting increasingly to authoritarianism, a diminishing of societal access to plural views, and a reduction of the role of rights of nature to a mere political ploy. The remainder of this introductory chapter situates this debate in Ecuador and then outlines how the succeeding chapters add nuance to elements of it.

SOCIAL MOVEMENTS AND THE PETRO-STATE
IN ECUADOR DURING THE LATE TWENTIETH CENTURY

The debate over multicultural versus pluralist rights in Ecuador's environmental movement is complex. In this section (and in more depth in the following chapter) we consider the neo-liberal approach to environmentalism and development in the 1990s. We then consider the era of indigenous rights dominance, from 1999 until about 2006, when the powerful Confederation of Indigenous Nationalities of Ecuador (Confederación de las Nacionalidades Indígenas de Ecuador, CONAIE), the indigenous social movement, and its political party, Pachakutik, dominated Ecuador's political landscape, articulating their view of this third way of harmonious living (*sumak kawsay* in Kichwa and *buen vivir* in Spanish). Upon discussing the contours of this debate and how they have evolved over the last twenty-five years, we then discuss the contribution of this book, which is to disaggregate the usual interest group analysis down to the level of individuals to understand the views of ordinary citizens on these issues at a moment in time, in 2014—the high point of the influence of Correa's "extractive populism." We relate the methodological strengths of our approach, which combines survey analysis with extensive interviews, and then outline our argument and presentation of findings in the rest of the book.

　　Any story of environmental rights in Ecuador, and particularly in the Amazon, must start with the leftist-statism of José María Velasco Ibarra in the 1970s and his efforts to colonize the Amazon and increase oil production as a means of financing social reforms. The country's Trans-Ecuadorian pipeline was completed in 1972, when Gulf Oil began pumping oil from the Amazon to the Pacific and then shipping it out. Velasco Ibarra took

3. The increase in prices in 2017 changed this trend somewhat under Moreno's administration, although Ecuador had contracted most of its medium-term future oil revenues to China at lower prices under Correa.

unpopular economic measures at a moment of worldwide economic volatility and was overthrown by a military junta, which ruled from 1972 to 1979 before transitioning back to an elected government. The oil embargo of 1973 caused oil price spikes, as inflation caused prices of most goods to soar, even as Ecuador joined the Organization of Petroleum Exporting States (OPEC) in 1973.

New social movements began to emerge in Latin America in the 1990s, including those that mobilized indigenous rights issues and mineral extraction. The diminishment of the size of the state in Latin America in the 1980s has been widely documented (see, for example, Margheritis and Pereira 2007; Molyneux 2008; Weyland 1998). As nations opened up politically and economically, the old corporatist ties, under which groups that supported authoritarian governments got rewards (O'Donnell 1973; Eisenstadt 2004), gave way to a new system under which interest groups competed for government and civil society support. Simultaneously, the fall worldwide of the commodities prices that drove Latin American economies in the early 1980s and already overleveraged borrowing by Latin American leaders under lax terms set by enthusiastic international lenders led to a fiscal retreat by fragile new democratic governments.

In the late 1980s and early 1990s, newly empowered citizens took to the streets to proclaim their new rights of assembly and participation and to contest massive public sector job layoffs around the region, the diminishment of government benefits, and regional governments' failures to regulate the economy to reduce income inequality. A new cohort of extremely wealthy business leaders emerged, profiting from privatizations by which former public institutions, like telecommunications providers, airlines, and railways, were sold at heavily discounted rates to the rich and influential and inequality skyrocketed. Urban and rural workers, whose unions had previously been used to receive modest social benefits from the state, found that labor unions no longer really mattered, and the state had few benefits left to distribute. Among the poor, most did not find new means of successfully asserting their agency to receive attention and services from weakened and reorganized states. However, indigenous communities were an exception.

Ecuador increased its reliance on oil for export revenue, which soon surpassed revenue from traditional exports like bananas. In 1989, Ecuador's para-statal oil company was renamed Petroecuador. Controversy ensued, as in 1993 a coalition of indigenous people and *campesinos* from the northern Amazon region (near the oil city then called Lago Agrio) filed the largest oil damage lawsuit ever (to that date), a $1.5 billion lawsuit against Texaco, arguing that that company's cleanup after the termination of its

1976-negotiated contract had destroyed the environment and created a massive public health threat.

Texaco officially left Ecuador in 1992, and the government absolved it of any further responsibility. Although criticized for leaving the cleanup unfinished, Texaco officials maintained that fault rested with the Ecuadorian government because it lacked a comprehensive set of environmental laws while the company operated. However, the government's deal did not include third-party claims, meaning the people of the land still had their legal right to sue. The quincentenary anniversary that year of Columbus's first voyage to the New World also witnessed the emergence of indigenous rights movements around the Americas, with Ecuador's perhaps the strongest to emerge in the late 1990s. Multicultural rights were increasingly observed in Ecuador and around Latin America, meaning that indigenous citizens regained titles to lands they had lost over the centuries and claimed autonomy in how they governed their own communities. As discussed more extensively later in this book, the Kichwa people of the Andes' central corridors, who were populous, centrally located, and politically connected, were able to gain these rights, while the Amazonian people, who were few, isolated, and in sparsely populated areas, were—with the exception of the Sarayaku people—unable to claim their multicultural rights, which were first mentioned in Ecuador's 1997 Constitution, but given great authority in 2008.

While the Texaco/Chevron case might have acquired added multicultural rights pressures had the Waorani and other Northern Amazon groups mobilized rather than dispersing and migrating, a *campesino* group did organize seeking indemnities. In 2011 an Ecuadorian court found Chevron—which had merged with Texaco in 20000—guilty, issuing an $8 billion fine (the largest ever). But Chevron, which had ceased operations in Ecuador, promptly filed an appeal.

The pre-1990s environmental movement was mostly one of Andean Kichwa peoples, joined forcefully by Amazonian peoples, as they marched in opposition to the oil damages. The Kichwa people of the Andean Corridor had provided the demographic basis of the indigenous political party Pachakutik that had played an important role in felling two presidents in the late 1990s (discussed further in chapter 2). By the first decade of the twenty-first century, Andean and Amazonian leaders came to rely on Pachakutik and the CONAIE to mobilize supporters for environmental causes, which came to include anti-mining and anti-oil protests, conflicts over water distribution, and a range of other concerns. President Correa was elected in 2006 in a politically important alliance with Pachakutik, which had, just years earlier, controlled around 20 percent of nation's votes in an alliance with the Partido Sociedad Patriótica (PSP). While the Chevron case lingered, Correa accepted a controversial 2012 Interamerican Human Rights Court ruling against the Ecuadorian government for its failure to conduct a prior consultation in Sarayaku before allowing an international oil company to initiate exploratory drilling in the 1990s.

In 2008, the president accepted the Constituent Assembly's proposal to make Ecuador the first nation in the world to grant explicit rights to nature. The 2008 Constitution launched a great debate over whether and how to implement *sumak kawsay*. On the one hand, the progressive pro-multiculturalist Correa integrated indigenous rights, such as of land titling and prior consultation, into his early political agenda. On the other hand, as Correa's ambitious social programs increasingly demanded revenue, the "extractive populist" president increasingly turned to oil (and mineral) royalties, which were politically much more popular than raising taxes. As Correa expelled foreign-capital providers like the World Bank and bilateral assistance donors starting in 2008 and 2009, oil royalties became Ecuador's best form of liquidity, and by 2014 and 2015, Correa was also selling Chinese para-statals "guaranteed" contracts of oil exports well into the future, albeit at prices that were often lower than those of the free market. A true populist, Correa was mortgaging Ecuador's future oil proceeds in order to maximize funds available for short-term social programs that would guarantee his legacy.

"WHO SHOULD SPEAK FOR NATURE?" TOWARDS MORE EFFECTIVE FORMS OF INTEREST ARTICULATION

While 80.2 percent of our national Ecuadorian survey sample believes that Mother Nature has rights, that percentage climbs to 85.7 percent for those who self-identify as indigenous, consistent with existing theories about how indigenous identity relates to environmentalism. However, belief in the rights of Mother Nature increases to 85.9 percent for those without plumbing, 94.1 percent for those in areas where there are active mines, and 95.5 percent for those who live in areas with a history of oil extraction (see appendix A, Table A.1). In other words, vulnerability matters more than ethnic identity in the formation of interest groups to address environmental issues. We show this statistically in the next several chapters and take stock of the implications. Then, in the conclusion of this book, we use the implications of these findings to propose that in Ecuador's political setting of extractive populism, "polycentric" pluralism may be a more successful means of aggregating environmental interests—even for indigenous communities—than the traditional format taken of multicultural rights.

Along these lines, in their pathbreaking new research, Kauffman and Martin (2017) show that while societal groups, government agencies and officials, and courts and legal advocates have all formally presented cases to the Ecuadorian courts representing the rights of nature, the judicial route—especially when not highly politicized—has had the greatest ability to protect the rights of nature, via pro-nature court rulings. While it may be that political rulings are less prominent and far-reaching (and thus judges are able to reach controversial rulings "under the radar"), it appears that multicultural rights advocacy has reached its limits. We argue that it is time for broader advocacy across groups, and we propose that we should place the concept of "polycentrism," coined by scholars of environmental interests, into a pluralist interest group framework.

As will be more evident in the chapters ahead, environmentalists, Amazonians, Andeans, indigenous and non-indigenous parties and movements, oil companies, miners, and the Ecuadorian government all claim to speak for nature. The problem is that no one has spoken effectively enough to spare some of nature's most sacred domains from some of the more avaricious aspects of development. As elaborated more in this book's conclusion, chapter 7, the proper question may not be 'Who speaks for nature?' but 'Who should speak for nature, and how?' Indigenous communities have, through their strong—and largely legitimate—claims of being more engaged stewards of nature, managed to attain multicultural rights where other groups have achieved only individual rights. And in the neoliberal era, which struck particularly hard in Latin America, service provision diminished in nations where natural resource extraction could not save national coffers. While Ecuador suffered a neoliberal turn in the 1990s, the country's increasingly potent indigenous rights movements managed to secure an important domain of political action through the implementation of multiculturalism, from the international level on down.

We address this question in part by broadening a debate about the possible form that multicultural rights versus polycentric pluralism should take in Ecuador, but also beyond. Indeed, "many multiculturalisms" exist, according to Lucero (2013), who argues that such movements have in some cases empowered indigenous movements much more than in others, depending on the democratic legitimacy, elite strategic calculations, and international development agency policies from above, and social movement pressures and transnational activist networks from below (Lucero 2013, 20–22). However, despite the apparent variation in forms taken by multicultural arrangements in Latin America, Lucero acknowledges that these forms of recognition have often represented "tokens to indigenous people rather than substantive changes to the political and economic structures of Latin American societies" (Lucero 2013, 23).

To wit, Mexico's multicultural rights movements do not seem to have improved services or people's standards of living, at least not relative to other groups. In Oaxaca, where multicultural customary law was legalized in the early 1990s, women, religious minorities, and citizens from out-lying hamlets rather than the main municipal population centers have been summarily disenfranchised from participation (Eisenstadt 2011). Furthermore, research shows that multicultural rights recognition there actually increased conflicts after elections related to representation and also to the preferential distribution of federal resources to more-affluent municipal population centers at the expense of more marginalized outlying hamlets (Eisenstadt and Ríos 2014).

We regard the Mexican case as a cautionary tale, as Oaxaca has been ex-tensively studied, making the shortcomings of multiculturalism quite evi-dent, especially as customary law elections are legal in Oaxaca but mostly illegal elsewhere in Mexico. While most of this book is about Ecuador, we want to briefly convey the comparability of findings across nations with a brief discussion here of the shortfalls of multiculturalism in Oaxaca, followed by a presentation of some of the successes of polycentric plu-ralist forms of interest articulation in rural Bolivia. This will lead us back to Ecuador, in chapter 2, where multiculturalism in the environmental issue area has failed to get indigenous communities (or others) a substan-tial role in determining whether oil and minerals should be extracted from their lands and how dividends from such extraction should be divided. Specifically, we demonstrate in chapter 2 that in the formation of abstract attitudes about the importance of the environment, variables indicating rational self-interest, ecological vulnerability, and exposure to oil drilling are very important. However, variables manifesting more-structural conditions like ethnic identity and post-material values—the variables tra-ditionally used to explain environmental attitudes and movements—have no significant impact on Ecuadorians' opinions. Upon demonstrating this statistical relationship, we interpret it using interviews in Ecuador. But first, we consider the cautionary tale offered by the Mexican case.

THE PARADOX OF MULTICULTURALISM IN OAXACA, MEXICO: CUSTOMARY LAW, CORPORATISM, AND CONFLICT

Formed precisely to diminish tensions surrounding elections, Oaxaca's unicameral state legislature (in partnership with the governor) has

instead manipulated customary law election outcomes (henceforth referred to as UC, their Spanish abbreviation referring to *usos y costumbres*).
In fact, the state legislature dissolved hundreds of Oaxaca's 570 municipal governments and named interim mayors over the last two decades on
grounds that the irregular conduct of customary law elections had rendered
them politically divided to the point of being "ungovernable." The centrist
ruling Party of the Institutional Revolution (PRI), which narrowly defeated
a left-right coalition in the 2004 gubernatorial race and lost the governor-
ship to a left-right alliance in 2010, used the state legislature before 2010
to dissolve local governments and substitute non-elected administrators
named by the governor (Eisenstadt 2011; Eisenstadt and Ríos 2014).
Although multicultural rights recognition allowed communities to do as
they wished locally while receiving little or no national attention, the rules
also created discretion that governors could exploit by pressuring local political operatives. Goodman and Hiskey (2008) reported that UC community turnout in national elections actually dropped, meaning that national
and statewide politicians had fewer incentives to consider indigenous community concerns. Federal and state electoral authorities were slow to cor-
rect the abuses in Oaxaca's local elections, which, at least prior to 2010,
helped garner the state's reputation as a premier hemispheric bastion of
subnational authoritarianism, or local governance that was not democratic
(Giraudy 2015; Gibson 2005).

The justification that customary law diminished post-electoral social
conflicts was also not borne out by empirical evidence. The number of
post-electoral conflicts (where electoral losers contested results through
protests and mobilizations and via legal appeals) in Oaxaca's UC elections
actually doubled between 1995 and 2004, before trailing off subsequently
(Eisenstadt 2004; Eisenstadt and Ríos 2014). While the conflicts have diminished greatly over the last decade, such conflicts still occur in every
three-year electoral cycle, with more than four hundred deaths resulting
from these conflicts over the last thirty-five years. Part of the problem, not
present in the Andean cases, is that post-electoral conflicts catalyzed more
deep-seated land tenure conflicts (Eisenstadt 2009).

A perspective emphasizing "polycentric pluralism" might indicate that
the Mexican focus on UC to achieve short-term indigenous autonomy may
have also been a distraction from the broader issue of rural sustainable development, as autonomy does nothing to develop interest group voices to
lobby for change and resources. Efforts to survey and title all lands during
the presidential administrations of Vicente Fox (2000–2006) and Felipe
Calderón (2006–2012) did not succeed in rural southern Mexico as in the
more private sector–oriented North. Most presume that Mexico's interest

in using land reform as a redistributive mechanism has ended. This has meant that rural dwellers, without state supports for agriculture, increasingly sold their parcels and migrated within Mexico or to the United States. Additionally, Oaxaca's agricultural lands were not of good quality, meaning that government officials did not bother hurling the "dog in a manger" epithet against them as they did in the Andes, where former Peruvian president Alan García used that phrase, referring to the indigenous communities in Peru, who were presumably begrudging others the gains from development they did not want for themselves (García 2007).

Mexico's history of corporatism is partly to blame for the lack of indigenous capacity for sustainable development there. This was a system of interest representation in which certain groups are officially recognized by the state in exchange for acceptance of state control or limits on their expression of interests and demands. The corporatist system that had held mythical sway in rural Mexico (Eisenstadt 2004; Reyna and Wienert 1977; Rus 1994; Fox 1994) was disbanded in the 1990s with the end of land reform, the discontinuation of state price supports for corn and other agricultural products, and the advent of international competition and market opening under the North American Free Trade Agreement (NAFTA). However, given this withdrawal of the state and absent a new framework for interest articulation in the countryside, the rural poor, including indigenous communities, tried to organize to fend for themselves. But absent state-guaranteed human rights and resources—that is, absent rights beyond those that accrued to indigenous citizens but not to other peasants, and without the attention that comes with electoral representation and citizen engagement (as opposed to autonomy)—customary law social organizations could not help channel the state's welfare safety net or represent citizen demands. And, contrary to early hopes, the indigenous communities in Oaxaca have not been able to substitute their own safety nets and social capital for state provision of benefits and services.

Generally speaking, corporatism is "a general system of interest representation in which specified groups are awarded monopoly status with regard to their clientele and, in one form or another, brought into official recognition as the central bases for decision-making" (Chalmers 1977, 34). Corporatism is not always anti-democratic (see Katzenstein [1985] on inclusionary corporatism in the "small states of Europe"), but has tended to develop this way in Latin America. Corporatism, where peak associations are officially recognized by the government to represent the interests of groups like labor and business, contrasts with pluralism (as exemplified by Dahl's rendering of the United States, for example), under which all groups are said—at least hypothetically—to have equal status, or at least equal access. Polycentric pluralism, as emphasized by Ostrom and others, emphasizes pluralism that simultaneously engages a range of sectors with common interests (here relating to the "umbrella" issue of the environment) across local, regional, national, and international arenas or some combination of these.

Bureaucratic authoritarianism was corporatism's most common Latin American expression when it was conceived in the 1970s. This was a relationship between capital, corporatist social groups, and authoritarian states that co-opted labor by alternately co-opting and repressing individual leaders at the top of the hierarchy, rather than having to persuade mass organizations, as democratic pluralism would have required (Schmitter 1974). In the Ecuadorian rainforest communities, we might interpret corporatism as the expression of favoritism by public officials to pro-extraction communities offering carrots of social programs to such groups and sticks of repression to groups who refuse to cooperate. And as this book demonstrates, such practices have been commonplace in areas where the Ecuadorian government has bolstered pro-extractivist groups and repressed anti-drilling and anti-mining interests.

Ecuador also features examples of polycentric pluralism, although these were more limited, especially during the Correa administration, which for the most part was characterized by the authoritarian shut-out of independent voices—such as the media, NGOs, and other interest groups—from environmental politics. Though environmentalism started out as a central pillar of Correa's electoral platform in 2006, a decade later it had been all but abandoned in favor of the petro-state development model. Oil drilling was viewed as the principal means through which Ecuador could pay for the grandiose social programs Correa pledged (and often delivered). The administration went from seeking a progressive red-green alliance to settling for a crude black one.

In Mexico, some of the internal contradictions of UC in Oaxaca—caused by corporatist imposition of local leaders on indigenous communities—were at least partly resolved by Mexico's national courts (Sonnleitner and Eisenstadt 2013). While conflicts regarding extractivism in Mexico have been limited by the fact that the main extraction of oil has been conducted by the state oil company rather than by outside interests, little oil has been discovered on indigenous communal lands to date. However, its discovery would create additional stress between the state and local communities, particularly since the country's 2013 energy sector reforms could presumably open some of Mexico's oil fields to outside interests. In the sections that follow, we contrast multicultural rights recognition in Mexico (mostly relating to customary law elections and governance) with the polycentric pluralism of Bolivia's "prior consultations." We argue that Bolivia's approach has done more to prevent socio-environmental conflicts between indigenous groups and the state over natural gas concessions (but not in mineral extraction).

PRACTICING POLYCENTRIC PLURALISM? PRIOR CONSULTATION IN BOLIVIA

As in Mexico, Bolivia also recognized UC at subnational levels, and multiculturalism there represented a break from inclusionary corporatism's long history during the country's authoritarian era, when tin miners, peasants, and others received social program benefits in exchange for supporting the government. Following the neoliberal multiculturalist trend of the 1990s, the Bolivian government reformed the 1994 Constitution, recognizing indigenous and peasant rights to "exercise functions of administration and application of their own norms as an alternative solution in conflicts" (Alberti 2013, 1). UC was extended by the new 2009 Constitution created during Morales's administration as an exercise of "communitarian democracy" by indigenous communities (Article 11). The new constitution replaced the multiculturalism of 1994 with *interculturalismo*, and acknowledged legal pluralism as a guiding principle. Article 1, chapter 1 of the Constitution of 2009 states that: "Bolivia is unitary, social, plurinational and communitarian. It is free and sovereign, democratic, intercultural, decentralized and with autonomies. Bolivia is based on political, economic, legal and linguistic pluralism, within a national integrating process" (Constitution of Bolivia 2009, version taken from Political Database of the Americas 2011).

Indigenous rights in Bolivia were reformulated to coincide with geopolitical and economic transformations, introducing new territorial jurisdictions for indigenous groups. The new autonomous regions (*autonomías*), multicultural institutions to be sure, were allowed to elect their authorities via UC as in Oaxaca. However, they were also granted the same legislative powers as subnational departments and municipalities (Bascopé 2012, 382). Bolivia acknowledged legal pluralism, but also individual rights and enforcement of these rights, unlike in Oaxaca. For instance, while recognizing the right to elect authorities according to indigenous practices, the Bolivian government established a quota for women to ensure gender equality (Fernández 2010, 52). The state has regulated UC more than in Mexico, but in Bolivia too, political co-optation has fostered authoritarian clientelism and political dependence by local organizations on the president's political party, the Movement Towards Socialism (MAS).

Alberti finds variation across UC practices, from authoritarian to more democratic indigenous local administrations, depending on the type of indigenous organizations and their connections with the national party-state (Alberti 2013, 7).

In this mix of new pluralism and autonomy with "old school" corporatism, the right to prior consultation—which we discuss further in chapter 3— was introduced as a legal figure promoting bounded pluralism in the 2009 Constitution as a mechanism of "participatory democracy" (Article 11). Prior consultation (PC) was mandated in all state decisions over project implementation on indigenous territories (Articles 15 and 345), and this practice was largely limited to multicultural rights areas. However, another conflict, that of the Indigenous Territory and National Park Isiboro-Sécure (Territorio Indígena y Parque Nacional Isiboro-Secure, TIPNIS), which would have bisected a fertile forested region of Bolivia, does convey the powers of polycentric pluralism, sometimes despite efforts by President Morales to stifle opposition voices. The ability of a coalition of indigenous groups, *campesinos*, and environmentalists from local, national, and inter-national levels to stop construction of this highway after seven years of mobilization is indicative of the force that polycentric pluralism.can have (but usually does not). In August 2011, the Bolivian government received a loan of US $332 million from the Brazilian government to construct the road Villa Tunari–San Ignacio de Moxos, connecting the Amazonian re-gion (lowlands) with Cochabamba (highlands). Indigenous groups headed by the Indigenous Federation of Bolivian East (Confederación Indígena del Oriente Boliviano, CIDOB) and Assembly of Guarani People (Asamblea del Pueblo Guaraní, APG) contested the project, arguing that it would bisect and despoil the 11,900-square-kilometer TIPNIS reserve.

According to the protestors, the 306-kilometer-long road would pro-mote Andean immigration and colonization, causing harm to the fragile Amazonian environment. On the other hand, the government assured that the road would bring development, connecting the Andes with the Amazon and allowing more commercial activity. Indigenous organizations from the lowlands CIDOB and APG, but also highlands indigenous organizations, supported by international NGOs and domestic civil society, pressured the Congress to constrain the executive; the three organizations formed a col-lective initiative to discredit government-executed consultations ("CIDOB, APG y CONAMAQ asestan un duro golpe al proyecto de ley de Consulta gubernamental," 2013). In this case, construction was started without the mandated prior consultation.

However, extended mobilization by indigenous communities and non-indigenous allies in the lowlands for over two months blocked construction.

At the height of the conflict, some two thousand people from local, regional, and national indigenous groups and national and international environmental allies marched from Trinidad in the Amazon to the highlands capital of La Paz. The protesters arrived in La Paz in October 2011 and were received as heroes and gifted food and clothing, as Amazonians are not used to the elevation and cold of the highlands ("Indígenas bolivianos llegan triunfantes a La Paz pidiendo anular proyecto de carretera," 2011). Nonetheless, one week before the protestors' arrival, the federal Chamber of Deputies in La Paz had already suspended construction of the highway (the Ley Corta 180). After eleven hours of debate, the Congress had suspended construction to protect the 26,000 people there, divided among three ethnic groups: the Yuracaré, Mojeño, and Chiman.

Congress was instrumental in providing legal protections to ethnic groups living in the TIPNIS area until the consultation was implemented the following year. The consultation was carried out from July through December 2012 amid protests accusing the government of trying to divide Amazonian organizations and manipulate the outcome. Even when the official results of the consultation yielded majority support for the road, indigenous leadership rejected these results as fraudulent. Meanwhile, indigenous resistance against the highway continued through 2014—including protests against the results of the "consulta"—with the president losing needed pledges of international funding for the road, which has not been built. Critics (Flores Castro interview) accused President Evo Morales of playing politics with the prior consultation (PC), refusing to stage it in the TIPNIS case until he had waged a publicity campaign in favor of the highway, and then conducting the PC, with an outcome favorable to his position, but which he could nevertheless not implement because of the social conflict the highway construction would seemingly exacerbate.

The Bolivian government's strength in negotiating with indigenous communities was due in part to the creation of political institutions during the first years of Morales's administration, designed to extend the state's presence among marginalized groups. As soon as Morales took power after winning election in 2005, he nationalized hydrocarbons and increased Bolivia's tax base, distributed pensions and scholarships to indigenous communities and other rural dwellers, and increased the nation's share of extractive industries' profits. Morales redistributed lands to indigenous population and fostered food self-sufficiency within indigenous communities. Between 2006 and 2012, 318,460 property deeds were granted to rural communities, twelve times as many as had been granted before 2005, with 982,089 individual beneficiaries. As a consequence of the reform, 37 million hectares were distributed to indigenous populations (see "Tierras en manos indígenas llegan a 37 millones de ha" in *Cambio*). The new constitution of 2009 was approved by a broad majority of the population and a quota for indigenous representation was established in the Congress. A Ministry of Autonomies was created in 2009 to regulate the process of political and economic decentralization, as was a Vice Ministry of Decolonization to implement *interculturalismo*, where autonomy rights were granted on a regional basis relating mostly—but not entirely—to ethnic rights. Despite politicization of a few cases (notably TIPNIS), prior consultation helped cement fortified roles for indigenous negotiators in a system where they already had great power and an unprecedented ability to defend their interests.

Contrary to the Mexican case, Bolivia mostly represented *interculturalismo*, which is closer to polycentric pluralism than the autonomy rights accruing strictly and entirely to indigenous people (as in Mexico). In Bolivia, multiculturalism still predominated with regard to prior consultation (PC), but the TIPNIS struggle, where PC was politicized to the point where mass mobilization and contention came to have a meaning beyond the sphere of ethnic autonomy, was a case where polycentric interests rose up and wedged open pluralist spaces for political maneuver. Ecuador has been a battleground between these two impulses: multicultural rights recognition, as in Oaxaca, Mexico, with its attendant limitations on group power and on individual rights, versus polycentric pluralism, as in the TIPNIS case (although it still involved mostly indigenous communities from different groups and regions). Polycentric pluralism defines groups by the societal interests they advocate, rather than limiting group scope to peoples' level of identification with indigenous communities near impacted areas. Recall that polycentrism refers to a form of pluralism in which "multiple benefits are created by diverse actions at multiple scales" (Ostrom 2014, 121).

In practice, multicultural rights grant people with fixed identities autonomy from the dictates of the state, allowing them dominion of their own resources and to set their own objectives and strategies. The problem, as we demonstrate in this book, is the lack of coordination between the state and indigenous communities caused when these communities detach themselves from secular state politics. As a result, these communities lose their say in national political debates for several possible reasons. First, if the indigenous communities vote less frequently or otherwise fail to pay tribute to the broader state, they risk being disregarded by the state as clients rather than citizens. Second, if most citizens are representing themselves following a pluralist logic, where groups are fluid and represent dynamic issue positions rather than static and immovable ethnic identities, then those relying on ethnic identity representation fall short in the marketplace of interest articulation. Third, a side effect of being stewards of their own resources often means failing to consider resources beyond their finite jurisdiction. In other words, by getting to administer their own territories, the communities themselves turn inward and may ignore opportunities available beyond their autonomous area.

The neoliberal reforms, which vastly reduced the ability of the state to redistribute in Bolivia, Ecuador, and Mexico, weakened the already weak and cast aside the role of the state as their champion. But multicultural movements did not greatly influence extant political structures beyond their immediate sphere of influence, as we will show. Rather, they gave the state a reason to ignore the rural, indigenous poor. These groups were viewed as asserting their "autonomy," assuming jurisdiction over their own problems and giving the state an excuse to withdraw. Latin America's democracy-era pluralist institutions, such as fortified legislative branches that respond to constituents, accountable bureaucracies that provide information allowing citizens to make informed judgments, improved government technical capacity, and sophisticated means of gathering citizen input, have yet to be fully implemented (and will be extremely difficult to implement in rural areas in any case). Prior systems of authoritarian-corporatist peak association representation and hierarchical decision-making with some public input (or at least from a select few labor leaders, albeit frequently co-opted) have only been partially dismantled with the advent of democracy.

We use the term "extractive populism" to represent the governing style of Correa, and to emphasize how Correa's political success depended upon the extraction of mineral resources. Politically, populism is the "mobilization of mass constituencies by personalistic leaders who challenge established elites" (Roberts 2006, 217). Populists bypass traditional elites to gain support directly through the public by granting favors, programs, and material benefits. In the economic tradition, populism is the "extensive intervention usually intended to favor inclusion, with some cases of genuine achievements but with self-destructive regard of the constraints necessary for a functional economic system" (Sheahan 1987, 29). Correa fit the political definition, coming from outside the established elite and hence needing to form a new electoral—and then governing—coalition that included indigenous communities and environmentalists. He also fit the economists' definition, as his policies disregarded the fiscal constraints needed for long-term economic solvency, and instead grew increasingly dependent on the short-term expenditure of oil royalties, which could be generated without having to make the difficult political decision to raise taxes. Correa's blend of extraction and populism was epitomized by the oil-funded public works projects he developed across the country, which he deemed the "Revolución Ciudadana" ("Civic Revolution") in reference to his direct appeal to Ecuador's people.

In Ecuador, socioeconomic conditions did improve under President Correa's "extractive populism" as more of the state's resources were redistributed. And while the Andean indigenous peoples did benefit some, as their fates were much more intertwined with those of the rest of the nation's political class, the Amazonian indigenous peoples remained distant, marginalized, and "autonomous." The challenge, as we argue in chapter 2, regarding several Latin American countries and then in greater detail regarding Ecuador, is that the indigenous communities, and the rest of the nation's citizens, may benefit from embracing pluralism, and then insisting that a range of interests be allowed to flourish. Under Correa, NGOs, newspapers and TV stations, and educational institutions were weakened and shut down, as the range of interests freely allowed to compete for support diminished. As considered extensively in the chapter 4 discussion of the evolution of Pachakutik and the CONAIE, the Ecuadorian indigenous communities' main interest aggregators, pluralist interest articulation, based on individual material interests rather than multicultural group identities, is the de facto form that the articulation of interests necessarily takes beyond indigenous communities. So regardless of how indigenous citizens wish to interact among themselves, if they do not adopt the logic of interest aggregation from the individual level up when interacting beyond their ethnic enclaves, they will lose in negotiations such as those with the highest stakes, when they most wish to speak for nature to resource extractors.

We are recommending a move from isolating multiculturalism to polycentric pluralism in addressing the broader socioeconomic rights of indigenous communities, whose interests have traditionally been grossly underrepresented in the past. The conclusion drawn in this book is that treating them as "separate but equal," which we loosely consider to be the objective of multiculturalism, has reached its limits. While we do not advocate that outsiders meddle in the internal affairs of indigenous communities (unless internal norms violate universal human rights), it is time for indigenous communities to more forcefully speak for nature in the environmental issues space, but in alliance with other affected citizens. Recall the classic theorist of pluralism, Dahl, who, in *Who Governs?* explains pluralism as the array of groups beyond the electorate that contribute positions and resources to the governmental framework. By Dahl's rendering, pluralism improves representation but also slows down policymaking, as groups adverse to political processes obstruct implementation (Dahl 1961, 1–8).

O'Donnell, an astute scholar of Latin America's political systems, added that in most of the region's Third Wave democracies, interest groups existed, as did branches of government beyond the executive, but without much authority. In his words, there was no "horizontal accountability" (2007, 49), and executive reserve domains predominated in most important arenas of contestation.

Correa curtailed what little horizontal accountability had existed in Ecuador, to be sure, and truncated what had been, just a decade earlier, Latin America's most powerful indigenous rights movement. This book explores state-society relations between President Correa and indigenous civil society. We discuss efforts to install and maintain pluralism in the face of clientelist relations between government and indigenous groups, especially in chapters 3, 4, and 6, but seek to end this chapter on a normatively positive note; mainly, that we also argue that the polycentric pluralism arguments made by scholars of environmental politics are synonymous with a pluralist approach to interest articulation. We proceed in chapter 3 to present cases of multicultural failure and pluralist success elsewhere in Latin America, and then home in on the ambiguous failures of non-interest approaches adopted by indigenous communities seeking to speak for nature through their environmental movement. Then we focus more extensively on how survey respondents in Ecuador have much stronger pro-environment positions when they are articulating individual interests than when they are expressing group identities. It does seem that indigenous citizens can speak for nature, and do care more about the environment than non-indigenous survey respondents. But they can more effectively speak for nature if they first are allowed—and encouraged—to speak for themselves as individuals and as members of groups.

CHAPTER 2

⌒⌒

Multiculturalism Versus Polycentric Pluralism

Vulnerability Challenges Post-Materialist Values
on Ecuador's Oil Extraction Frontier

L atin America is said to be responsible for a large proportion of the world's extractive conflicts (Özkaynak et al. 2015). Within this region, Ecuador has an extensive representation, with perhaps the highest number of conflicts per capita. Although Ecuador has only 4 percent of Latin America's population, it is the site of some 8 percent of the region's extractive conflicts. Moreover, it is a quintessential neo-extractivist state where a leftist president has financed extensive social welfare provision through extraction (Falleti and Riofrancos 2013; Kauffman 2017; Martínez Novo 2013). The leftist populist Ecuadorian government has harnessed the gains from extraction there by using oil revenues—around 53 percent of total exports—to nearly double social spending from 5 percent of GDP in 2006 to 9.8 percent of GDP in 2011 (de la Torre and Ortiz Lemos 2016, 227–28). In this chapter, we explain how environmental politics have been a central part of the public discussion during the Correa presidencies (2007–2017), especially debates about extraction and its effects on some of the world's most varied ecosystems present in Ecuador.

Most studies of extractive mobilizations have been carried out at the national level, and, only much more recently, at the level of the individual. As noted by Cederman et al. (2013, 208–9): "By leaping from country-level analysis to individual-level investigations, an entire class of phenomena involving group-level mechanisms has been left understudied. A large and important class of civil wars [and other internal conflicts] unfolds primarily in constellations featuring ethnic groups and governments." Still, neither national-level conditions nor individual-level characteristics alone fully explain protest behavior (see Cederman et al. 2013, 208–9). In this chapter, we investigate individual-level attitudes toward the environment and development, taking into account community and group-level factors; we further elaborate on those factors in chapter 3.

Deploying data from our 2014 original nationwide survey in Ecuador, we find that respondents do not adapt their concern for the environment in accordance with predictions of economic structuralist norms such as post-materialism. In the following sections, we formalize hypotheses to argue why the poor, like their affluent nation post-materialist counterparts, often care deeply about the environment. We then discuss how we use an original survey of environmental attitudes in Ecuador to conceptualize objective vulnerability—such as access to water and reliance on ecotourism—and proximity to extraction. Ecuador is a true laboratory for such questions because the northern part of the Amazon region has been drilled extensively for oil but with notorious environmental degradation along the way,[1] the central part of the Amazon region is in the process of being leased in oil blocks for drilling, and the southern part of the territory is a pristine rainforest untouched as yet by oil extraction.[2] In other words, Ecuador affords variation in respondent exposure to environmental vulnerability and extractivism, and we were able to exploit this in our survey sampling strategy (discussed in appendix B). After operationalizing our hypotheses and discussing our statistical findings, we utilize extensive interviews with leaders to further support our arguments.

At the individual level of analysis, our survey offers extensive evidence that extraction is conflictive and polarizing, justifying more dramatic forms of protest. However, it is important to consider that extraction is complex, and there are winners and losers, and degrees of support. For example, while 74 percent of those surveyed approved participation in legal demonstrations, only 17 percent approved of blocking freeways, a much more dramatic and contentious form of mobilization. However, fully 56 percent of respondents approved of blocking entrances to mines or oil drilling sites, a contentious form of protest that should arguably be comparable to blocking highways. As per Table 2.1, close to 65 percent of

1. The disastrous oil extraction by Texaco/Chevron in Ecuador's northern Amazon has been extensively documented. See Yanza 2014.
2. However, mining is an extractive industry at work in the southern Amazon, such as in the Napo province where concessions have been given to Canadian and Chinese companies mining for gold.

Table 2.1 APPROVAL OF PARTICIPATION IN DEMONSTRATIONS

	"Do you approve of people participating in legal demonstrations?" PROT1.			"Do you approve of people blocking highways as a form of protest?" PROT4.			"Do you approve of people organizing to block mining and oil companies from entering the community?" PROT8.		
	Agree	Disagree	NR/Depends	Agree	Disagree	NR/Depends	Agree	Disagree	NR/Depends
Has No Plumbing	249	63	11	69	237	17	219	77	27
Percent	77.1	19.5	3.4	21.4	73.3	5.3	67.8	23.8	8.3
Oil Debated or Drilled	280	72	19	65	282	4	234	91	51
Percent	74.5	19.1	5.1	17.3	75	10.6	62.2	24.2	13.6
Mining Debated or Underway	235	67	16	49	243	26	204	71	43
Percent	73.9	21.1	5	15.4	76.4	8.6	64.2	22.3	13.5
Self-Identified as Indigenous	558	107	50	149	533	33	494	137	84
Percent	78	15	7	20.8	74.5	4.6	69.1	19.1	11.8
Identifies with Pachakutik	102	11	16	23	100	6	97	21	11
Percent	79.1	8.5	12.3	17.8	77.5	4.7	75.2	16.6	8.5
Overall National Average	1,322	371	88	303	1,379	99	991	546	244
Percent	74.2	20.8	4.94	17	77.4	5.5	55.6	30.6	13.7

Note: Percentages do not add up to 100 because some respondents did not reply, or responded "Do not know."

respondents in areas of oil and mining debates approved of blocking extraction sites; the percentage increased to 68 percent among vulnerable
respondents without plumbing and to 69 percent among self-identified
indigenous respondents. Furthermore, as we elaborate in chapters 3 and
4, extraction in Ecuador has become a highly politicized issue, as illustrated by the 75 percent of those identifying as members of the opposition Pachakutik political party who support physically blocking entrances
to extractive companies. Clearly, an overwhelming majority of respondents
did not believe that blocking extractive sites carried any moral ambiguity,
particularly in the current political context where they feel that major economic extractive interests get the government's attention more than
victims of the resulting environmental degradation.

Many neo-extractivist governments claim to promote what has been
deemed a "democratic developmental" state, which in addition to expanding
the economy also "builds human capabilities, promotes sustainable development, and seeks feedback from civil society" (Hochstetler and Tranjan
2016, 498). In Ecuador, as discussed in chapter 1, the administration of
President Rafael Correa claimed to implement a democratic developmental
model by including the rights of Mother Nature (*Pachamama*) in the 2009
Constitution, evaluating environmental impacts, and respecting the rights
of communities by utilizing prior consultation and environmental impact
assessments before undertaking extractivist activities. Indeed, Correa
claimed to adopt a developmental model based on the indigenous concept
of *sumak kawsay* (*buen vivir* or harmonious living). As aptly summarized
by Kauffman and Martin (2014, 43), this concept bypasses the Western
duality where humans dominate or conserve nature, because humans are
believed to be an active part of nature rather than separate from it. Under
sumak kawsay, "[r]ather than a linear progression of accumulation, development is understood as the attainment and reproduction of the equilibrium state of *buen vivir*, which refers to living in harmony with nature"
(Kauffman and Martin 2014, 43).

However, scholars questioned the democratic nature of contemporary
Ecuador, at least under Correa (see, for example, de la Torre and Ortiz
Lemos 2016; Conaghan 2015; Martínez Novo 2013). We thus propose that
Ecuador's model is better conceptualized as "extractive populism" to account for President Correa's increasingly authoritarian "populist polarization" (de la Torre and Ortiz Lemos 2016, 222). Given the emphasis that
Correa placed on *sumak kawsay* and harmonized development (Kauffman
and Martin 2014) and his populist tendencies, Ecuador is an excellent
case for analyzing the extent to which developmentalism mitigates environmental concern. Using the results of our survey, we find that Ecuador's

extractive-led developmental model has done little to balance environmental concerns with economic demands—or attain *sumak kawsay*—in the minds of the public.

Building upon the arguments that we presented in chapter 1, we will now formalize hypotheses to argue why the poor and vulnerable, like their affluent nation post-materialist counterparts, often care deeply about the environment. We then discuss how we use our survey to conceptualize objective vulnerability—such as access to water and reliance on ecotourism—and proximity to extraction. In the process, we show that ethnic identity, anticipation of material benefits, and post-materialism really do not explain environmental attitudes.

NEOLIBERALISM, THE RISE OF INDIGENEITY IN THE TWENTY-FIRST CENTURY, AND THE ERA OF SUSTAINABLE DEVELOPMENT

Considered as peasants during the corporatist era in most nations, including Bolivia, Mexico, and Peru (Eisenstadt 2011, 5–11, 163–170), as well as Ecuador (Pallares 2002), indigenous peoples actively asserted ethnic identities in most nations starting in the early 1990s. As related by Burguete (2013, 40–46), indigenous intellectuals started rejecting treatment by the United Nations as mere minorities in the 1980s. Instead, they sought consideration in legal settlements as autonomous groups with separate land rights. As pointed out by Lucero (2013, 23) and others, the International Labor Organization's Convention 169 recognized multicultural rights in 1991. However, Lucero (2013, 24) critiques the "perversity" of multiculturalism, arguing, as does Hale (2002), that "rather than creating more egalitarian and inclusionary political orders, multiculturalism conspires with neoliberal market reforms to weaken, divide, and ultimately thwart challenges for radical reform" (Lucero 2013, 24). The linchpin of this argument is that the richness of indigenous communities may be recognized in the abstract, but in fact they are not given any public resources or legally implemented means of executing these rights. These communities were rich on paper but poor in practice.

In general, scholarship on ethnic mobilization in Latin American in the 1980s still emphasized the corporatist nature of rural life and characterized citizens as clients who received goods and services in exchange for votes and political support. That changed in the 1990s, however, as the Zapatista agrarian movement in southern Mexico in 1994 adopted an ethnic frame (Eisenstadt 2011, 88) to broaden their scope of grievances and supporters, so that "interest groups . . . far from the Zapatista epicenter, were not necessarily loyal to [the leader, Sub-commander] Marcos and his balaclava-clad insurgents in the jungle, but they certainly seized upon the political opportunities presented" (Eisenstadt 2011, 89). This insurgency, symbolic and rhetorical more than empirical, was joined by other adoptions of indigeneity by groups around the hemisphere who realized that as autonomous groups they could be buffered from the destabilizing effects of neo-liberalism (Yashar 2005). As observed by Engle (2010), indigenous peoples compensated for their political frailty by making urgent claims to cultural distinction and calls for protection. Indigenous leaders presented "authentic" traditions at international meetings to gain recognition, and "however valuable this recognition [from the international community] might be . . . the costumes and dances are what are remembered" (Engle 2010, 153). Besides Mexico, the other Latin American nation where the indigenous rights movement gained the most traction in the 1990s was Ecuador.

ECUADOR'S INDIGENOUS MOBILIZATION AND THE *SUMAK KAWSAY* THIRD WAY

Indigeneity was gaining traction as a social movement frame in Ecuador at the same time it was appearing in Mexico and elsewhere around the Americas, but without a lot of success until the very end of the twentieth century. The country's 1998 Constitution codified indigenous and Afro-Ecuadorian territorial circumscriptions, but these administrative units were never activated through implementing legislation (Lucero 2013, 23). Indigenous-led agencies for development (Consejo de Desarrollo de las Nacionalidades y Pueblos del Ecuador, CODENPE) and intercultural bilingual education (Dirección de Educación Intercultural Bilingüe, DINEIB) were created in the late 1980s and representatives of the Confederation of Indigenous Nationalities of Ecuador (Confederación de Nacionalidades Autónomas Indígenas de Ecuador, CONAIE) were given important roles in management of these organizations, although these agencies did not achieve extensive reforms. By the early 1990s, Ecuador's indigenous movement, despite its overall weakness, was "considered stronger than others in the region because it was able to unify organizations from the community to the national level, and because its massive uprisings were able to deeply affect state policy" (Martínez 2013, 115).

The movement further consolidated in 1996 when it formed a political party, Pachakutik, to serve as its electoral arm, immediately winning some 10 percent of the seats in Congress and an important role in the 1998 Constituent Assembly to draft the new constitution (West n.d.). Parallel to this rise in indigenous power, the 1992 United Nations Conference on Environment and Development provoked interest in biodiversity and sustainable development, with Ecuador playing an important role in transnational efforts (Lewis 2016, 87–89). However, "'problems that affect Ecuadorians' immediate quality of life, such as air, land and water pollution and urban issues" (Lewis 2016, 90), were left off the international agenda, even though issues such as the Texaco/Chevron oil pollution (which ultimately resulted in lawsuits totaling well over US $1 billion) in the northern Amazon, and water shortages through much of the Andes, were among the true causes of indigenous mobilization.

The indigenous movement continued to have influence into the new millennium, although it remained at least somewhat removed from the environmental agenda as national economic policies took precedence. Politically, the CONAIE effectively helped oust President Abdalá Bucaram in 1996 and led opposition in January 2000 to the neoliberal economic policies of President Jamil Mahuad, a Harvard-trained technocrat who made unpopular decisions to freeze bank deposits, ban withdrawals, and dollarize the Ecuadorian economy to try to help stave off an economic crisis. The CONAIE and Pachakutik supported President Lucio Gutiérrez in his role as military leader in the 2000 social movement to overthrow Mahuad, and then in his election to power in 2002. However, the indigenous interest groups found themselves out of power by 2003, even after gaining two cabinet posts in the Gutiérrez administration. CONAIE's crisis coincided with what Lewis describes as the "organizational bust" of Ecuador's environmental movement (2000–2006), as international funding for environmental initiatives diminished, the crude oil pipeline to carry heavy crude from Lago Agrio across the Andes to the port of Esmeraldas was constructed over the objections of many, and the Brazilian company Petrobras was granted permission to construct a road through the Waorani Ethnic Reserve in Yasuní National Park in 2005.

CONAIE leadership throughout the 1990s had been centered in the densely populated Andean region, where Kichwa leaders worked with the Ecuadorian state, often as loyal opposition, but sometimes also as co-opted allies. Then in the 2000s, leadership moved toward the Amazon, where the Sarayaku People won a landmark legal case at the Inter-American Commission on Human Rights in 2012 (see chapter 3). Despite these small victories, neither groups in the Andes nor those in the Amazon region had much luck sustaining an indigenous environmental movement during this period but, as noted by Lewis (2016, 161), "the lessened influence of transnational [environment project] funders created space for alternative development visions." This political space gave rise to the adoption of the philosophy of *sumak kawsay* under the leadership of Rafael Correa, whose savvy platform simultaneously filled gaps in indigenous *and* environmental leadership. Gutiérrez's ouster in 2005 on corruption charges paved the way for Correa, who ran a strong campaign in 2006 and captured the presidency in the second round of balloting (Conaghan 2011). Correa was able to take advantage of the indigenous movement's weakness following their ouster from the Gutiérrez government (West n.d.), and although indigenous leaders were hopeful that Correa—one of the first candidates to address the nation in Kichwa—would represent them, they were hesitant to unite with an outsider once again.

As part of the Pink Tide of Latin American leftists (as they were not quite "Red" like the Cold War communist and socialist revolutionaries, who traced their ideological roots to Che Guevara and Regis Debray), Correa was a capitalist, but he believed in a more equitable distribution of wealth. His regional counterparts in Bolivia and Venezuela led the Bolivarian Alliance for the Peoples of Our America (ALBA), an inter-Andean alliance based on trade but also ideology, which reached its first trade agreement, between Ecuador and Venezuela, in 2010. Venezuela's Hugo Chávez was widely regarded as the charismatic leader of the movement, representing a change for the Latin American left, which had been led by Fidel Castro for nearly half a century. Ultimately, Evo Morales in Bolivia and Correa in Ecuador proved to be the group's most effective banner wavers, as Chávez's successor in 2013, Nicolás Maduro, faced economic hardships, including double-digit economic contraction and an annual inflation rate well over 500 percent as a result of the oil price collapse of 2014. Correa and Morales identified as "post-neoliberal," or neoliberal in sourcing income from extractive rents, but redistributive and environmentalist in development strategies.

Lewis identifies five platforms that define this position in the Ecuadorian case (2016, 165): 1) a new social role for the state as differentiated from the market-led laissez-faire approach of the 1990s; 2) the translation of economic gains into social gains; 3) prioritization of social inclusion and participatory democracy; 4) economic growth fueled by state profits from extractive royalties rather than by the private sector; and 5) the establishment of new regional institutions seeking to shift geopolitical power away from the United States and toward these economically emboldened nations themselves. Correa lost no time in implementing his agenda of increased social welfare paid for by accelerated oil drilling and an increase in mining activity. However, as the Correa objectives of environmental conservation and resource extraction came into conflict, the public debate widened, and Ecuador became polarized over a range of environmental issues.

COOPTATION OF *SUMAK KAWSAY* BY RAFAEL CORREA
(2007–2013)

At the center of Correa's political strategy was the formal incorporation of *sumak kawsay*, which had been part of the Kichwa vernacular for some time, into the 2008 Constitution. As per Article 275 (Constitution of Ecuador 2008), "the development structure is the organized, sustainable and dynamic group of economic, political, socio-cultural and environmental systems which underpin the achievement of the good way of living (*sumak kawsay*)." This concept (*buen vivir* in Spanish) is quite plural and definitionally imprecise, meaning that to some it opens up a whole new pathway for an ethical, ecological, dignified, and socially just form of development (Escobar 2010, 23), while for others it is rhetorical and self-serving by indigenous leaders who want to ensure their control by keeping outsiders away (for example, Coka and Pinos interviews). Martínez Dalmau, who advised drafters of the Bolivian (2009), Ecuadorian (2008), and Venezuelan (1999) constitutions, argued, along with Gudynas (2009, 34–46) that "affirming that nature has its own rights separate from human appraisal goes beyond the classic approach. . . . Nature goes from an *object* of rights assigned by human beings to a *subject* of rights and therefore possessed of intrinsic value . . . The great challenge Ecuadoreans have before them is to create the conditions for a true implementation of *sumak kawsay*, which could collide with both the use of extractivist policies that exhaust natural resources and pollute the very nature of historical change in the political process" (Martínez Dalmau 2016, 170). Other elements of the constitution fortified executive power over the legislative branch (Conaghan 2011, 271–73) and granted Ecuadorians the right of consultation over activities on their land. However, as further addressed in chapter 3, contrary to the United Nations Declaration of the Rights of Indigenous Peoples (adopted in 2007), Ecuador's constitution did not require the consent of these groups before the government commenced extractive projects (Lewis 2016, 180).

This tension between recognition of the rights of nature and its implementation, noted by Martínez Dalmau (2016), Gudynas (2009), and others including Lewis (2016), Kaufman and Martin (2016), and Lalander (2014), is central to this book because it has become a centerpiece of the public debate in Ecuador, and it is reflected in our survey of public opinion. President Correa's initial position was strongly supportive of the rights of nature, although Lalander (2014, 3) noted that the "strategic economic and political interests of the State clash[ed] with indigenous and environmental rights."

Correa epitomized populism, such as through the use of a constitution-making process in 2008 for the populist ends of building a new coalition on clientelism and symbolic politics, like "the rights of nature." His staff proposed the first-ever constitution granting "nature" human rights (even though, as Gudynas [2009], Kaufman and Martin [2014], and Martínez Dalmau [2016] all note, there was no evident way to implement this). At the same time, he designed an extensive new program of welfare and redistribution, based entirely on royalties obtained through extractive industries.

Soon after his initial election in 2006, Correa presented his effort to protect the biodiverse and lushly forested Yasuní National Park from imminent oil drilling by asking international donors to pay Ecuador to offset the oil revenues the nation would forgo by leaving the oil in the ground. This campaign to "leave the oil in the soil," discussed more extensively in chapter 6, contributed to prominent calls worldwide to "strand" fossil fuel deposits in hard-to-drill areas as a means of preserving nature and mitigating climate change. Together with the important symbolism of the "rights of nature" in Ecuador's constitution, Correa quickly became an environmental champion on the international scene, whose administration took the lead worldwide of what was conveyed as a "third way" alternative means of development. The administration sought, at international and domestic fora (Kauffman 2017), to add a new development philosophy where nature was a subject and part of a holistic ecosystem that also included humans.

The Ecuadorians (along with Bolivians who adopted similar constitutional language in 2009) sought to broaden the debate between development through neoliberal extractivist capitalism and environmental conservation where the environment was an object, separate from humans. Sustainable development, promoted in the 1990s to cushion neoliberal extractivism and make it more humane, was also different from *sumak kawsay* and the rights of nature in that it still treated nature as the means to the end of human prosperity. The *sumak kawsay* movement, in its original form (as described by Acosta and Gudynas and its other public intellectuals), sought to include humans and their interactions with nature as endogenous to the whole (Lewis 2016). As aptly summarized by Kauffman and Martin (2014, 43), under *sumak kawsay*, "[r]ather than a linear progression of accumulation, development is understood as the attainment and reproduction of the equilibrium state of *buen vivir*, which refers to living in harmony with nature" (Kauffman and Martin 2014, 43).

Ostensibly to help foster this "third way" of development, in 2011 the Ecuadorian government created Ecuador Estratégico, a public agency to mediate between community residents and extractivists. One official at the agency (Pinos interview 2014) acknowledged that "there are two interpretations [of the organization]. Some think we are buying consciences with projects, but others think we demonstrate how serious the state is [about redistribution] as before the extractive operators came and took away everything. Now many say that some benefits stay in the zone of extraction." But this "squeaky wheel approach" of giving resources to citizens in areas of extraction to offset environmental damage has been controversial. Critics argue that Ecuador Estratégico offers projects without coordinating with subnational provisional governments (Arruti interview 2014), fails to follow through (Arruti interview 2014), offers populist "Santa Claus" gifts without coordinating with local governments to make service provision cost-effective and rational (Laurini interview 2014), and does not offer culturally sensitive projects (Vallejo interview 2014), focusing instead on just "breaking ground" on populist projects to placate publics and keep them from protesting.

BETRAYAL OF *SUMAK KAWSAY* ENVIRONMENTALISM BY "EXTRACTIVE POPULIST" CORREA, 2013–2016

Perhaps the decisive moment in Correa's shift to "extractive populism" was the battle over Yasuní, which had been a cornerstone of his administration for his first several years in office. After collecting a few million US dollars— only a fraction of the funds sought—the Correa administration decided in the summer of 2013 to discontinue the campaign and drill for oil in the national park. Many, including the parents of countless schoolchildren from around Ecuador who had sent in small donations to save jaguars and freshwater dolphins and never got their donations back, were frustrated, and legal advocates tried, in vain, to use the constitutional rights of nature to protect Yasuní. Implementing legislation was never passed for those rights, however, and Correa seemed to have lost interest in what had become a political "nonstarter" pitting his "rights of nature" constitution and platform against the funding source for his entire economic program: oil royalties.

People came to expect the gains from oil revenue when, starting in about 2014, the drop in international oil prices made social spending much harder to obtain. However, oil prices fell by nearly two-thirds between 2014 and 2016, and Ecuador financed much of these increases in social programs through true extractive populism. Ecuador literally mortgaged probable future oil price increases by selling crude at low 2015 and 2016 prices (which bottomed out at US $33 per barrel in February 2016 before nearly doubling by 2018) years into the future. Ecuador reaped the liquidity advantage of immediate cash advances but at the cost of future oil guaranteed at what will likely be much lower than the market rate. Coming into office in the summer of 2017, President Moreno started his term with greatly diminished spending options as a result of President Correa's reckless populism.

President Correa had already foreclosed other liquidity and financing options. In 2008 he stopped paying international creditors, thus defaulting on loans from international institutions like the World Bank and Inter-American Development Bank. The Chinese government stepped into this breach to become Ecuador's leading source of public financing. By 2011, China was purchasing 50 percent of Ecuador's oil (Ray and Chimienti 2015, 9), creating a great trade imbalance between the two countries, and by 2013, borrowing from China accounted for over a third of Ecuador's public debt (Ray and Chimienti 2015, 13). In 2016, China's new oil concessions in Ecuador consisted of Blocks 79 and 83, drilling sites near Yasuní National Park, where drilling is still heavily contested by the Sápara People, who claim, in part, that the government never consulted them regarding plans to drill there (Ray and Chimienti 2015, 30). The Ecuadorian government's failure to consult the Sápara People prior to drilling, combined with the dubious environmental record of the Chinese parastatal companies Andes Petroleum (north of Yasuní, in Waorani, Secoya, and Siona communal land areas) and PetroOriental (in the Sápara area), generated great controversy over oil exploitation.

Against this backdrop, poor indigenous communities are sometimes consulted prior to the initiation of extractive projects, but, as chapter 3 extensively documents, prior consultation is usually perfunctory rather than substantive, and results of such consultation can be summarily ignored. Part of the problem is that most citizens, represented by two-thirds of our national sample, have never even heard of prior consultation. When they do know the concept, they are "consulted" as individuals but—especially in indigenous communities—they act in groups. This book seeks, perhaps for the first time, to address this gap between individual and group rights by considering both individuals and their attitudes, and how these are aggregated through historical, social, and political contexts.

We will now outline the methods used in this study, first by reviewing the literature on social movements and particularly, environmental social movements, as collective action, but then by considering how we also address this as an aggregation of individual views. In addition to demonstrating the aggregation problem of summing individual choices into group behavior, we hope to demonstrate that the type of aggregation also matters, and claim that rather than following a logic of multiculturalism (organization according to ethnicity), that perhaps a geographically based logic of polycentric pluralism should be invoked.

VULNERABILITY ON THE FRONT LINES OF EXTRACTION AND CONCERN FOR THE ENVIRONMENT

Our analysis differs from prevailing theories of indigenous and environmental mobilization. Specifically, we argue that extant theories ignore individual-level incentives for collective action. Here, we critically review explanations that have been marshaled in recent years to account for indigenous and environmental collective action and demonstrate their limits for explaining the emergence of the new movements in the Amazon. We then introduce hypotheses that account for individual-level incentives that lead to indigenous environmental collective action. We argue that these individual attitudes are essential for understanding when citizens engage in environmental conflicts.

Unlike in previous research, we argue that indigenous identity is not a sufficient condition for environmental protest. Early work on ethnic mobilization emphasized the importance of shared ethnic identities for collective action among minority populations (see, for example, Horowitz 1985). However, most scholarship today rejects essentialist views of ethnic identity, instead recognizing that ethnicity is both socially constructed and used instrumentally to achieve political goals (Eisenstadt 2011). We build upon this research and challenge the traditional view that indigenous identity alone leads individuals to care more about the environment and act on its behalf. Instead, we argue that vulnerability to environmental change—particularly in the form of proximity to extraction—is more important in determining environmental attitudes and corresponding action on behalf of the environment.

In addition, previous theories of indigenous mobilization cannot explain the full variation in collective action for the environment. Scholars have gone a long way in discovering the effects of indigenous movements (Selverston-Scher 2001; Zamosc 2007) and the importance of political opportunities, resources, and capacity for indigenous movement emergence—key factors in social movement theory (Yashar 2005). However, because this research focused on national-level variables—such as democratization and neoliberal reforms—it cannot explain why some individuals participate in collective action while others do not. In this chapter, we fill this gap in the literature by focusing specifically on individual attitudes that we argue are essential for collective action on behalf of the environment.

We also argue that the post-materialist thesis cannot explain mobilization by Latin America's impoverished communities, such as the indigenous. An explanation that, at least for a time, held "hegemonic status" (Guha and Martínez-Alier 1997, xiv) in the study of comparative environmental movements is Inglehart's (1997) theory of post-materialist values. Post-materialism originally aspired to explain value-shifts in the affluent European economies. The initial argument, as articulated by Inglehart and Flanagan (1987), sought to explain leveling in the curvilinear relationship between economic development and income inequality that occurred in "mature industrial societies" (1987, 1291) only. That argument, based loosely on Maslow's Hierarchy of Needs,[3] was that after basic needs were met (as they most frequently were in affluent nations), they were free to address "less basic" issues like environmental protection (as well as quality of life, women's rights, etc.).

However, in his 1995 piece, Inglehart expanded the scope of his argument beyond affluent Western Europe; he appropriately criticized scholars of the "boom" in worldwide environmental interest, through a statement which holds equally true today: "Much of this research is limited to the tip of the iceberg, focusing on what people think about environmental problems without probing into why they think it or how deeply they are committed" (1995, 57). Using cross-national World Values Survey data from forty-three countries at the time, Inglehart's conclusions were two-fold: 1) that post-materialist cultural factors—defined as "emphasizing self-expression and . . . quality of life"—were critical, but that 2) "people are concerned about the environment because they face serious objective problems [such as air and water pollution]" (1995, 57). If Inglehart's argument is valid, we would expect these arguments to hold not just at the aggregate level of countries, but also for individuals within countries. In other words, affluent individuals—despite living in developing areas—should be able to "afford" to care for the environment and should also be capable of holding other post-materialist values. However, we believe that post-materialism is an inadequate explanation of environmental concern in developing countries such as Ecuador, and as such, we posit the following hypothesis:

Hypothesis 1—The Post-Materialist Hypothesis: Post-materialist living conditions and the associated post-materialist values are expected to have no relationship with concern for the environment.

Although Inglehart argued that post-materialism was only partially responsible for explaining the prioritization of the environment over development, his work was unable to explain all varieties of environmentalism. For example, Brechin (1999) critiqued the "post-materialism plus objective problems" theory, arguing that while it was true that citizens from poor countries were more concerned with local environmental problems,

---

3. Brechin makes the connection between "post-materialism" and Maslow's hierarchy (1999, 794).

there were no patterns of difference in views of more abstract and global problems between the respondents in rich nations and those from poor ones. Recent research using cross-national survey data raises doubts about Inglehart's theory but also does not provide an alternative explanation for why poor people value the environment (Dunlap and York 2012). Carrying these concerns further, we seek to more systematically explain differences in the attitudes of survey respondents, but as being related more to matters of environmental vulnerability and local extractivist debates.

To Adger (2006, 268–69), vulnerability ("the susceptibility to be harmed," as defined in chapter 1) is the flip side of resilience, "the magnitude of disturbance that can be absorbed before a system changes to a radically different state as well as the capacity to self-organize and the capacity for adaptation to emerging circumstances." In his 2006 review of the literature, Adger emphasizes the need for giving greater consideration to human factors in vulnerability, as "the common property resource tradition, for example, stresses the importance of social, political, and economic organizations in social ecological systems, with institutions as mediating factors that govern the relationship between social systems and the ecosystems on which they depend" (269). Still, Adger states that there has been little in the way of a synthesis of social and ecological factors into considerations of vulnerability, and he acknowledges the challenges of "developing metrics that incorporate both human well-being and recognize the relative and perceptual nature of vulnerability" (274).

As mentioned in chapter 1, the clearest pathway out of living in vulnerable circumstances is through development—such as with increased infrastructure and greater job opportunities. Therefore, for vulnerable individuals, development should take priority over the environment. Our second hypothesis is thus:

> **Hypothesis 2—Vulnerability Hypothesis:** An individual's objective vulnerability to environmental change—or the extent to which his/her livelihood depends on the environment—is expected to increase environmental concern.

A corollary to vulnerability is the effect that the presence of resource extraction may have on individuals' concern for the environment. The extractivist debate is based on claims (Kurtz 2004; Silva 2009) that 1990s neoliberal reforms in Latin American demobilized labor and other traditional groups, but may have opened spaces for the mobilization of other groups, such as indigenous communities, in their efforts to control natural resource extraction (Arce 2014; Yashar 2005). Protests to resist oil extraction reached their zenith near the Peruvian town of Bagua, in 2009, where thirty-two people were killed and hundreds were injured. Clearly, that event galvanized the debate in Peru, and authors like Arce (2014) and Vasquez (2014) have claimed that localized debates over whether to open up environments to extraction have a great effect on public opinion and citizen mobilization.

Indeed, extensive oil production has been found to hinder nations' environmental performance, possibly due to the expectations such oil production brings for economic development and how that production gets distributed (Eisenstadt, Fiorino, and Stevens n.d.). Additionally, in the Andean region, "the negative environmental and social externalities brought about by the boom in the exploration and development of hydrocarbons reserves, and the impact these have had on local communities, constitute the main trigger of local conflicts today" (Vasquez 2014, 5). Beyond triggering actual conflicts, we believe that the possibilities of hydrocarbon production—with all of the attendant environmental, political, social, and economic complications this may bring—become a focal point in communities, which then frame their attitudes on environmental issues.

Hypothesis 3—Extractivist Debate Hypothesis: Respondents in localities where debates over hydrocarbon and/or mineral extraction frame views on the environment are more likely to express concern for the environment.

Extractivist efforts can harm the land and water that poor, rural, and indigenous communities depend upon for their livelihoods, but extractivism is also promoted by developing-area governments as a means of economic advancement. Mining and oil contracts often stipulate that a percentage of royalties be redistributed back to local communities as development projects (Becker 2012). Indeed, the increasingly state-dominated neo-extractivist efforts across the Andean region have restructured the economies of these countries, creating an unprecedented level of development driven by royalties from the extraction of natural resources for export. The focus on development across Latin America has increasingly shifted "from the industrial ambitions and actors of earlier developmentalism to instead seek to build human capabilities and address sustainability" (Hochstetler and Tranjan 2016). Deeming this new form of state-focused development "democratic developmentalism," Hochstetler and Tranjan (2016) recognize that states are increasingly concerned with broad-based monitoring and feedback from civil society. Given these efforts, we might expect there to be little tension between developmentalism and environmental concern, even for extractive-led development. If the state is mitigating environmental damage, then concern for the environment can coexist with the desire for developmental benefits drawn from extraction.

As noted, the administration of President Rafael Correa in Ecuador certainly implemented an extraction-led developmental model by distributing unprecedented public services—such as roads, schools, and clinics—using funds received from the oil export surplus. Correa also undertook a range of symbolic gestures to win support of the indigenous community, whose lands contain much of the mineral wealth in Ecuador, and who united in 1998 and 2000 to overthrow two separate presidents. Along these lines, Correa advocated recognizing the rights of Mother Nature (*Pacha Mama* in the indigenous language of Kichwa) in the 2008 Constitution, developed mechanisms to evaluate environmental impacts, and sought to respect the rights of communities by implementing prior consultation before undertaking extractivist activities.

However, Correa's use of extraction-led developmentalism was largely viewed as motivated by populism and as propaganda by a variety of communities facing the threat of extractivism. As such, oil drilling and mining are highly politicized in Ecuador. Because Correa did not successfully promote "environmentally friendly" extractivist development, we posit that individuals who expect extraction to reward them with economic benefits—in the form of employment opportunities, development projects, or even community-level cash transfers—to still be wary of the environmental costs associated with the practice. Given the divisive nature of extraction, we develop the following hypothesis:

Hypothesis 4—Role of Expectation That Extraction Has Benefits: Individuals who believe that extraction has benefits for Ecuador are no more or less likely to have concern for the environment.

Within the broader, overarching debate between proponents of economic development and advocates of environmental protection, these hypotheses are separate, at least in international debates. However, at the local level, the hypotheses have some conceptual overlap. It bears mention also that vulnerability represents those who depend inordinately on the environment for their livelihoods or feel endangered by threats to the habitats where they live, and that while not excessively correlated with the extraction variables, poorly regulated extraction can contribute to respondents' sense of vulnerability.

DATA AND VARIABLES

To test all four hypotheses, we conceptualize citizens' concern for the environment as our dependent variable. We rely on one measure developed from citizen responses during focus groups and extensive field tests. The question involves two stages. First, we provide individuals with a list of concerns, including basic needs (employment, ability to buy basic goods, health problems, and security), as well as arguably higher-order or abstract concerns (ability to obtain or pay for education, interpersonal relations, the overall situation of the country, and the environment), and ask them if they are worried about each of these concerns with a simple "yes" or "no" response. We then follow up with a question: "Taking into account the previous list, how much do you worry about the environment? Not at all, less than most other concerns, more than some of the other concerns, more than the majority of the other concerns, more than any other concern?"[4]

The responses capture concern for the environment relative to other concerns that, in theory, should matter to affluent individuals as well as to vulnerable populations. The response to the question is ordinal, where 0 represents that the environment is not at all a concern compared to other problems, 1 indicates that the environment is less of a concern than some problems, 2 indicates that it is more of a concern than some other problems, 3 is that the environment is more than a majority of the problems, and 4 indicates the environment is more worrisome than any other problem. We coded individuals who answered "no" to the initial question of whether they worry about the environment as 0. In the sample, the mean response is 1.93 (meaning that on average the environment is more of a concern than some other problems), and 25.15 percent of the citizens indicate they are concerned about the environment more than the majority of other problems (3) or more than any other problem (4). (See Table A1 in appendix A for a description of the survey items, question wording, and coding of this and all other variables included in the analysis, and Table A2 for the descriptive statistics of this and all other variables.)

Several elements of the survey instrument allow us to develop measures of what we consider to be post-materialist dispositions. The first set of these variables measure an individual's propensity toward what Inglehart (1995; 1997) classifies as higher-order values, such as human rights, equality, and democracy. In an effort to capture these values, we include the variable *Human Rights*, which indicates whether a respondent ranks human rights among the six most significant problems facing the country (1 if yes, 0 otherwise); *Indigenous Leader*, which codes whether the respondent disagrees that the indigenous do not make good leaders

---

4. See appendix A for the survey question used to create this variable, and other survey-based variables.

(1 if no, 0 otherwise); and *Democracy vs Development*, which is coded as 1 if individuals believe that democracy is more important given the choice between democracy and development. The breakdown of these indicators in our sample is as follows: 4.9 percent rank human rights as one of top six problems, 52.1 percent disagree that indigenous cannot be good leaders, and 31.3 percent think that democracy is more important than development. We also included a variable that coded whether individuals believe that *Climate Change* exists (1 if yes, 0 if no), which 91.8 percent of our sample does. Finally, we included a measure of whether respondents thought that one of the most important characteristics of a local government should be to *Promote Modernity*. We coded this variable as 1 if respondents agreed that "promoting the modernity and development of the town" is most important, and 0 otherwise. About 48.1 percent of the sample agreed that promoting modernity and development is most important for local governments.

We further developed a measure of *Social Media* use, which indicates whether an individual has used a social media outlet like Facebook or Twitter in the past week (1 if yes, 0 otherwise). Among our respondents, 38.1 percent said that they had accessed social media in the past week. We argue that social media use should have a positive relationship with environmental concern if post-materialism is indeed the source of such concern. Another potentially important correlate of post-materialism is an individual's position in society. We include the *Professional* variable, which indicates whether an individual is a professional, intellectual, scientist, technician, or mid-level professional (1 if yes, 0 otherwise) and expect that it should also have a positive effect on concern for the environment based on classic post-materialism. Around 4.2 percent of our sample claims to be a professional.

Finally, according to post-materialist theory, a key expression of higher-order values is a respondent's ability and willingness to donate for the cause. The *Eco Donation* variable indicates whether an individual has ever donated to an ecological organization (1 if yes, 0 otherwise). Again, if post-materialism predicts concern for the environment, then we would expect this donation to have a positive relationship with our dependent variable. In our sample, only 3.5 percent of respondents have ever made such a donation.

We also consider the importance of international networks for influencing attitudes toward the environment. We include the measure of *International Networks*, which combines two questions about whether the respondent knows of anyone who has met with 1) representatives of international foundations; and/or 2) international scientists, technicians, or academics. In our sample, 11.6 percent of respondents said they knew someone who had met with one or the other type of international representative (in which 6.2 percent of our sample said they knew someone who had met with both).

Recall that our main argument is that vulnerability to ecosystem change influences individual attitudes toward the environment. Our survey assessed the extent to which individuals are *actually* vulnerable to environmental damage—because they rely primarily upon rain or river for water—as well as their *perceived* vulnerability to such damage. Survey respondents were asked about their water source, and we created the measure *Rain/ River Water Source* to indicate when individuals are dependent primarily on rain or river for water (coded 1 if they depend on rain or river; 0 otherwise). Approximately 18.1 percent of our sample claims to rely upon rain or river water as their primary water source. The second question that we use to measure vulnerability is how often respondents had water available to use in their home. We used the question to create the *Water Scarcity* measure (coded 1 if they never have water available, or have it available only a few times a month or few times a week; 0 otherwise). Approximately 10.82 percent of our sample claims to live with scarce access to water. We expect individuals faced with water scarcity to be particularly vulnerable to ecosystem changes resulting from climate change and/or extractive activities.

Another objective measure of vulnerability to environmental damage is the extent to which an individual's livelihood is derived from the environment. The variable *Ecotourism* indicates whether an individual directly benefits from ecotourism in their community (1 if yes, 0 otherwise), of which 13.5 percent of our sample does. We expect individuals who rely upon ecotourism to express high levels of environmental concern.

Vulnerability to environmental damage can also be assessed from the *perceptions* of individuals. We designed questions on our survey to capture whether Ecuadorian citizens perceive themselves to be vulnerable to environmental changes. The variable *Climate Change Concern* indicates the extent to which individuals worry that events related to dramatic climate change, such as droughts and floods, could affect themselves or their families in the next six months (ordinal scale where 1 represents not worried and 4 very worried). By our reasoning, the more worried citizens are about the impact of climate change (37.5 percent of the sample are very worried), the more vulnerable they perceive themselves to be to environmental damage, and the more likely they should prioritize the environment over development.

We used several measures to capture individual political orientations. The first variable is individual affiliation with the Pachakutik party—an indigenous political party that is active in its opposition to government extraction for environmental and cultural reasons (1 if affiliates with the party, 0 otherwise). We expect those who identify with the Pachakutik party to be more likely to express environmental concern. About 7.2 percent of our sample identifies with the Pachakutik (opposition) party. We also include a variable that measures trust in the national indigenous movement organization (CONAIE). Like the Pachakutik party, the indigenous movement has been critical of the government, and in doing so, has adopted a pro-environment stance against state extractivism (Becker 2012). This variable is coded 0 (no trust) to 3 (high trust), and the mean in the sample is 1.1 (between little and some trust in the movement).

Finally, in Ecuador's presidential system, the president—Rafael Correa—and his party—Alianza PAIS—were the biggest promoters of using oil and mineral wealth to develop Ecuador. We include a variable that measures whether an individual identifies with the PAIS party (1 if so, 0 otherwise), and about 9.6 percent of the sample does. We would expect affiliation with the PAIS party to decrease an individual's likelihood to express concern for the environment, following Correa's priority for extraction-led development.[5]

We argue that a respondent's proximity and experience with extraction should be among the most important factors influencing their attitudes toward the environment versus development. We therefore developed three measures that code for proximity to extraction. The first, based on the Ecuadorian government's list of mining projects and the map of their locations (Agencia de Regulación y Control Minero, ARCOM 2012) assigned a value of 1 if the respondent's locality is within about 30 kilometers of an active mine, and 0 if not. About 17.8 percent of our respondents lived in localities where mining occurs. Two other variables were used to code whether the respondent's locality was within about 30 kilometers of an area where oil is actively being extracted or not, and whether, if oil is not yet being extracted, the area is in an oil block that the Ecuadorian government was considering for concession to an oil company. The *History of Oil Extraction* variable is coded a 1 for areas where oil is being actively extracted, while the *Oil Debate* variable is coded a 1 if the locality is part of an oil block under consideration by the government. About 6.5 percent of our sample lives in areas

---

5. Ecuador has a weakly institutionalized party system, and party identification is correspondingly low. The majority of respondents in our sample (77.7 percent) claimed they did not identify with any political party. The PAIS governing party and the opposition Pachakutik party—as the most established parties—have the highest percentages of party identifiers in the sample.

of active oil extraction, while about 14.9 percent of our sample lives in areas where oil extraction is under debate. The information was taken from government oil block maps given by the Ecuadorian Secretary of Hydrocarbons (Secretaría de Hidrocarburos del Ecuador, SHE n.d.). Please see Figure 2.1.

To assess our final hypothesis, we include a variable that measures the extent to which a respondent agrees that *Extraction Benefits Ecuador*, coded 0 if the respondent disagrees that allowing access to land to extract resources benefits Ecuador; 1 if they believe that maybe it benefits Ecuador, or that it depends; and 2 if they agree that allowing businesses access to land to extract resources benefits Ecuador. Around 35.7 percent of our sample agreed with this statement, 49.4 percent disagreed, and 14.8 percent said maybe/it depends. We expect that individuals who believe extraction has benefits will be no more or less likely to express concern over the environment, given the divisive nature of extraction in Ecuador.

Our survey included a series of questions that also allow us to measure the extent to which individuals share in the perspective of indigenous cosmovisions. One question—*Indigenous Closer to Nature*—asks whether respondents agree that the indigenous are more connected with Mother Earth than non-indigenous (1 if agree, 0 otherwise). We also asked how much respondents agree with the idea that *Mother Earth Has Rights*. About 80.1 percent of our sample said that they agree (coded 1), while the remaining 19.8 percent said that they either did not agree or that it depends (coded 0). We also controlled for whether an individual self-identified as indigenous (1 if yes, 0 otherwise). About 40.2 percent of our sample self-identified as indigenous.

We also include control variables that the literature identifies as having a potential effect on concern for the environment. We control for *Media Access* (coded as 1 for never having access to any media outlet, and 5 as daily access to media outlets) and *Popular Knowledge* (an index created by asking respondents if they have ever heard of a list of fourteen different phenomena prevalent in the media). Average media access is 4.2, and popular knowledge ranges from 16.8 percent familiarity (respondents who had heard of the 169th Convention of the International Labor Organization) to 81.5 percent familiarity (respondents who had heard of the Confederation of Indigenous Nationalities of Ecuador, CONAIE). We controlled for *Religiosity* by asking how important it is to an individual's life (1 is not at all, 4 is very important, with the sample mean being 3.5). We also controlled for several demographic factors, such *Education* (ordinal variable, where 1 is no education and 8 is postgraduate education, with mean of 4.2, where a 4 corresponds to incomplete secondary education) and *Age* (continuous variable ranging from 16 to 85, mean of 37.5). The *Income* variable is an ordinal variable that indicates an individual's self-reported monthly income level

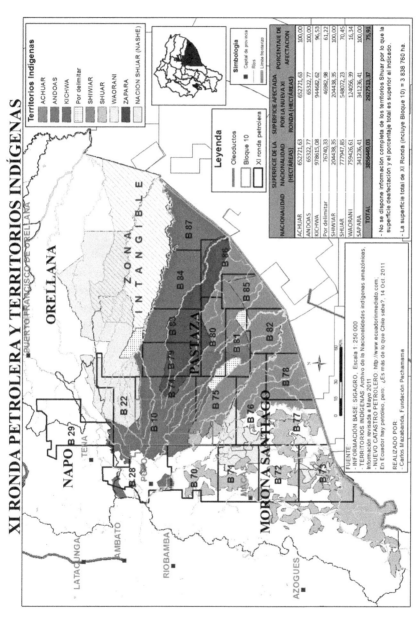

Figure 2.1 Map of Oil Blocks and Indigenous Territories in the Ecuadorian Amazon. Graphic provided by Carlos Mazabanda of Amazon Watch-Ecuador

(0 represents no income, 5 represents \$301 to \$500, and 10 represents an income of over \$2,000 per month, with a mean of 4.67 indicating that our average respondent has a monthly income between \$200 and \$500). According to classic post-materialist theory, income should have a positive effect on concern for the environment, because more affluent individuals can "afford" to care about the environment.

ANALYSIS AND RESULTS

To analyze the relationship between our multi-level independent variables and our ordinal dependent variable, we used an ordered logit model with standard errors clustered at the level of the *parroquia* in Ecuador. We cluster our standard errors at this level because that is where the extraction variables are measured, and thus the observations at that level are not independent. There are several trends that emerge from our analysis, presented in Table 2.2, which we highlight here.

First, only two of the correlates that we use to measure post-materialism are found to be significant determinants in prioritizing the environment over development. This is true for measures of post-materialist values (such as human rights and modernity) as well as for more objective measures of post-materialist lifestyles (such as professional occupations, social media usage, and donating to ecological organizations). Not surprisingly, the one measure that does have a positive relationship with environmental concern is a belief in climate change. As we will discuss further, worry over climate change as an indicator of perceptions of vulnerability is also a powerful predictor of environmental concern. By contrast, prioritizing democracy over development—a key value-based question included as a post-materialist measure on the World Values Survey—has a counterintuitive negative relationship with environmental concern, the opposite of what post-materialism would predict. Based on these findings, we feel confident rejecting the idea that post-materialism plays a role in shaping the prioritization of the environment over development in Ecuador.

Furthermore, we find that integration into international networks is a significant factor in determining the prioritization of the environment. Individuals who had experience with international foundations and international scientists were significantly more likely to express concern for the environment. As we describe later in this chapter and in others, communities that were concerned with environmental degradation often had intimate contact with international organizations that reinforced environmental concern in a multitude of ways.

Table 2.2 FACTORS THAT DETERMINE CONCERN FOR THE ENVIRONMENT

Post-Materialism

Human Rights	−0.054
	(0.2544)
Promote Modernity	0.128
	(0.118)
Climate Change	0.614**
	(0.310)
Indigenous Leader	0.156
	(0.116)
Democracy vs. Development	−0.335***
	(0.120)
Social Media	0.075
	(0.116)
Professional	0.231
	(0.238)
Eco Donation	−0.277
	(0.284)

International Networks

International Networks	0.107**
	(0.046)

Vulnerability

Rain/River Water Source	0.128
	(0.180)
Water Scarcity	0.529*
	(0.291)
Ecotourism	0.397**
	(0.175)
Climate Change Concern	0.600***
	(0.085)

Political Orientations

Pachakutik Affiliate	0.623***
	(0.169)
Trust in Indigenous Movement	0.011
	(0.072)
PAIS Affiliate	−0.076
	(0.228)

Extraction

Mining	0.199
	(0.167)
History of Oil Extraction	−2.490***
	(0.386)
Oil Debate	0.663***
	(0.192)

(*continued*)

Table 2.2   CONTINUED

Extraction Benefits Ecuador	−0.040
	(0.063)
Cosmovision	
Indigenous Closer to Nature	0.258*
	(0.138)
Mother Earth Has Rights	0.360**
	(0.152)
Indigenous ID	−0.205
	(0.2066)
Controls	
Media Access	−0.017
	(0.073)
Religiosity	−0.066
	(0.078)
Knowledge Index	0.070**
	(0.036)
Education	0.093
	(0.057)
Income	−0.072
	(0.051)
Cut 1	−1.443*
	(0.842)
Cut 2	2.203***
	(0.686)
Cut 3	4.188***
	(0.682)
Cut 4	5.803***
	(0.710)
N	1,441

*$p < 0.1$; ** $p < 0.05$; *** $p < 0.01$
Note: The dependent variable is coded a 0 if the environment is not at all a concern compared to other problems, 1 the environment is less of a concern than some problems, 2 if it is more of a concern than some other problems, 3 more than a majority of the problems, and 4 the environment is more worrisome than any other problem.

Ultimately, however, our analysis highlights the relevance of the two key variables we emphasize through this book: vulnerability and extraction. Additionally, our analysis also demonstrates that conventional economic structural explanations—such as affluence or post-materialism—do not predict environmental concern. The individuals who are most vulnerable to environmental damage are indeed likely to express the greatest concern over the environment. Among the measures of vulnerability, water scarcity and ecotourism are both factors that make a respondent more likely to worry about the environment. Using our model results to estimate predicted probabilities, and holding all other variables at their means, we find that respondents with scarce access to water are 7 percent more likely to express the greatest level of concern for the environment than no concern for the environment. By comparison, respondents with regular access to water are only 3 percent more likely to express the greatest level of concern for the environment than no concern for the environment. This means that respondents with scarce access to water are more than twice as likely to express the greatest level of concern for the environment than are respondents with regular access to water, demonstrating the powerful influence that vulnerability has on respondents' prioritization of the environment. That change in likelihood is similar for respondents who are directly impacted by ecotourism: respondents who directly benefit from ecotourism are about twice as likely to express high levels of environmental concern than are those who do not benefit from ecotourism.

Not only are objective measures of vulnerability relevant predictors of environmental concern, but *perception* of vulnerability is also significant. Recall that we measured perceptions of vulnerability by asking respondents how worried they are about climate change. Again using predictions derived from our model, respondents who were very worried about climate change had a 0 percent probability of stating that the environment was of no concern to them and an 8 percent probability of stating that the environment is more worrisome than any other problem. Contrast those predictions with respondents who are not at all worried about climate change, and had an 8 percent probability of stating that the environment is not at all a concern, and a 1 percent probability of stating that the environment is the greatest concern. Respondents concerned about climate change were eight times more likely to prioritize the environment than those not worried at all about the climate—a powerful distinction. Clearly, respondents' perceptions of their vulnerability to climate change strongly shaped the level of concern that they expressed for the environment.

Furthermore, orientations toward the environment are also clearly influenced by an individual's experience with extraction—particularly oil extraction. In fact, living near an active mining operation was not a significant determinant of environmental concern in this analysis. Mining is still relatively new and has received much interest from international NGOs that have educated individuals about the adverse effects of mining operations where it is taking place. Instead, living in a community where oil is being debated is a robust predictor of concern for the environment. As with other forms of vulnerability, respondents living in an area where extraction is being considered were more than twice as likely to express the highest level of concern for the environment than were respondents who were not living in such an area, based on predictions from our models. As we elaborate in further chapters, oil negotiations can have a very powerful impact on the affected communities, and not just because they will experience the environmental impact of extraction. Indeed, communities can become politically divided by the negotiation process itself. The results of this analysis suggest that negotiating with the government can even determine the extent to which individuals prioritize the environment overall.

By contrast, a history of oil extraction has a *negative* relationship with environmental concern. This is perhaps one of the most interesting findings of our analysis, and coincides with the experience specific to Ecuador. Oil extraction that is already underway for some areas began decades in the past and has left the environment already devastated. In areas with a history of oil extraction, and where the environment is already quite degraded, individuals are much less likely to express concern over the environment. Individuals who live in localities with a history of oil have a minuscule 0.51 percent probability of being concerned about the environment over any other problem, and instead have a 12.31 percent likelihood of being not at all concerned about the environment. This powerful finding is something that we hope to examine in more detail in future research.

Our final set of independent variables measures the effects that beliefs consistent with indigenous cosmovision have on attitudes toward the environment versus development. Two variables have significant positive effects on prioritizing the environment: a belief that the indigenous are closer to nature, and a belief that Mother Nature has rights. Respondents who believe that Mother Nature has rights have a 2 percent greater likelihood in prioritizing the environment over those who do not believe that Mother Nature has rights. Respondents who believe that the indigenous are closer to nature are only slightly more likely to express the highest level of concern for the environment than those who do not believe the indigenous are closer to nature, with a 5 percent and 4 percent probability respectively, holding all other variables at their means. Together, these variables give credence to the idea that indigenous cosmovision is consistent with valuing the environment over other priorities.

We do not, however, find that the self-identification as indigenous has a significant relationship with environmental concern. This further validates the central claim of this book about the need to move beyond multiculturalism to a perspective of polycentric pluralism. Finally, only one of our control variables—*Popular Knowledge*—is significant. The effect of this variable is positive, suggesting that more knowledgeable individuals are also more likely to express higher levels of concern for the environment.

QUALITATIVE SUPPORT FOR RESULTS: COMMUNITY RESPONSES TO PETRO-STATE DEMANDS

More than one hundred open-ended interviews at over a dozen localities throughout Ecuador between June 2014 and July 2017 strongly confirmed these statistical findings. Not only was the post-materialist argument disconfirmed by the fact that vulnerable populations demonstrated stronger views on the environment than more affluent respondents, but we also found that those in rural communities (indigenous groups and *campesinos*) whose livelihoods depended on the environment and were thus more vulnerable to its shifts appeared equally concerned. For example, a Sápara leader said, "[f]or us there is no capitalism. Everything is collectivism. Anyone can harvest what they want, but the land belongs to everyone" (Ushigua interview). He further added that money was not important to his people. Rather, what mattered was "living well with the richness of the earth." Indeed, to Ushigua, having lots of money and living in harmony with the environment were almost incompatible. The mayor of Puyo, de la Torre, argued similarly that what matters is development in harmony with nature, rather than monetary wealth, adding that "development cannot be measured by meters of freeways built . . . It is when one has a way to get up and work in something useful that fills the basic needs of his/her children" (de la Torre interview). In this way, the environment forms an integral part of citizen livelihoods, and is valued for the role that it plays in meeting the most basic needs of rural, indigenous, and impoverished citizens. In the minds of these citizens, development is not beneficial if it also harms the environment.

The rural respondents surveyed were especially vocal in relating their material (and spiritual) outlooks to their attitudes toward the environment. According to one Santa Isabel activist, "Ecology has become fashionable . . . but . . . the underlying problem is inequality and we need to focus on that" (Arpe interview). Some, like a federal government official in Sucumbios, argue that oil and mineral extraction is what will diminish vulnerability to poverty and the elements, even if it does carry some inevitable environmental costs. "There is social remediation," he said (Sallo interview). "Petroleum extraction helps us attend to peoples' basic needs." That sentiment was echoed by dozens of interviewees—that environmental exposure to oil drilling may make people vulnerable in some ways, but that it does help them meet their basic needs. This argument is highly controversial, however, and scores of interviewees also argued for restricting extractivism, but based on perceived detriments of pollution to the economy of poor rural residents more than on any innate post-materialist position in favor of the environment.

In the Amazon region, interviewees were much more divided regarding their views of the environment, and those living near the already-exploited northern oil fields had much more sanguine views. Further to the north, the focus was more on mitigating environmental damage already done, and interviewees seemed to place a higher priority on more tangible and immediate needs when compared to the environment. For example, the Waorani indigenous group, centered in Lago Agrio where Texaco/Chevron left hundreds of open pits of oil that drain directly into the water supply, strongly criticized the central government's failure to attend to environmental degradation, but were divided over whether to further explore and drill for oil. Indeed, the national president and vice president of this group openly disagreed in a joint interview over whether they should allow the national or provincial governments to extract more oil from Waorani land (Cahauigia and Moi interviews), although others, like the Andwa peoples, said they would accept reasonable compensation for oil drilling on their lands (Proaño interview).

Further south in Coca and Puyo, where oil concessions are more recent, and in some cases still being negotiated, Kichwa, Shuar, and Waorani leaders conveyed ambivalence about whether to cooperate with further oil extraction efforts (Ampush, Grefa, Omentoque interviews). In the pristine rainforest areas of the far south (near Macas), Achuar and Shuar leaders say they are completely against oil drilling and have more strongly articulated pro-environmental attitudes (Callera, Paes, Tibi, Wachapa Atsau interviews). The geographic relativity of community positions was summarized by a Sápara leader near Lago Agrio: "Those whose lands have been polluted are in favor (of more extraction). They live in that reality. Those who are opposed are those of us whose lands have not yet been contaminated, and above all, those of us who do not live near a paved highway" (Ushigua interview).

This distinction in attitudes toward the environment, based on individuals' locations vis-à-vis Ecuador's extractive frontier (the northern, drilled lands, the central drilling-contested lands, and the southern "yet undrilled" lands) rather than on indigenous identities, is crucial to our argument. Recall that the central claims of this book are: first, that peoples' attitudes regarding saving the environment vary according to their perceived vulnerability rather than with regard to class or ethnic iden-tity; and second, that groups should be encouraged to aggregate based on their interests—here represented by whether an area has been drilled or not—rather than on ethnic, indigenous lines. The fact that attitudes follow this "extractive frontier" pattern rather than an ethnic one confirms both arguments. Having demonstrated this pattern in the central analysis above, we offer illustrative examples below, and then offer different evi-dence of these claims in the chapters to come.

Indeed, having demonstrated statistically that rational explanations—such as location along the extractive frontier—are more important to Ecuadorians than post-material "values-based" arguments for their valu-ation of environment versus development, we have also offered at least an introduction to the public debates—revealed extensively to us in interviews—which strongly corroborate our causal claims. In the concluding section of this chapter, we briefly discuss Ecuadorian intellectuals' efforts to create a materialist argument, but on a different premise from that of Inglehart and his colleagues. As discussed in chapter 1, the formula-tion of a "good living" philosophy (referred to most often by its Kichwa name, *sumak kawsay*, and in Spanish *buen vivir*) seeks to better define a pro-environmental worldview that also involves elements of vulnerability and development (to diminish vulnerability). This opens up the subject of chapter 3, on mobilizations relating to the rights of prior consultation (where indigenous communities get to approve extractive projects before these are allowed), and chapter 5, where we directly compare respondent attitudes about this indigenous worldview with respondent attitudes about Western science, regarding how people perceive climate change. It also offers explanation, presented in chapter 4, of the types of justifications given by indigenous leaders in negotiating terms of oil and mineral extrac-tion and, in less common cases, decisions to "leave the oil [and minerals] in the soil."

CONCLUSIONS: *SUMAK KAWSAY*, INDIGENOUS SYNCRETISM, AND VULNERABILITY

Over the last decade, a movement to syncretize a strong position on envi-ronmental rights has emerged in Ecuador and elsewhere in the Andes, based loosely on Kichwa worldviews. A few of the movement's features will be briefly delineated here, as they address the need for a new non-materialist representation of environmental issues within worldviews of the poor, the rural, and those vulnerable to environmental catastrophes and human development setbacks. Giving better framing to the issue than what is possible through survey responses, dozens of interviewees offered perspectives on the meaning of *sumak kawsay*, which relate to the claims we articulate above. We wish to offer a composite of how indigenous respondents crafted their own articulation of an anti-materialist worldview revolving around environmental issues, which strongly contradicts post-materialism and reaffirms vulnerability theory. We briefly present the autarkic version, focused entirely on inward-looking dynamics, but then mention a more internationalist variant. Note that it is presented as an indigenous worldview, but is compatible with that of other environmentalists, especially those living in environmentally vulnerable circumstances. Normatively speaking, the international variant holds the greatest hope for the protagonism of indigenous peoples in helping resolve environmental degradation in their lands, which are among the most biologically varied, resource rich, and unspoiled lands remaining in the world.

The purist view holds that *sumak kawsay* is based on ancestral views; people find their place in nature, and this generates personal harmony and well-being in relation to other natural living entities in the forest, and with Mother Earth (*Pacha Mama*) as a whole. As tersely summarized: "*Buen vivir* is to live with our own riches, the waterfalls, nature, and [ancestral] knowledge. Any development has to be consistent with these times" (Tibi interview). Outsider involvement interferes with the direct bond between humans and nature. The Western introduction of money, carcinogens in food, and environmental degradation have caused the links between human beings, the forest, and nature more broadly, to uncouple. "Growing up with chemicals in your body is not good," said one *sumak kawsay* adherent. "I grew up without pain or sickness, but everything is changing . . . now we have to buy everything with money . . . we have to raise only corn and then sell it on the market" (Chimbo interview).

Some advocate for a modernizing of *sumak kawsay* to allow Ecuadorians to integrate with the outside world. For example, one indigenous government official argued that: "We have to meld traditional health practices with Western ones, just as in justice there is a uniting of indigenous and state forms of law. However, the ancestral knowledge does not have human talent [to give it full expression]. We need to develop that talent" (Tumink interview). Others accuse *sumak kawsay* practitioners of using that philosophy as an excuse to undermine deals with the state and extractive companies that would give poor communities clinics and schools, even at the expense of an ethereal link between people and their natural environment. Those arguing that indigenous communities accept contracts for oil extraction on their lands view *buen vivir* in more conventional development terms: "Here you have to buy [things] and if you don't have money, you die of hunger. That is poverty. . . *Buen vivir* means to have nutrition, health, and live in a collaboration between man and nature" (Santi interview).

While our analysis of survey results could not offer nuanced casual explanations, we have found that it identified key problems in prior interpretations of interest in environmental issues. Field research showed that these attitudes are outward manifestations of values formed in relation to critical and even acerbic debates in many parts of Ecuador (and in the Andean region more broadly), relating to the role of the state in using extraction as a development tool as it simultaneously tries to protect the nation's people living in or near its fragile and unique ecosystems. The state propels economic growth, and, more importantly, a strong boom in public spending, by staking the nation's public spending on oil royalties and those that can be derived from extracting other resources, like hydroelectric power and gold and copper mining. The oil frontier in Ecuador, moving south and east from the heavily damaged area contaminated in the past by egregious oil spills from wells run by Texaco/Chevron and the Ecuadorian state into virgin rainforests, polarizes citizen attitudes strongly as it extends, giving even greater credence to the vulnerability explanation for their positions.

Overall, our analysis of individual-level survey data discounts the relevance of post-materialism as a source of prioritizing the environment in developing countries like Ecuador. Furthermore, it illustrates the importance of the fierce conflict between development and environmentalism missing from developed country debates. That conflict in Ecuador—as well as in other Andean nations mentioned—is between citizens seeking to use the environment as a stepping-stone out of poverty, and environmentalists seeking to preserve nature. The survey identified key problems in prior interpretations of interest in environmental issues—namely, the tension between economic development and the vulnerability to environmental threats, including extraction. Ultimately, we find that individuals in Ecuador prioritize the environment when they are objectively vulnerable to environmental damage and live in areas where oil concessions are being debated. Furthermore, we find that individuals living in areas where oil extraction has already occurred are ambivalent toward the environment, as it has lost not only its economic but its spiritual value as well.

This debate occurs not only in many parts of Ecuador, but across the Andean region of Latin America more broadly, and Correa's "populist extractivism" was not dissimilar to that of Morales in Bolivia, or models adopted in Colombia, Peru, and Venezuela. Populists like Correa sought to implement new social programs funded directly by the very extraction that created the damage. The state propels economic growth by staking the nation's public spending on oil royalties. The oil frontier in Ecuador, moving south and east from the heavily damaged area contaminated by the infamous Texaco (now Chevron) oil spills and then into virgin rainforests, polarizes citizen attitudes as it extends, giving even greater credence to the ambivalence people feel, particularly when they live in the areas of extraction.

Part of Ecuador's extractivism debate seems to be driven by diverse interpretations of *sumak kawsay/buen vivir* as a development approach. Though President Correa claimed to desire a developmental approach in harmony with ecological cycles and which promoted solidarity and dignity among living things, he instead prioritized extraction, perpetuating the dichotomy between development and the environment, "a false dilemma posed by Western ideals" (Kauffman 2016, chapter 8, 5). For example, the Ecuadorian state in December 2015 amended the constitution to remove the ability of local communities to regulate extraction, doubling down on the populist "extractive development" side. In interviews, many indigenous leaders openly expressed consternation over Correa's abuse of the *sumak kawsay* concept (Tibán interview 2014) and even went so far as to create alternative Spanish terminology (*vivir bien* instead of Correa's *buen vivir*) to present a more mainstream version of the indigenous belief of development in harmony with nature (Cueva interview 2014). Correa's successor, President Lenin Moreno, elected on Correa's Alianza PAIS label, is less obvious in his abuse of *sumak kawsay.* One of his first moves as president was to abolish the Ministry of *Buen Vivir,* created under Correa to give the appearance that harmony with nature was important (*El Universo*, May 17, 2017). However, the ministry had come under harsh criticism for lacking a clear mission and for failing to actually protect "harmonious living" in Ecuador.

Moreno's environmental policies, while less pronounced than Correa's, seem to veer back to Correa's earlier and more impassioned years of support for the environment. Moreno environmental adviser Esteban Falconi, agreeing that much of Correa's politics were "demagoguery," said that the government is trying to enforce the laws in place, where they were often ignored after their creation early in the Correa administration. "A lot of environmental principles have been dead letter [unimplemented] because there was no national will," Falconi said (interview). "Our intention is to be respectful of human rights and makes sure new laws are consistent with these principles and with the constitution." The contradiction between Correa's early environmental advocacy and protection of indigenous stewardship, and his later deregulation of mining and oil and support for economic development at the expense of environmental protection, is quite stark. The Moreno administration seems to recognize these contradictions and is working to resolve them in favor of indigenous rights and the environment.

Having demonstrated statistically that vulnerability and location along the extractive frontier are more important to Ecuadorians than socioeconomics for their environmental concerns during the height of the Correa administration in 2014, we have also offered at least an introduction to the community-level debates that corroborate our causal claims. Our interviews also reinforced relationships found in Peru (Ponce and McClintock 2014; Arce 2014) and Bolivia (Mähler and Pierskalla 2015) that citizens in extractive areas experience conflicts not just over extraction itself, but over allocation of the riches from that extraction. Chapters 3 and 4 directly explore those conflicts with greater precision. For now, we conclude with the observation that in Ecuador and Peru, and the other Andean economies, extraction provides the single biggest source of tax revenue and thus public spending; therefore the existence of such conflicts is not surprising. Extractive-area residents seem to perceive they are withstanding environmental damage to generate national social spending, without being compensated at a differential rate for the damages they must tolerate. Consistent with these statistical analyses of our survey, Ecuador's community leaders affirmed the strong effect that living near extraction has on environmental concern. Indeed, community leaders across Ecuador expressed such concern in response to President Correa's prioritization of mining. For example, in the Íntag valley, a rare cloud forest in the heart of Ecuador's mineral-rich Andean region, citizens have mobilized to prevent mining explorations. As summarized by community leader José Cueva, mining is "on the environmental side, disastrous because of the contamination of the water, of the air . . . but there is also a grave social impact, and the worst of all would be the relocation of four communities and almost 200 families . . . that would obviously lose their way of life" (Cueva interview 2014).

Clearly, for these communities, President Correa was not adhering to a model of democratic development, nor standing by the commitment to developing in harmony with nature (*sumak kawsay*). President Moreno may do a better job of protecting environmental rights. In February 2018, Moreno held a popular referendum that contained two questions related to restricting extraction in Ecuador: Question 5, which asked about amending the Ecuadorian Constitution to prohibit all phases of mining in protected areas and urban centers; and Question 7, which asked about reducing the area of oil extraction in Yasuní National Park (CNE

2018).[6] Although both measures overwhelmingly passed with nearly 70 percent of the vote (Tegel 2018), environmental activists remain skeptical of Moreno's administration. As Cueva responded, "It's only a sedative and it's not going to solve the problem of mining. The government is conscious that there is citizen demand resulting from fear and worry around the topic" (*La Hora* 2018). In reality, according to Cueva, Moreno's administration has sped up granting mining concessions, registering more than 90,000 hectares in Íntag alone (*La Hora* 2018). Clearly, in response to extraction, concern for the environment as well as for individual livelihoods is very strong.

Reconciling respondents' personal needs to address vulnerability to environmental changes—which could worsen poverty—with efforts to insert their communities into regional, national, and global debates about resource extraction and climate change and the equities related to these, may be the attitude-defining debate of the next decade in resource-rich developing nations in the Andes. Even the poorest and most remote Ecuadorians have positions on these issues, and their perceptions of the urgency of these matters may offer even further evidence of the need to bring vulnerability theory into political science.

Generalizing from our findings, it would seem that a disconnect exists between post-materialist values and the self-interest evinced by citizens in a developing country on the "front lines" of environmental degradation. Rather than prioritizing the environment because they can "afford" to, as Inglehart (1990; 1995) and others suggest, we find that individuals in developing countries like Ecuador prioritize the environment when they cannot afford to ignore the impact that environmental damage has on their livelihoods and their communities. In Ecuador, this is manifested through several controversies, such as rainforest pollution from oil spills, and the pitfalls of strip mining in the country's mountainous Andean region, where scarring of the land occurs and water is scarce even before the mining companies arrive. And as our statistical results demonstrate, individuals living where oil has already been extracted are less likely to agree that the environment should be protected, making environmental preservation even more important. Meanwhile, in areas where oil is debated, individuals are more likely than others to advocate for the environment, indicating the

6. Question 5: "¿Está usted de acuerdo con enmendar la Constitución de la República del Ecuador para que se prohíba la minería metálica en todas sus etapas, en áreas protegidas, en zonas intangibles, y centros urbanos, según el Anexo 5?" and Question 7: "¿Está usted de acuerdo en incrementar la zona intangible al menos 50.000 hectáreas y reducir el área de explotación petrolera autorizada por la Asamblea Nacional en el Parque Nacional Yasuní de 1.030 hectáreas a 300 hectáreas?"

importance that vulnerability to extraction has on concern for the environment overall.

Observation of the United Nations Framework Convention on Climate Change 2014 meeting in Peru revealed that the developing world is a macrocosm of the Ecuadorian people, as their positions regarding climate change policy are dictated in large part on how vulnerable they are to environmental changes exogenous to their national spheres of influence, where they are located on the carbon emissions "frontier," and what domestic actors have to gain or lose from engaging in the international debate.[7] Carbon emissions are not tangible, to be sure, but international efforts like the United Nations Collaborative Programme on Reducing Emissions from Deforestation and Forest Degradation in Developing Countries (REDD+) convert the abstract need to reduce emissions into concrete manifestations, like rainforest preserves, which directly affect resident livelihoods. Changes in the political importance of environmental issues are not just changes in esoteric values, but stem from peoples' rational dependence on the environment for day-to-day survival and the extent to which they feel that environmental change may be outside their direct control.

7. Eisenstadt observed the Lima, Peru, meeting from December 8 through 13, 2014.

cᴠᴐ

Does Prior Consultation Diminish Extractive Conflict or Channel It to New Venues?

Evidence From Ecuador and the Andes

L ocal communities around the world have mobilized to prevent mining and oil extraction on their lands, coming into conflict with both corporations and governments that seek to benefit from a globalized economy dependent upon mineral resources. Nearly half of the 346 extractive conflicts identified by Özkaynak et al. (2015, 12) worldwide between 2006 and 2013 were in Latin America, with 2009 Bagua, Peru, as an exemplar resulting in dozens of mortal conflicts. But not all conflicts result in physical violence. Lago Agrio, Ecuador, the site of oil spills from early drilling by Texaco/Chevron, represents the most heavily litigated conflict in the hemisphere for its widespread property damage and public health implications.[1] Worldwide, the primary means of reducing extractive conflict is the mechanism of "free, prior, and informed consent" (FPIC), which requires the organization of plebiscites or votes on whether communities should allow extractive projects in their communities. The process, mandated under International Labor Organization (ILO) Convention 169 (signed in the early 1990s), requires such approval in indigenous

---

1. Several studies point to dramatic adverse effects of oilfield proximity on public health in the area, such as Hurtig and San Sebastián (2002); San Sebastián and Hurtig (2004); and San Sebastián, Armstrong, and Stephens (2004).

communities, and national laws require this more broadly in some countries. Known in Latin America as *consulta previa* (CP), or prior consultation, dozens of such votes have been convened under the assumption that, as with environmental impact hearings in the United States and other countries, indigenous land stewards/owners (depending on particular national laws) will get access to all information and projections about revenue from extractive projects, adverse effects of drilling and mining, and then deliberate and decide—through a plebiscite or other voting—whether they want to accept proposed extractive projects, and if so, under what terms.

An exemplar of a practice grounded in multiculturalism, prior consultation has gained prestige as an increasingly mandatory process around the world to give indigenous communities choice in whether to allow natural resource extraction on their lands. Since the ILO approved the law of prior consultation with reference to indigenous communities, the norm of FPIC has become standard (Laplante and Spears 2008; McGee 2009; Sánchez Botero 2010). In Latin America, the practice has become commonplace as a sort of environmental impact hearing prior to the entrance of oil and mining companies into rural communities, especially in indigenous areas (First Peoples Worldwide 2013; Organization of American States 2009). Peru legally mandated prior consultation after the 2009 Bagua Massacre, while Ecuador spelled out prior consultation requirements in Article 57 of the 2008 Constitution, although these have not been consistently implemented. It is practiced in Peru (in oil and gas drilling, but not in mining), in Bolivia (in natural gas pipeline construction but not mineral extraction), in Mexico (only since 2014), and infrequently in Ecuador (Eisenstadt and Torres 2016).[2]

However, implementation has been marred by inconsistent application in much of Latin America (see, for example, Boanada Fuchs 2014 on Brazil and Schilling-Vacaflor 2014 on Bolivia). As a result of this inconsistency,

2. Only in Bolivia have consultations—required for natural gas extraction—widely occurred. And even there, the most important prior consultation, over the construction of a paved highway through the TIPNIS-area protected forest, was disregarded by the national government, which announced plans to proceed with construction (even though that construction has not yet started). Bolivia is a strong case in that conflict began earlier and extensive prior consultations have occurred over the last few years, but these have been widely studied in the secondary literature using the group as the level of analysis for protest (Perreault 2006; Spronk and Webber 2007; Schilling-Vacaflor 2014; Mähler and Pierskalla 2015). We seek to study the individual as the unit of analysis for the first time, and those countries with greater variation in the conduct of such consultations (Ecuador and Peru). We also will compare group-level protest data from these two countries with data from Bolivia and the rest of the Latin American cases.

the Kichwa community of Sarayaku in Ecuador won a US $1.8 million law-suit because they were not consulted prior to the initiation of oil drilling on communal lands a decade ago. The Inter-American Court of Human Rights mandated prior consultation in their Sarayaku decision, but as we elaborate below, Ecuador has yet to fully comply with this mandate. Overall, prior consultation has only been implemented in a minority of Latin American states, and even those countries exhibit wide variation in citizen knowledge and expectations regarding this international legal norm (Eisenstadt and Torres 2016).[3]

If FPIC is an international norm, why has its implementation been so inconsistent? Furthermore, why has *consulta previa* failed to resolve conflicts surrounding extraction? We argue that the process of FPIC has become politicized and is therefore implemented only in areas that are strategically relevant for extractive industries. Rather than serving as a genuine referendum over whether communities want to allow extractive projects, "consultations" have morphed into bargaining tables where indigenous communities negotiate multimillion dollar settlements in exchange for granting permissions to use indigenous lands for extraction, which is essentially a foregone conclusion. In each of the scores of cases studied where prior consultation occurs, permission is ultimately granted to extractive industries—but at a price. In cases where communities really do not want to allow extraction, governments never allow the prior consultation process to occur in the first place. After briefly presenting the history of prior consultation and its role in seeking to diminish some of the conflicts associated with extractive projects, we present evidence from our public opinion survey in Ecuador demonstrating that proximity to extractive projects and indigenous identity matter more for agreeing with the enforcement of prior consultations than do other factors like post-material predisposition and international networks. After discussing these findings, we show that actual prior consultation enforcement on the ground nearly always results in extractivism—and with indigenous community approval.

As we argued in chapters 1 and 2, contrary to post-materialist views, Ecuador's citizens, and especially those on the front lines of environmental

3. A possible exception is Colombia, where prior consultations have been upheld by the national constitutional court such as in *Critianía Indigenous Community vs. Solarte* in 1992, *Yanacona Villamaría de Mocoa Indigenous Community vs. Municipality of Mocoa* (Putumayo) in 2005, and the *Afro-Colombian Community of Barú vs. Sociedad Portuaria Puerto Bahía S.A.* in 2010, among others. However, we do not more extensively discuss the Colombian case, agreeing with Van Cott (2003) that indigenous rights have been upheld more vigorously there precisely because the small indigenous population does not threaten national elites.

change, have attitudes strongly shaped by their perceptions of vulnerability to environmental degradation and change. Building on those two chapters, this chapter further demonstrates the importance of vulnerability in practical matters like the conduct of prior consultations by analyzing public opinion while illustrating the connection between attitudes and practice with empirical cases. We argue that these conflicts around extraction have emerged because prior consultation has become a political tool for petro-states such as Ecuador's that pursue extractive populism to maintain power. As such, the factors that influence public support for prior consultation are largely political, and individuals who hope to genuinely protect the environment are less supportive of the process. However, because indigenous groups and the indigenous political party—Pachakutik—have hung their hopes on the use of prior consultation to provide them with a place at the bargaining table, we expect those groups to continue to support the binding nature of prior consultation. Using public opinion data as well as case studies, this chapter documents citizen support for prior consultation in Ecuador. Upon showing that this multicultural policy has become a tool of extractive governments, we consider reforms to the institution being considered in Ecuador and beyond.

THE POLITICS OF PRIOR CONSULTATION IN LATIN AMERICA'S EXTRACTIVE POPULIST SYSTEMS

In Latin America's most deadly extractive conflict to date, the promise of prior consultation and its procedural assurances contributed to the deaths of more than thirty people in Peru in 2009. Then in 2011 in Bolivia, protesters chanted "We demand . . . the right to consultation and participation" (Schilling-Vacaflor 2013, 208) as they halted construction of a freeway through the middle of Bolivia's Isiboro Sécure National Park and Indigenous Territory (TIPNIS). As of 2018, the freeway project appeared to be moribund. In both Peru and Bolivia, the gap was simply too large between indigenous citizen expectations of what these consultations might achieve—especially when framed against the paucity of other mechanisms for rural participation or representation—and what such consultations actually yield. The act of prior consultation alone does not alleviate conflict, particularly when the decisions made by the indigenous communities are not upheld. At issue are how well-informed citizens are prior to any vote, whether communities deliberate and discuss extractive proposals rather than just approving them, whether the consultations are binding, and what they mean for indigenous—and non-indigenous—citizens in extractive areas as well as other regions of extractive populist nations. In other words, how are the benefits of extraction distributed?

To date, scholars have not addressed this issue, nor have they investigated further the dynamics of prior consultation: whether such institutions for deliberation are open to all citizens or just to indigenous communities, and, in the case of the latter, who qualifies as indigenous. This is not a trivial matter, as defining ethnic indigeneity has been a contentious public policy debate in both Bolivia (Aguilar 2013) and Peru (Marapi 2013). Worldwide, indigenous identity has been correlated with low levels of economic development and human capital (Roberts 1995; International Work Group for Indigenous Affairs 2009), and from a legal standpoint, indigenous communities tend, more than others, to be the ones who hold their lands collectively—not for private sale—without clearly defined borders or titled owners (Colchester and MacKay 2004, 8). However, as the neoliberal reforms of the 1980s and 1990s stripped away state programs in the countryside (and with them the need for corporatist relationships between the state and rural citizens), the non-indigenous rural-subsistence poor were also left without a voice (see, for example, Holzner 2010). The scope of prior consultation, and whether it should be applied only to indigenous communities or expanded to all communities affected by extraction, is thus also a central issue in weighing the effectiveness of FPIC in mediating conflict.

The irony may be that ethnic identity can be malleable. Consistent with Chandra (2012), we accept the constructivist definition of ethnic identities as being empirically evident but fluid, and we assume that such identities can be activated and deactivated. For example, Mähler and Pierskalla (2015) have argued for Latin America's most indigenous nation—Bolivia— that "in the presence of valuable natural resources, usually under control of the national government, local indigenous identity frames become less malleable, due to the fusing of indigenous and territorial identity" (323). Interviewees in Ecuador, such as Coka and Thurber (interviews 2014), mentioned that indigenous leaders utilized their representation of entire groups in part to "venue shop" for how to effectively bring the collective identities they represented into negotiations. When such groups extend their considerations beyond multicultural primordial concerns, they are conveying the polycentrism of their quests for support, whether to drill or not to drill. Indeed, stark divisions along the extractive fault line within the Shuar and the Waorani convey that cultural heritage does not determine peoples' political positions as the theory of multiculturalism would expect.

Questions about the effectiveness of *consulta previa* are particularly relevant in the political landscape of Latin America today. Across the region, democratic states under neoliberalism provided fewer services to citizens, especially remote rural citizens, than the strong authoritarian states that preceded them. Prior systems of inclusionary corporatism, where rural peasants (*campesinos*) were given agricultural inputs and social services in exchange for loyalty and mobilization for ruling parties and governments, have been replaced by a system, perfected in Evo Morales's Bolivia and Rafael Correa's Ecuador, where redistribution toward sustainable development is supported by extractive industry royalties. These royalties may be negotiated directly by governments, such as President Morales's dramatic takeover of international natural gas mining equipment pending renegotiations of more favorable royalties for his public coffers. In some cases, such as Peru, where the Ministry of Energy and Mines directly oversees environmental impact investigations (Laplante and Spears 2008, 100)—much like a fox overseeing a henhouse—there was until recently no national prior consultation law, meaning that polycentric international and domestic NGOs wield tremendous authority as standard-bearers of democratization and social capital formation. Given the new importance of these groups, we conclude by comparing prior consultation to other exercises in deliberative democracy, such as participatory budgeting, noting that such institutions seeking "democracy between elections" need to answer questions of whether such exercises are binding and who is entitled to participate before they can become arenas where conflicts are settled rather than escalated.

Despite all the international attention to prior consultation, only in Bolivia have consultations widely occurred, and that is because they are required for natural gas extraction. And even there, the most important prior consultation denying the construction of a paved highway through the TIPNIS area of protected forest was disregarded by the national government, which announced plans to proceed with construction anyway (though plans for that construction had been halted by court order in 2018). Bolivia is an important case for understanding prior consultation because conflict began earlier and extensive prior consultations have occurred over the last few years. However, these have been widely studied in the secondary literature using groups—rather than individuals—as the level of analysis for protest (Perreault 2006; Spronk and Webber 2007; Schilling-Vacaflor 2014; Mähler and Pierskalla 2015). Many consultations have been heeded, but as argued by Torres (2016), the willingness of communities to even hold prior consultations tends to mean that they are disposed to work with mining companies and provisional and national governments, as those who do not wish to allow extraction protest extensively and even violently, and anti-extractive communities block prior consultations altogether.

Perhaps the most notable prior consultation in the hemisphere resulting in a halt to territorial intervention was over the Belo Horizonte Dam in Brazil, slated to be one of the world's largest hydroelectric plants when it becomes fully operational. In 2011, Brazilian president Dilma Rousseff ordered a cessation of relations with the Inter-American Commission on Human Rights (IACHR), the first instance body whose decisions are appealed to the Inter-American Court of Human Rights. The IACHR recommended that provisional measures be taken to stop dam construction until local indigenous groups could be consulted, as it was estimated that the dam could flood 195 square miles of Amazon rainforest and displace some 50,000 people. Analyst Boanada Fuchs (2014, 19) summarized the prior consultation process executed in the Belo Horizonte case as a "faulty and incomplete process of consultation" that "ended up working as an instrument that facilitated and legitimized the opening up of indigenous territories . . . instead of actually fulfilling the requirements of national and international law in the matter of the protection of indigenous rights." Licensing of another Brazilian hydroelectric dam on the Tapajós River has been stalled also as a result of complaints by indigenous communities, but also, according to officials, because the years of political wrangling required to get Belo Monte under construction is deterring investors in the Tapajós project.

In 2016, the Brazilian government introduced legislation seeking to diminish the scope and authority of prior consultation, which had an important role in national and international rulings that slowed Belo Monte construction and threatens to end subsequent projects. This was never a problem in Ecuador, where prior consultations, while mentioned in the constitution, have never been binding in practice. As in Bolivia, extraction is relied upon to provide populist social programs, and these needs seem to overwhelm claims to progressive environmental policies, even though the Correa administration claimed to speak for nature.

The prior consultation about whether to extract oil in Yasuní-ITT was not accepted by the Ecuadorian government, even though such consultations have legal status in the Ecuadorian constitution because of that document's acceptance of international legal instruments like ILO 169 (Ávila interview 2014). In the sections that follow, we first demonstrate statistically that the factors influencing public support for prior consultation are largely political, and then we show, through case studies, that the government utilizes a political logic to stage prior consultation processes to fulfill procedural obligations and win support for extractive projects, rather than to undertake a deliberative and democratic exercise. For example, in 2014 the Ecuadorian government discredited an extensive national plebiscite on whether to drill for oil in Yasuní and ignored the inability of "uncontacted" peoples to even participate in a prior consultation there. Correa's administration also disregarded demands by citizens in the country's principal mining project to conduct a prior consultation, and in true corporatist tradition, dismantled independent anti-extractive groups and discredited their votes in favor of those by government-assembled pro-extractive groups. The current president, Moreno, has continued the use of prior consultation with the referendum in February 2018 that asked about drilling in Yasuní and the restriction of mining operations in urban centers and protected areas. Although both items passed, it remains to be seen whether these public mandates affect the extractive activities pursued by Moreno's government. However, we commence by studying the factors that influence public support for prior consultation and the assertion that these are largely political. Demonstrating that the public understands the politicized nature of prior consultation may help demonstrate that President Correa's administration used the technique in a political fashion.

To be sure, prior consultation is only one indicator of cooperation between the state and citizens in extractive communities. However, it is the legal instrument generally available to communities offering the best single indication of whether these communities are part of the process of negotiating extractive projects. For those reasons, we expect indigenous citizens and their affiliated party to be largely supportive of the binding nature of prior consultation, because it is the primary mechanism by which these groups are given a voice.

We show that prior consultation is not an instrument that creates a negotiating arena of dynamic polycentric pluralism, but rather a static state-corporatist bargaining table following traditional multiculturalist assumptions that indigenous community leaders can have a say, but only if they are already in agreement with extraction. While prior consultation has gained acceptance as an international legal norm in the United Nations (codified in 2007) and in the World Bank (adopted in more vigorous form in 2017), and among some Andean governments, Ecuador still does not respect this legal figure. In this chapter we demonstrate the Ecuadorian government's failure to open up this pluralist realm—although President Moreno has thus far expressed a stronger disposition for pluralism—and also argue that this failure has carried costs. Indigenous communities have fragmented over the corporatist consultations that have occurred, as indigenous groups invariably splinter when one group wants the benefit of state resources while another refuses to acquiesce to extractive projects. This lack of consensus within indigenous groups disconfirms the assumption of primordial group unity of multiculturalism. Yet it is precisely because prior consultation provides a formal mechanism of bargaining that we expect indigenous individuals to be among the strongest in favor of the binding nature of prior consultation. Furthermore, *mestizos* and other "non-indigenous" residents near extractive sites also lose, and without even having their positions represented.

THE HIGH STAKES OF THE PRIOR CONSULTATION DEBATE IN ECUADOR

Contrary to Colombia and Peru, where prior consultation is legally required, and Bolivia, where it is at least required in the mining industry, prior consultations in Ecuador have not carried the force of law. As in the other Andean nations, extraction is relied upon to provide populist social programs, and this imperative overwhelmed claims to progressive environmental policies, even though the Correa administration claimed to speak for nature. In this section we briefly elaborate on the precedent set by the Sarayaku community, explained more extensively in chapter 4, and on the Yasuní referendum, which, while not a prior consultation, claimed the legitimacy of one. We then consider a highly conflictive controversy stemming from a lack of prior consultation in the mining sector before proceeding to analyze our public opinion data on prior consultation.

The July 2012 Inter-American Court of Human Rights (IACHR) award to the Kichwa people of Sarayaku, in the central Amazon, of $1.25 million, after a seventeen-year battle against Argentine extractive interests, had the effect of generating extensive interest in prior consultations. As elaborated further in chapter 4, the Sarayaku people used these funds to generate scholarships and economic development in their region, and to encourage the CONAIE and other regional and national indigenous organizations to advocate more forcefully for consultation of indigenous communities. This was in large part because the formal decision handed down from the Inter-American Court of Human Rights mandated that prior consultation must be conducted and respected in Ecuador (Gualinga interview). Indeed, as part of the Eleventh Round of oil contract leases, Shuar and Achuar assemblies in the southern Amazon were to be consulted by the government regarding their granting of permission for extraction to occur. However, as also presented more extensively in chapter 4's evidence of corporatist "dividing and conquering" of indigenous interest groups by the "extractivist populist" state, the national government in 2013 and 2014 retracted official recognition from anti-extractivist indigenous groups and granted it to those groups that were more supportive of the government's agenda.

However, prior consultation is far from the norm in Ecuador. Guillermo Loza, director of Environmental Control in the Napo province—where Oil Blocks 7, 19, 21, and 29 have been leased—stated the perspective of Correa's government most clearly: "Prior consultation is not binding" (interview). He argued that although the redesigned 2008 Ecuadorian Constitution guarantees prior consultation, there "needs to be a period of transition" before the constitution can really be put into effect (Loza interview). Loza argued his position by stating that the government has developed other formal ways of ensuring that citizens participate in the extractive process. For example, for what he calls "Category 3" extractive efforts—those that have the greatest environmental impact—the state formally incorporates citizen participation in the regulatory process. However, the participatory nature of the process that he described was vague. He said that his depart- ment "facilitates a process of social participation that is obligatory, that registers facilitators of the process, and that registers the consultants in the process" (Loza interview). He stated clearly that the state "does not pay" participants, but that they do engage primarily with professionals, and that they focus on areas with "strategic interest" to the state (Loza in- terview). His disregard for prior consultation was made more evident when he explained that the Sarayaku people were contradictory in their efforts to ensure prior consultation, because they personally "benefited" from the lawsuit in other ways and were not genuinely interested in environmental regulation (Loza interview).

Smaller indigenous groups in the Amazon are grateful to the Sarayaku for promoting prior consultation and yet recognize that it has been implemented unfairly and has not always been respected. As Fernando Santi, president of the Shiwiar Nationality, described, "The extractivists entered our zone in 1995 and we have had a very negative experience. We do not want the contamination in the river where we drink our water, where all our fish have died out. . . . We have solidarity with the Sarayaku and the Achuar" (interview). However, for him, prior consultation has thus far been meaningless in his area. "We have fourteen communities. They held consultations in only five of them, and manipulated them [the people in the consultations]" (Santi interview). Santi also said that when communities deny extraction, the government "rejects the consultation" (interview). In all instances, he described what he views as a "form of de- ception" carried out by the subsecretary of hydrocarbons during consul- tation processes: "They offer money and manipulate the communities" (interview). For Santi, prior consultation is beneficial in theory but has not borne any tangible benefits for his community.

In 2014, the loose-knit YASunidos civic group, composed of many university students as well as longtime social activists, sought to extend prior consultation to the population at large. In other words, they sought to expand multicultural rights into broader citizenship rights, arguing that because the figure of the referendum was recognized in Ecuador, one should be held to decide whether the government should end its eight-year pledge to not drill for oil in the Yasuní National Park. YASunidos collected some 850,000 signatures, or 25 percent more than were needed by law to launch a public referendum (Vidal 2014), but the National Electoral Council (Consejo Nacional Electoral, CNE) disqualified more than half of them, canceling the referendum and the effort. YASunidos representative Bonilla (interview) said there was aggression against the signature collectors, consistent with the crackdowns against activists that had been ongoing for several years, and in 2016 oil started pumping from Yasuní.

The YASunidos referendum effort galvanized the country, but Ecuador's nascent mining sector was even more controversial than oil drilling, as Shuar mobilizations against the entry of the copper industry prompted forced relocations, deaths, and government reprisals with helicopters and tear gas. Analysts have pointed out that oil drilling procedures and cleanliness have improved markedly, precisely because of Texaco/Chevron, and that the adverse impacts now are mostly at refineries in the United States and other consumer countries (Thurber interview). Gold mining was launched by Fruta del Norte, a British firm that adhered to international standards, although that mine ceased operations; the current mine in operation is the open pit copper mine in the south, Mirador el Condor, operated by EcuaCorriente, a Chinese state-owned conglomerate. "A non-pit mine in the desert is not that bad" Thurber (interview). "Mining in a tropical environment is dangerous (high precipitation rates, landslides, biodiversity, and rural forest or farming communities)." As a result, mining projects require greater regulatory attention and larger investments. The Correa government devoted extensive resources to opening the mining sector during the final years of his presidency. If the government continues to demonstrate impulses towards Mazzuca's "absolutist temptation" (Mazzuca 2013, 111), it may be in the government's plans to expand the economic base of extractive populism but with the participation only from government allies. In 2017 Lenin Moreno openly broke with Correa, seemingly to redirect the government's efforts toward a more moderate position balancing environmental protection against oil extraction.

The conflict over whether open pit copper mining was to be allowed at Mirador has displaced dozens of people and yielded at least four deaths. The most recent seem to have been in November 2014, when Shuar anti-mining activist José Isidro Tendetza Antún's body was found in a grave marked "no name," and the slaying of police officer José Mejía in melees that broke out in November 2016. At that time, the Shuar community mobilized and, upon being forcibly expelled from the Nankints community in August 2016, retook the village occupied by some thirty-two people in November 2016. The residents hunkered down when the government entered with tanks and helicopters to remove them, and instead expelled the Chinese-owned EXSA (Aguilar 2017). The government arrested Shuar community leaders, including the Inter-Provincial Federation of Shuar Centers (FISCH) president Agustín Wachapá, and tried to shut down the NGO Acción Ecológica, renowned for its critical reporting on government mining operations.

According to analyst Martínez Novo (2017), presidential aspirant Guillermo Lasso promised to restrict the oil frontier to protected areas, to stop persecuting social leaders like Wachapá, and to implement prior consultation beyond international norms requiring only consultation, and in addition making this last item binding. Koenig (2017) states that the lack of any consultation at all helped precipitate tensions in Nankints. Even when consultation does occur, Koenig writes, the process is "rarely informed, usually consisting of a single meeting and PowerPoint presentation in a non-native language by a partisan government ministry about the economic benefits of the project, with little to no information or disclosure about environmental or social impact, or risk" (Koenig 2017, 2). The Shuar-EXSA–Ecuadorian government conflict did garner attention for prior consultation, making it an important issue in the 2017 presidential campaign. Our survey considered these issues prior to the campaign, as we elaborate in the following sections, when only about half of the population knew the meaning of prior consultation.

And just as whether to allow extraction has generated conflict within indigenous communities, such as the Achuar and Waorani, belying the multiculturalist thesis, notable conflicts have occurred among the Shuar. While the Shuar largely agree about the conduct of prior consultations, there is great disagreement about whether such consultations amount to a "sanction" of extraction. Vicente Tsakimp, president of the Shuar Arutam Peoples in the Province of Morona Santiago (the site of San Carlos Ponanza), argued strenuously that his people do not want extraction and that prior consultations do not reflect the will of the people because they only seek support of a few people, and based on government offers of clientelism rather than on policy discussions (2017 interview). The leader of Tsakimp's "umbrella" group, Elvis Nantip, president of the Inter-Provincial Federation of Schuar Centers (FISCH), likened Tsakimp's group to "children," and argued (2017 interview), to the contrary, that "natural resources and mining are the pillar of development." Clearly, the results of prior consultation are controversial, meaning that the process itself is open to being discredited. As with the Waorani in the north and the Sápara in the central Amazon, as documented in chapter 4, this divide among the Shuar shows that fundamental differences exist within indigenous groups about the role of extraction in local economic development. These differences manifest in procedural arguments about the role of prior consultation as groups try to validate such consultations post hoc depending on the outcomes, whereas human rights and environmental activists argue that uniform policies need to be set and followed.

PUBLIC OPINION ON PRIOR CONSULTATION ENFORCEMENT: DATA AND VARIABLES

As is the case in many other Latin American countries, we argue that prior consultation in Ecuador has become a political tool used by the government to legitimize extractive activity. Furthermore, we believe that sectors of informed citizens are aware of this manipulation of the institution, and as such have conflicting views on the extent to which prior consultation should be binding. To assess public opinion on prior consultation, we turn to our nationwide survey of Ecuadorians to analyze whether and why prior consultation has popular support. In this section, we describe the survey questions that we use to measure public opinion toward prior consultation. We argue and show that citizen attitudes toward prior consultation are determined by their political affiliation, their beliefs with respect to the environment and nature, their location on the extractive frontier, and their indigenous identity. By contrast, measures of post-materialist beliefs and objective measures of vulnerability are not relevant for determining attitudes toward prior consultation.

We conceptualize citizens' support for prior consultation (the dependent variable) through a single measure we developed based on citizen responses during focus groups and extensive field tests of the survey instrument. First, we educated our respondents on prior consultation by stating: "The following questions refer to the fact that when a group wants to explore for oil or minerals, it should be subject to prior consultation (convocation of an assembly) of the residents of the affected zone."

We then asked respondents: "Should the government obey prior consultation, whatever it says?" Respondents were asked to select one of the following responses that best reflected their opinion: "1—it does not have to obey it; 2—depends on how informed the people are; 3—depends on how difficult the conditions are for the people; and 4—yes, without conditions." We coded the dependent variable 0 for the "do not have to obey" response; 1 for responses that offer conditions on when it should be obeyed; and 2 for the "yes, without conditions" response. As per Table 3.1, a majority of our sample (63.5 percent) believed that prior consultation should be obeyed without conditions. The other third of the sample believed that there should be some conditions for when prior consultation is obeyed (35.1 percent), while only 1.2 percent of respondents believed that the government does not have to obey prior consultation. (See the description of the variable *Prior Consultation* in Table A1 of appendix A for a description of the survey items, question wording, and coding of this and all other variables included in the analysis.)

Public opinion in Ecuador relating to prior consultation does not coincide with the law, which encourages prior consultation (such as in the constitution) but does not establish it as binding. Besides believing by a two-thirds majority in the binding nature of prior consultation, some two-thirds of the population also believes that all Ecuadorian citizens should participate, rather than just those who live in affected areas (see Table 3.1). Not surprisingly, this percentage diminishes somewhat among indigenous respondents, particularly those in areas of mining debate and among Amazon indigenous citizens. This is because indigenous groups have been the primary beneficiaries of prior consultation, and because of the controversies and conflicts by citizens in areas where prior consultation has not occurred, such as for mining in Mirador and oil drilling in Sarayaku. Reflecting the probable outcome of consultations—which the extractive populist state no doubt wishes to force by holding prior consultations— over 60 percent of respondents also conveyed, uncategorically, that "mining is unacceptable for the damage it causes."

Consistent with the rest of this book, we control in the statistical anal ysis that follows for post-materialist dispositions, which includes eight elements of the survey instrument that allow us to develop measures of post-materialist values and objective conditions. As in chapter 2, we include the variables *Human Rights* (respondent includes human rights as one of the six most important problems facing the country); *Promote Modernity* (respondent believes that promoting modernity and development are the most important characteristics of good local government); *Indigenous Leader* (respondent disagrees that the indigenous do not make

Table 3.1 SCOPE OF PRIOR CONSULTATION PROCESSES

	"Should the government obey prior consultation, whatever it says?" CP6.			"Should all Ecuadorian citizens participate in prior consultation, or just those who live in the affected area?" CP5.		"The perforation of the earth by mining is unacceptable for the damage it causes."		
	Without conditions	Conditionally	No	Agree, all Ecuadorians	Disagree, only those in the affected zones	Agree	Disagree	NR/Depends
Has No Plumbing	214	84	7	212	99	176	115	32
Percent	70.2	27.5	2.3	68.2	31.8	54.5	35.6	9.9
Oil Debated or Drilled	227	126	8	254	115	250	92	34
Percent	62.9	35	2.2	68.8	31.2	66.5	24.5	9
Mining Debated or Underway	181	111	2	170	134	216	62	40
Percent	61.6	37.8	0.6	55.9	44.1	68	19.5	12.5
Self-Identified as Indigenous	462	193	8	419	276	435	194	86
Percent	69.7	29.1	1.2	60.3	39.7	60.8	27.1	12
Indigenous from Amazon	261	82	6	217	147	256	74	41
Percent	74.8	23.5	1.7	59.6	40.4	69	20	11
Indigenous from Andes	252	114	2	239	147	232	121	46
Percent	68.5	30.9	0.54	61.9	38.1	58.1	30.3	11.53
Identifies with Pachakutik	101	20	1	80	47	98	22	9
Percent	82.8	16.4	0.8	63	37	76	17	7
Agrees with Blocking Freeways*	194	81	41	184	107	184	86	33
Percent	68.5	28.6	14.4	63.2	36.7	60.7	28.3	10.8
Agrees with Blocking Wells or Mines**	611	302	17	596	368	642	260	89
Percent	65.7	32.5	1.8	61.8	38.1	64.8	26.2	8.9
Overall National Average	1066	590	21	1103	617	1096	496	189
Percent	63.6	35.2	1.2	64.1	35.9	61.5	27.9	10.6

Note: Based on responses to the statement: "For the following questions, please tell me if you agree or disagree with the following:"
* "That people participate in blocking roads as a form of protest."
** "That people organize to prevent the entry of mining or oil companies in their community."
Percentages do not add up to 100 because many respondents did not reply or responded "Do not know."

good leaders); *Democracy vs. Development* (respondent believes that democracy is more important than development); *Climate Change* (respondent believes in climate change); *Social Media* use (respondent has used social media in the past week); the *Professional* variable (respondent's occupation is professional); and the *Eco Donation* variable (respondent has donated to an ecological organization). As with chapter 2, we do not expect any of these variables measuring post-materialist dispositions to be significant determinants of attitudes toward prior consultation. Instead, we expect more concrete characteristics—such as political affiliations and proximity to extraction—to influence support for prior consultation.

We also include a variety of independent variables that we used to capture a respondent's vulnerability in our statistical analyses. Specifically, we include the variables *Rain/River Water Source* (respondent gets their water primarily from rain or the river), *Energy Scarcity* (respondent has less than twelve hours of regular access to electricity per day), *Climate Change Concern* (scale of respondents' worry over climate change), and *Ecotourism* (respondent directly benefits from ecotourism in their community). If prior consultation were implemented in Ecuador in its purest form—to allow communities to protect their lands from extractive incursions—then we would expect these variables—especially *Climate Change Concern* and *Ecotourism*, the two variables that also predicted greater environmental concern in chapter 2—to have positive relationships with support for prior consultation. However, because we argue that prior consultation is employed primarily as a political tool used by the state to validate extractive efforts, we do not expect a significant relationship between these variables and support for prior consultation.

As we summarize in chapter 1 and show further in chapter 4, the indigenous movement and its affiliated political party—Pachakutik—had contentious relationships with President Correa (although this has changed somewhat under President Moreno). Indeed, Pachakutik leaders recognized that Correa manipulated forms of prior consultations—such as the YASunidos effort to prevent drilling in Yasuní Park—and are highly critical of this (Tibán interview). Nevertheless, Pachakutik has been one of the strongest advocates of prior consultation to protect indigenous lands. Indeed, the success of the Sarayaku case, and the strong affiliation that the Sarayaku people have with Pachakutik,[4] are key reasons why

---

4. The Sarayaku community has been a stronghold of the Pachakutik party, even serving as a refuge in early 2014 for Pachakutik affiliates that fled prosecution by Correa's administration for insulting the president.

Pachakutik continues to advocate for prior consultation to preserve indigenous rights. Of course, the more cynical perspective on Pachakutik's adherence to prior consultation is that they also use the mechanism as a strategy to undermine support for the Ecuadorian government's extractivist agenda, using it as a means to achieve political ends of their own. Regardless, given the consistent advocacy of Pachakutik for prior consultation, we expect that *Pachakutik Affiliates* will be more likely to support the binding nature of prior consultations. Given the politicized nature of prior consultation, we also control for trust in the national indigenous movement organization Confederation of Indigenous Nationalities of Ecuador (Confederación de Nacionalidades Autonomas Indígenas de Ecuador, CONAIE), and whether an individual identifies with the PAIS party. We do not expect these two political variables to influence attitudes toward prior consultation.

We also argue that an individual's experience with extraction should influence their attitudes toward the binding nature of prior consultation. We therefore include our three measures that code for proximity to extraction: *Mining* (2 = respondent lives within approximately 30 kilometers of an active mine, 1 = respondent lives in an area where mining is debated, 0 = otherwise), *History of Oil Extraction* (respondent lives in an oil block where oil has been extracted), and *Oil Debate* (respondent lives in an oil block where oil drilling is being negotiated). We expect individuals in these areas to be particularly attuned to the politicization of prior consultation—especially those living in areas where oil extraction is actively being debated. Therefore, we expect *Oil Debate* to have a negative relationship with support for the binding nature of prior consultation because individuals in these areas will fear manipulation in the process. As we did in chapter 2, we controlled for expectations that *Extraction Benefits Ecuador*, as those attitudes may play a role in support for prior consultation.

Several elements of the survey instrument allow us to develop measures of how cosmovision, or adherence to a worldview reflected by indigenous beliefs, may affect support for prior consultation. We included *Indigenous and Nature* (respondent agrees that the indigenous are more connected with Mother Earth than non-indigenous), of which about 73.1 percent of our sample agreed (coded 1), while the remaining 26.8 percent said that they either did not agree or that it depends (coded 0). We also include the variable *Mother Earth Has Rights*, for which about 80.18 percent of our sample said that they agree (coded 1), while the remaining 19.8 percent said that they either did not agree or that it depends (coded 0). If prior consultation was genuinely an instrument used to protect the environment, these variables would have a positive relationship with support for the binding nature of the institution. However, given the political manipulation of prior consultation, we expect these beliefs to have a negative relationship with support that all prior consultations be binding without conditions. We also control for *Indigenous ID*, or respondents who self-identify as indigenous (1 if self-identified as indigenous, 0 otherwise). As with Pachakutik affiliation, we expect indigenous citizens to be more supportive of the binding nature of prior consultation because it is one of the only legally mandated processes that require input from indigenous groups, despite the manipulation of the process.

Because prior consultation is a formal mechanism for constraining extractive activity, we believe that attitudes toward protest may also determine support for the binding nature of prior consultation. We argue that individuals who believe in legal forms of protest—who approve of legal demonstrations as a form of protest—are more likely to agree in the binding nature of prior consultation because they view it as a legal mechanism. By contrast, we argue that individuals who believe in more radical forms of protest—who approve of invading private property and land as a form of protest—will be less likely to respect the binding nature of prior consultation. In order to measure those attitudes, we include two variables: *Protest by Invading Private Land* and *Protest Through Legal Demonstrations*. These variables are based on the following two questions, respectively: "Do you agree or disagree with the following: 1) that people invade private property or land as a form of protest; 2) that people participate in legal demonstrations." For both variables, we coded those that agree with the statement a 1, and all other responses (disagree, depends/maybe, don't know) a 0. The majority of our sample (74.2 percent) agreed with legal demonstrations as a form of protest, but only a very small minority (5.8 percent) of our sample agreed that invading private property is an acceptable form of protest.

Finally, we include several controls: *Media Access, Knowledge Index, Religiosity, Education,* and *Income*. In addition, we control for whether respondents have *Heard of Prior Consultation* (1 if yes, 0 if no). Around 34.6 percent of our sample had heard of prior consultation. This proportion is substantially larger among our sample of indigenous living in the Amazon, of which 41 percent had heard of prior consultation. We have no clear expectations for how these variables relate to support for prior consultation, especially given that increased media access and advanced education may lead to conflicting knowledge or beliefs around the implementation of prior consultation.

RESULTS AND DISCUSSION

To analyze the relationship between our multi-level independent variables and our dependent variable of support for prior consultation, we used an ordinal logit model with standard errors clustered around the locality in which respondents live. We did this because our *History of Extraction, Mining,* and *Oil Debate* variables are coded at the level of locality, meaning that observations at that level are not independent. In this section, we briefly review and discuss the results of our analyses. In interpreting our results, positive coefficients mean that respondents are more likely to support the implementation of prior consultation, both with and without conditions.

The results of our analysis are presented in Table 3.2. The discussion here refers to results for Model 1 in Table 3.2, unless otherwise noted. First, as we expected, the majority of correlates that we use to measure post-materialism are not significant determinants in attitudes toward prior consultation. This is true for measures of post-materialist values (such as human rights and democracy) as well as for more objective measure of post-materialist lifestyles (such as professional occupations, social media usage, and donating to ecological organizations). Based on these findings, we feel confident in rejecting the idea that post-materialism plays a role in shaping support for prior consultation in Ecuador. Integration into international networks is also not a significant factor in determining support for the implementation of prior consultation, with or without conditions.

As we expected, the strongest predictors of support for prior consultation are respondents' political orientations. Affiliation with the Pachakutik party is highly significant and substantively powerful, suggesting that prior consultation has become a political issue in Ecuador. Using probabilities predicted by our model, Pachakutik adherents are fully 21 percent more likely to believe that prior consultation should be obeyed without conditions than non-Pachakutik respondents. As we argue above, Pachakutik has been one of the strongest advocates of prior consultation to protect indigenous lands. Indeed, the success of the Sarayaku case, and the strong affiliation that the Sarayaku people have with Pachakutik, are key reasons why Pachakutik continues to advocate for prior consultation to preserve indigenous rights. Of course, the more cynical perspective on Pachakutik's adherence to prior consultation is that they also use the mechanism as a strategy to undermine support for the Ecuadorian government's extractivist agenda, using it as a means to achieve political ends of their own.

Table 3.2 SUPPORT FOR WHETHER PRIOR CONSULTATION SHOULD BE OBEYED IN ECUADOR

	Model 1	Model 2
Post-Materialism		
Human Rights	−0.034	0.074
	(0.273)	(0.269)
Promote Modernity	−0.172	−0.197*
	(0.119)	(0.116)
Climate Change	0.143	0.084
	(0.250)	(0.244)
Indigenous Leader	0.181	0.136
	(0.119)	(0.116)
Democracy vs. Development	0.058	0.086
	(0.127)	(0.125)
Social Media	−0.020	−0.036
	(0.133)	(0.130)
Professional	0.182	0.178
	(0.314)	(0.313)
Eco Donation	−0.202	−0.208
	(0.307)	(0.301)
International Networks		
International Networks	0.038	0.049
	(0.049)	(0.049)
Vulnerability		
Rain/River Water Source	0.152	0.106
	(0.182)	(0.179)
Energy Scarcity	−0.611	−0.612
	(0.389)	(0.389)
Climate Change Concern	0.186**	0.143*
	(0.079)	(0.077)
Ecotourism	−0.272	−0.248
	(0.169)	(0.166)
Political Orientations		
Pachakutik Affiliate	1.056***	1.095***
	(0.303)	(0.302)
PAIS Affiliate	0.240	0.203
	(0.202)	(0.199)
Trust in Indigenous Movement	0.080	0.085
	(0.072)	(0.071)
Extraction		
Mining	0.104	0.026
	(0.130)	(0.128)

Table 3.2 CONTINUED

	Model 1	Model 2
History of Oil Extraction	0.386	0.395
	(0.299)	(0.295)
Oil Debate	−0.583***	−0.480**
	(0.191)	(0.187)
Extraction Benefits Ecuador	−0.078	−0.089
	(0.066)	(0.065)
Cosmovision		
Indigenous Closer to Nature	−0.344**	
	(0.138)	
Mother Earth Has Rights	−0.416**	
	(0.163)	
Indigenous ID	0.490***	0.371***
	(0.148)	(0.144)
Perceptions of Protest		
Protest by Invading Private Land	−0.154	−0.107
	(0.259)	(0.254)
Protest Through Legal Demonstrations	0.401***	0.402***
	(0.134)	(0.131)
Controls		
Heard of Prior Consultation	−0.009	0.018
	(0.129)	(0.128)
Media Access	0.092	0.076
	(0.063)	(0.062)
Religiosity	0.138*	0.138*
	(0.083)	(0.082)
Knowledge Index	−0.027	−0.040
	(0.034)	(0.033)
Education	0.068	0.068
	(0.054)	(0.053)
Income	0.012	0.017
	(0.040)	(0.039)
Cut 1	−2.673***	−2.347***
	(0.619)	(0.597)
Cut 2	1.255**	1.517***
	(0.578)	(0.558)
N	1,377	1,404

$^{*} p < 0.1;\ ^{**} p < 0.05;\ ^{***} p < 0.01$

Note: The dependent variable is based on the survey question: "Should the government obey prior consultation, whatever it says?" with ordinal responses coded 0 for the "do not have to obey" response; 1 for responses that offer conditions on when it should be obeyed (depends on how informed the people are or depends on how difficult the conditions are for the people); and 2 for the "yes, without conditions" response.

Also, as we expected, one of the extractive conditions has a significant effect on individual attitudes toward prior consultation. While mining and a history of oil extraction have no effect, living in an area where oil is debated makes it *less* likely that an individual will support prior consultation with or without conditions. We argue that this is because respondents in areas where oil is debated are currently involved in the negotiating process with the government, and are highly aware of the political nature of the process. As we described in the context of the Mirador mine, communities and their leaders become acutely aware of the manipulation of prior consultation as extractive projects move onto their territory.

Another set of independent variables measures the effects that beliefs consistent with indigenous cosmovision have on attitudes toward prior consultation. These variables have significant effects on attitudes toward prior consultation, in the direction that we would expect if prior consultation is frequently manipulated. The belief that Mother Nature has rights has a *negative* effect on support for prior consultation. In addition, the belief that the indigenous people are closer to nature also corresponds with *less* support for prior consultation. Together, these findings provide support for how beliefs based in indigenous cosmovisions affect support for prior consultation. These findings result from the fact that prior consultation has become a political tool for imposing development on communities, rather than one that genuinely protects the environment. In other words, we argue that in areas where respondents knew of prior consultation, they associated it with oil and mineral extraction (as prior consultation has overwhelmingly tended to lead to extraction), rather than as a means of evaluating *whether* to extract.

It is important to note that it is not only indigenous individuals who adhere to beliefs consistent with indigenous cosmovision. For both measures—that Mother Nature has rights and that indigenous people are closer—the majority of indigenous respondents as well as the majority of non-indigenous respondents agree with these statements. This helps explain why indigenous individuals differ in their support for the binding nature of prior consultation, and like Pachakutik, take a more positive perspective on the institution. It is not because of a cultural distinction— that they are indeed much more protective of the environment than other groups—but instead because they have also politically benefited from the multicultural nature of the process.

The findings with respect to beliefs about protest further support the idea that support for prior consultation is based upon whether it is viewed as a legitimate legal mechanism, or whether it is viewed as an instrument of manipulation. Individuals who agree with legal demonstrations as forms of protest are more likely to agree with the implementation of prior consultation. However, individuals who agree with the invasion of private property or land are no more or less likely to agree with the implementation of prior consultation. These findings reinforce the argument that attitudes toward prior consultations are based on the sense that it is legally and fairly implemented. We believe that the division is between those who think that prior consultation is a step along the policy path to extraction versus those who see it as a means of questioning or contesting extraction.

One of our measures of vulnerability is also significant in shaping attitudes toward prior consultation: concern over climate change. Interestingly, concern over climate change has a positive relationship with support for prior consultation. Individuals who are concerned about climate change are a diverse group, including a large proportion of people in urban areas. Not all of them may be aware of the politicization of prior consultation. No other measures of vulnerability have an effect on attitudes toward prior consultation. But if citizens in extractive areas believed that prior consultation was simply a bureaucratic requirement of extraction, this would explain the apparent inconsistency.

Where prior consultation is not required, survey respondents believe that the results of such consultations should be respected only when they have a propensity toward respecting legal forms of contestation, and when they believe in the true purpose of prior consultation, as do affiliates of Pachakutik. We turn now to a broader discussion of how this highly sought outcome of respected consultations is manipulated in practice. That is, we study cases in Ecuador and in other nations where the institution of prior consultation is used as a bargaining process means rather than as an approval-granting end. Having established the importance of prior consultation plebiscites, we first reiterate this by summarizing the most famous case of when such a plebiscite was not held, and how, in Sarayaku, Ecuador, this resulted in the Ecuadorian state's loss of a lawsuit and payout of over US $1.25 million to fewer than 1,000 Sarayakus. After considering this defining case, we explore cases of negotiation in prior consultations, cases where consultations do not occur because extraction is not favored. We next seek to recenter the issue of prior consultation within a broader problem, that of how interest groups attain recognition within the liberal multicultural framework. Finally, we conclude by framing an alternative framework for interest articulation, bounded pluralism.

PRIOR CONSULTATION AND ITS POLITICIZATION
IN PRACTICE: BARGAINING TABLES RATHER THAN
VETO POINTS

The Sarayaku people of Ecuador have made perhaps the best claim to speaking for nature of any group. Arguing that the Ecuadorian government's failure to consult them resulted in destruction of the forest for oil exploration, and thus erasures of their souls, was acknowledged and even embellished by the Inter-American Court of Human Rights (IACHR) in 2012. Indeed, the Court's acknowledgment of the "sadness and suffering" of the Sarayaku Kichwa people, because of the government's failure to consult them before allowing private oil exploration, prompted a close tracking of all subsequent consultation processes in Ecuador and around Latin America. The victory of the Sarayaku people versus the government of Ecuador may have yielded the most resounding victory and legal settlement for indigenous peoples to date, at least in Latin America.

The IACHR heard and reiterated strong testimonials by Sarayaku Kichwa leaders such as Patricia Gualinga, on the special relationship between the forest and the Kichwa peoples: "For us *Kawsak Sacha* [Living Forest] is the living forest, with everything this implies, with all its beings, with all its worldview, with all its culture with which we are intermingled . . . and, therefore, the Sarayaku defends its living space so ardently" (IAHRC 2012, 38). Sarayaku shaman Sabino Gualinga further argued that his people should speak for the fragility of nature, if not for nature itself: "The destruction of the jungle erases the soul; we stop being people of the jungle" (cited in IAHRC, 2012, 38).

The Inter-American Court of Human Rights agreed, ruling that "the failure to consult the Sarayaku People affected their cultural identity, since there is no doubt that the intervention in and destruction of their cultural heritage entailed a significant lack of respect for their social and cultural identity, their customs, traditions, worldview and way of life, which naturally caused great concern, sadness and suffering among them" (IAHRC 2012, 63). The settlement, issued in 2012, obtained US $1.25 million for the Sarayaku Kichwa community, which created scholarships for students, launched a micro-enterprise loan-granting agency, a computer center, and community-owned motorboat and airline transportation companies (Santi interview). The ruling was in large part because the Ecuadorian government had failed to conduct a "good faith" prior consultation that informed people about possible impacts of the oil extraction by PetroEcuador and did not share environmental impact assessment results. Since the events leading to the Sarayaku resolution, most of which occurred over a decade ago, the consultation process has only grown more controversial.

The Achuar people of Peru (who share lineage with the Ecuadorian Achuar people) held a prior consultation process and received payment in exchange for allowing extraction, as documented by Torres 2016 (120–22). In 2015, the contract between the Peruvian state and PLUSPETRO governing Oil Block 192 came to an end. A new process to find another operator had to be undertaken. The new legislative framework enacted in 2012, however, required that prior consultation with indigenous communities be executed in advance. Oil Block 192 is located in the municipality of Andoas, comprising the Achuar, Quechua, and Kichwa ethnicities. The state formally consulted with indigenous organizations before finalizing the contract with PLUSPETROL, commenced in May 2015 through the government parastatal oil company PERUPETRO, the same company charged with allocating concessions to oil companies. Indigenous representatives in July 2015 sought to create an endowment administered directly by the indigenous communities (Torres 2016, 120–22), financed by Block 192 production. Indigenous leaders also asked for state representatives to improve education and health services, as well as to create jobs for local communities. In August 2015, after months of negotiations, the Peruvian government created the indigenous fund (Torres 2016, 120–22), with the prior consultation serving as a starting gambit for the negotiations.

Like the Peruvian groups, Mexico's isolated Yaqui population also used prior consultation as a negotiating starting position. In 2014, the government decided to build the Sonora Gas Pipeline to transport gas from the United States to Mexican power plants. The projected pipeline crossed Yaqui territories, and the government pledged to hold a prior consultation. According to data cited by Torres (2016), the 33,000-strong Yaqui population is distributed across three different municipalities in Sonora: Guaymas, Bacum, and Cajeme. The prior consultation began in July 2014, with the Secretariat of Energy (Secretaría de Energía), or SENER, conducting the process. Only SENER, IEnova (the company hired to build the gas pipeline), and Yaqui authorities were initially allowed to participate, Torres writes, with SENER initially offering the Yaqui 36 million Mexican pesos (about US $2 million) in compensation for the gas pipeline.

The Yaqui were able to raise the amount to 76 million Mexican pesos (some US $4 million), and in the words of a Yaqui leader cited by Torres (2016): "The obstacles in prior consultation were mostly economic; it was hard to negotiate with the company. We had to make some concessions because the goal was to reach an agreement." Seven of the eight Yaqui delegations approved the project and the Mexican federal government agreed to pay half of the US $4 million indemnity in November 2015, and the other half by the time the construction of the pipeline had concluded. The government and the Yaqui leaders agreed that the funds were to be administered by the Yaqui leadership directly, in accordance with customary law norms. Indeed, Torres states that the Yaqui people agreed to distribute the funds among all eight Yaqui communities equally, granting each group discretion to spend the money where it was most urgently needed (Torres 2016, 127–30).

THE BROADER ISSUE: PRIOR CONSULTATION AND MULTICULTURAL RIGHTS IN NEOLIBERAL SOCIETIES

As the aforementioned examples show, a consensus in the literature is emerging that even a substantive recognition of the right to prior consultation, such as that of Bolivia, that grants veto power to indigenous communities results in approval of extraction (Falleti and Riofrancos 2014). Likewise, Mirna Cuentas, a Bolivian prior consultation specialist, argues that indigenous prohibition of extractive projects is unlikely as indigenous organizations know that the prior consultation procedure is designed to get their consent (Mirna Cuentas, cited in Torres 2016, 70). Communities are often divided over whether to take the funds, with that division often based in part on who stands to benefit economically from the extraction. These divisions within indigenous groups disconfirm the multiculturalist arguments implying a unity of these groups, and may offer some indirect validation of the efficacy of a polycentric approach seeking to unify all groups in prospective areas of extraction by their proximity to the extractive site rather than based on their ethnicity.

According to NGO employee Néstor Cuellar of the Peasant Development Research Center (Centro de Investigación y Promoción del Campesinado, CIPCA), who has worked with Bolivian Guaraní organizations for many years, prior consultation procedures consist of formal meetings between indigenous leaders and state officials. State officials tender an economic offer, as well as possible mechanisms to address environmental damages associated with the proposed extractive project, to indigenous representatives. These indigenous leaders take these proposals back to their communities and discuss them within their Community Assemblies (*Asamblea Comunal*). Collective assessment of the state's offer results in a counteroffer, which is handed back to state officials at a second meeting, and so on. Negotiations can last for several months and, in many cases, indigenous communities allow operations to begin before an agreement has been reached as prohibiting extraction is not their goal. However, in cases where reaching a final settlement takes longer than expected, and the state continues refusing indigenous demands, some groups adopt mobilization tactics, such as blockading oil wells and roads, to force the state to comply with indigenous counteroffers (Cuellar, cited in Torres 2016, 52).

The mobilization of indigenous communities requires that aggrieved people assume those identities. A fierce debate erupted in Bolivia over the 2010 census regarding who qualified as indigenous, deferring the release of that census by several years (Moreno 2011). Mexico may have pioneered the practice of diverting indigenous citizens into the peasantry (see Otero 2007) to connect them to corporatist agrarian and social benefits networks (Rus 1994; Eisenstadt 2011) and church members (Trejo 2012), rather than leaving them to their own autonomous devices as indigenous communities. As extensively documented by Mattiace (2003), the Mexican government undertook an extensive assimilation project to make indigenous-language speakers part of the PRI-supporting *"raza cósmica"* during the middle of the twentieth century, which lasted until the state lost its ability to provide clientelist largesse in the 1980s economic crisis, and the Zapatista uprising of 1994 brought fear of a more widespread indigenous uprising (see Inclán 2009). In many Latin American countries, then, the relative fluidity of ethnic identity was known and emphasized by governments, even as indigenous communities came to assert indigeneity as a means of preserving their lands during the 1990s neo-liberal era.

The return of multicultural indigenous identity has been largely a function of political movements of the last twenty-five years in Ecuador, Mexico, and Bolivia. A normatively better means of empowering citizens in these nations, and in others, might be for each to universalize the prior consultation mechanism among their entire populations, thereby recognizing the rights of all citizens to use that legal mechanism to guarantee their rights. Indigenous groups could still mobilize to guarantee constitutionally enshrined rights to territory and autonomy, but non-indigenous citizens might also use the mechanism as a focal point for mobilization. Such a move would put the Andean nations squarely within the movement toward participatory democracy in Latin America identified by Fung (2011), Pateman (2012), and Eisenstadt, LeVan, and Maboudi (2017) and illustrated, via Brazil's participatory budgeting, by Avritzer (2009), Spada and Allegretti (2013), Wampler (2012), and others. And in the environmental realm, it would approximate pluralism with Ostrom's polycentrism (2010).

In the case of Bolivia, legal tools provided to protect indigenous organizations in the 2009 Constitution have counterbalanced the increasing power of the executive and the party Movement Toward Socialism (Movimiento al Socialismo, MAS). Some minority lowlands indigenous groups have faced obstacles to forcing the Bolivian government to respect their territorial rights even when they are legally protected by ILO 169, the Bolivian constitution, and sectoral prior consultation legislation. As these communities grow increasingly disenchanted with the Morales government, they seek to express their discontent through new participatory governance institutions, like prior consultation "referenda." Such functions may not have been the intent of the creators of these participatory institutions, but they do bolster the autonomy, strength, and popularity of the institutions. As demonstrated through the Ecuador survey respondents, people want prior consultation results respected, but the mobilized also manipulate the forum to bargain rather than decide.

The commitment of indigenous communities and other rural citizens to prior consultation through their ability to see their input affecting the shape extractive projects take would no doubt improve relations between mobilized social movements and the state on issues "that are far more important to the lives of voters than the typical election of the next set of government officials" (McGee 2009, 574). In the case of Bolivia, the nearly fifty successful cases of prior consultation involving indigenous communities were possible because prior consultation was perceived as a useful mechanism to enable indigenous access to some of the returns on extractivism. Indigenous and governmental responsiveness to prior consultation filled the vacuum left by corporatist regimes and provided communities with a legal discourse ("We have the right to be consulted") to mobilize the population. We argue that this was an improvement of participatory governance institutions over traditional representative institutions such as the universal vote. However, the bigger quandary facing even progressive governments as they seek to implement prior consultation is the role of international corporations. Just as state-society relations are finding new arenas of bounded but pluralist democratic contention through the creation of new interest groups to represent community livelihoods and lands, international mining conglomerates, with seemingly infinite resources, are pre-negotiating concessions with states (as in the Peruvian case), and then, only when they must, submitting these forgone conclusions to perfunctory plebiscites.

Consideration of prior consultation as mere procedural requirements, rather than as exercises critical to participatory democracy, is detrimental to most normative definitions of democracy and democratization. However, new analysis indicates—surprisingly—that it would also be detrimental to the "bottom lines" of mining companies. Worldwide, some 250 large-cap extractive companies were found to be "exposed" to indigenous rights-related risks, according to Experts in Responsible Investment Solutions (Stefani 2009). First Peoples Worldwide (2013) reported that among the 370 extraction sites of its 52 US-based Russell 1000 extractive companies, some 92 percent posed medium or high risks to shareholders due to violations of indigenous peoples' rights. A few of the highest location risk sites—all but one of which were on indigenous peoples' lands—were in the Andean regions mentioned here, but others were in Argentina, Canada, Indonesia, Ghana, Nigeria, and New Guinea (First Peoples Worldwide 2013, 19–21). Only one of 52 companies analyzed had an explicit policy of abiding by the United Nations–advocated prior consultation policy (FPIC), and "all but four of the companies we analyzed were operating on or near Indigenous land and (. . .) have no agreements with Indigenous Peoples, are likely to be facing non-violent and violent protests, and most likely do not have an Indigenous Peoples policy informing them how to engage" (First Peoples Worldwide 2013, 4).

This brings us back to a central issue raised early in this chapter, the non-binding nature of prior consultation, as implemented to date in Ecuador and elsewhere in the Americas. Indeed, former World Bank Adviser to Indigenous Peoples Luis Felipe Duchicela argues that his institution's standards for consulting indigenous people before making infrastructure loans are high, but "the problem is the application of the policy because there is sometimes incompatibility between our policy and the legislative frameworks and constitutions and political willingness of national governments to recognize indigenous peoples and use the policy we have" (interview 2017). He also confirmed that most of the long-standing international standards on FPIC, like ILO 169 on the United Nations Declaration on the Rights of Indigenous Peoples, do not require community consent for World Bank projects (or oil drilling) to proceed; they only require that efforts be undertaken to try to achieve such consent.[5]

Companies seem to be following the examples of domestic governments, which have no policy requiring that prior consultations be taken seriously, rather than those of more conscientious international financial institutions. Extraction-reliant governments in Bolivia, Ecuador, and Peru have sought to have it both ways: to win constituent support for high-impact extractivist projects and others (like the TIPNIS highway), and at the same time to execute these projects, which generate government

---

5. Dulchicela pointed out (interview) that the World Bank is adopting a new policy in 2018 that does require loan borrowers to actually gain consent, rather than just strive to do so.

operating revenue without forcing hard choices about cutting budgets or raising taxes. Making prior consultation binding may appear democratic in that it would give authority to some of the region's underdog political actors, but on the other hand, putting individual and collective rights into the hands of a small group could also result in the repression of minority (and sometimes, even majority) views or positions. As with other forms of pluralism, preference is given to those with the resources to express their interests more boisterously. Furthermore, the structural inequality still pervasive in countries like Peru is reflected in the quality of public services. People's living conditions are among the poorest in the rural areas where the extraction occurs, generating human rights violations and contamination. Royalties from extractive industries should pay for the improvement of services on "front line" rural Peruvian towns as well as in the slums of Lima—and across the country—where these royalties are also desperately needed to pay for services.

CONCLUSION: THE PROBLEM OF PRIOR CONSULTATION AS A MULTICULTURAL RIGHT

Multicultural rights regimes are those where ethnic groups are given legal autonomy over their lands and self-governance and thus set their own terms of participation. These terms are not always inclusionary, as famously conveyed by the example of Oaxaca, Mexico, starting in the 1990s, where residents dictated the terms of inclusion and exclusion, discriminating overtly against women, citizens from population hamlets outside municipal population centers, religious minorities, and immigrants (Juan Martínez 2013; Eisenstadt and Ríos 2014; Lucero 2013; Sorroza and Danielson 2013). In the cases highlighted in this chapter, internal disputes emerged over whether prior consultation processes were adequate (if even undertaken), and the Ecuadorian government deepened divisions by recognizing and supporting some groups but not others. As also demonstrated in chapter 4, trans-indigenous unity, as sought by polycentric pluralism, may further encourage inter-ethnic unity rather than division.

The prior consultation mechanism (also known in international law as Free, Prior, and Informed Consent, FPIC) ensures that, even if citizen consultation referenda are manipulated by corporatist state actors or clientelist patrons, such actors would have to mobilize these resources for each and every consultation, which would involve different interests with different stakes. The likelihood of entrenched patterns of hierarchical clientelist relations between indigenous peasants and their patrons is lower than in the entrenched patron-client systems established during the twentieth-century heyday of state largesse and dismantled during the neoliberal 1980s and 1990s. While the extractivist bonanza of the twenty-first century has heralded a new era of state largesse in the Andes, ad hoc case-by-case consultations should help prevent a new round of corporatist entrenchment.

The scope of these consultations as a tool for diminishing conflicts and improving indigenous rights recognition—including between indigenous groups—remains contentious. Rodríguez-Garavito cites at least two prominent forms these claims have taken: a neoliberal multiculturalist approach and a counterhegemonic approach. The first approach, the neoliberal approach, argues that prior consultations establish a dialogue between indigenous people and the state on implications and consequences of projects (extractive industries in particular), seeking to persuade indigenous communities to approve them. By this interpretation, even when indigenous communities deny land use for such projects, the state can overrule them. The second approach—counterhegemonic—empowers indigenous interest groups more extensively. This position argues that indigenous people must consent to projects, and that without such approval, the state cannot proceed. By this logic, indigenous groups have veto rights over encroachments to their territories (Rodríguez-Garavito 2011). The counterhegemonic approach (where prior consultation is binding for government) is consistent with the view that prior consultation is a participatory governance institution, mandating direct citizen participation (and compliance with citizen will), whereas the neoliberal approach (where prior consultation is non-binding) considers prior consultation to be an extension of traditional forms of representative democracy. This is an insightful distinction, although we would argue that both ideal types of multiculturalism implicitly assume indigenous unity of position, which is far from granted, and explore this further in chapter 4 when we directly address negotiations between the state and communities over extraction.

Picking winners from prior consultation might be sidestepped if the process is implemented broadly, and over a range of issues. That is, the legal figure of prior consultation might be extended to the holding of public impact hearings across a range of participatory governance areas. This would make the process just one among many consultative processes to address a range of public policies, with the range of scope of Brazil's participatory budgeting, for example. Currently, the prior consultation mechanism, now commonly exalted but infrequently enforced, is being emulated by non-indigenous communities. In Ecuador, the nationwide Yasuní referendum, described in this chapter and discussed more extensively in chapter 6, offers an example, as does the 2013 municipal referendum in Tolima, Colombia, documented by McNeish (2017). In chapter 4, we further address the means used by the Ecuadorian national government to manipulate prior consultation processes to ensure favorable outcomes to oil drillers. As we will see, when the government did not anticipate a positive vote by an indigenous assembly, it divided and conquered the indigenous community, splintering "pro-extraction" groups, constructing and officially recognizing new assemblies, and then having those pro-extraction assemblies cast the votes.

Corporatist manipulation of state-society relations is not new, especially in Latin American politics. However, the manipulation of such processes does not entirely negate the progress indigenous interests have made in using prior consultation in order to gain representation over vital economic and environmental decisions. Throughout the region, given the inability of some Latin American congresses to subpoena witnesses critical of executive branch programs (or their unwillingness to do so), prior consultations could help bring transparency and accountability to government administration. And given the urgency of representation of the needs of increasingly isolated rural citizens, the practice of polycentric pluralism, more broadly, as elaborated further in chapter 7, may offer citizens the chance to express their opinions, rather than just receiving clientelist goods in exchange for supporting the government and ruling political party, as under antiquated corporatist systems. Indeed, even if prior consultation is a weak, non-binding, and exclusionary mechanism erratically applied and susceptible to co-optation by wealthy mining companies, the mere existence of this institution and the debate it has fostered create demands for a new form of participation and have enabled citizens in new democracies to imagine idealized processes of representation and deliberation, for perhaps the first time ever. That is no small achievement, and one worthy of much further consideration.

CHAPTER 4

⌒⌒⌒

Crude Bargaining

Indigenous Ambivalence Regarding Oil Extraction in the Ecuadorian Amazon

After decades of confrontation with oil companies and the Ecuadorian government over exploitation of the country's oil reserves—located on their lands—a coalition of indigenous groups, led decisively by New York lawyers and the California-based Pachamama Foundation along with several leading Ecuadorian lawyers and NGO leaders, filed class action lawsuits against the US oil company Texaco in 1993. While final verdicts were appealed in 2013, these cases may have influenced the Ecuadorian government's 2008 decision to seek a Solomonic solution to drilling in one delicate rainforest reserve: the government would prevent drilling on indigenous lands in the overlapping Yasuní National Park (one of the world's most biodiverse) if the international community purchased carbon offsets for the tropical rainforest lands saved (Narváez 2009). The international response was underwhelming, and Ecuadorian President Rafael Correa reneged on this extravagant pledge of conservation in 2013. However, Amazonian indigenous groups and their allies have obtained remarkable, albeit tentative, concessions. As we show in chapter 6 of this book, that movement was internationally led, although it did help the domestic originators of Ecuador's domestic knowledge-based movements, such as that in nearby Sarayaku.

This chapter is framed on three case study areas highlighting findings of chapter 2, that survey respondents have more strongly positive attitudes toward the environment in areas where the environment is still pure. We conclude, based on our survey and follow-up interviews, that respondents in areas of environmental degradation (like Ecuador's northern Amazon region) concern themselves more with resultant problems like public health, immigration, employment, and others subsidiary but related to environmental degradation. In the south, where the forest is pristine, indigenous—and other—citizens care more about the environment per se. And in Ecuador's central Amazon, where the forests are mostly intact and an important movement for environmental protection is centered in the Sarayaku area, respondents also have stronger pro-environment attitudes.

In the sections that follow, we report interviews in the degraded northern Amazon region; in the central Amazon, where the influence of the pro-environment Sarayaku movement is strongest; and in the south, where extraction has mostly not occurred but has commenced in some mining areas. Andean indigenous peoples also have strong views regarding the environment, but their histories are more intertwined with those of the country's ruling elites, and hence are not as distinct as those of the differentiated Amazon areas, which will be the focus of this chapter's case studies. We examine the political history of interactions between the Andean and Amazon groups and the Ecuadorian government, and the differences and similarities between these groups, before considering the differences in the north, the center, and the south and how the Ecuadorian state has mediated these interests.

The Waorani people in Ecuador's northern Amazon region have perhaps borne the worst of the oil drilling in Ecuador's northern region, in the provinces of Orellana and Sucumbios. In the words of Kemperi, a Woarani elder and shaman quoted by Kimerling (2013, 99):

> Many companies want to enter, everywhere. But they do not help; they have come to damage the forest. Instead of going hunting, they cut down trees to make paths. Instead of caring for [the forest] they destroy. Where the company lives, it smells nasty, the animals hide, and when the river rises the manioc and plantain in the low areas have problems. We respect the environment where we live. We like the tourists because they come, and go away. When a company comes, it does not want to leave. Now the company is in the habit of offering many things, it says that it comes to do business, but then it makes itself the owner. Where the company has left its environment, we cannot return. It stays bad.

The prevalence of cancer is high in this area, fish and fauna have dwindled and died, and groundwater has been contaminated with oil (Maldonado interview). Energy industry analysts compare the Texaco/Chevron "clean up" to the recklessness of the *Exxon Valdez* oil spill in Alaska. They say the oil industry has had to labor extensively to improve its image. Human rights activists offer "toxic tours" of the region where witnesses see firsthand the oil-contaminated tap water relied upon by residents for hygiene and hydration (Maldonado and Moncayo interviews) and stick gloved hands into tar pits created by Texaco/Chevron and PetroAmazonas.[1] Meanwhile, many of the Waorani and others had to wonder, as Texaco/Chevron left scores of small oil spills throughout the rainforest upon leaving the country as their contract ended in the early 1990s, if they were doing their best to speak for nature.

In the middle latitudes of Ecuador's Amazon forests, the Kichwa people of the environmentally clean Pastaza River watershed village of Sarayaku (in Ecuador's central Amazon region, being explored as part of the country's Eleventh Round of oil block concessions) fought more successfully to "keep the drilling out," and also sought to document climate change. In June 2012, two generations of Sarayaku's indigenous leaders— José Gualinga and Marlon Santi—traveled to Quito to meet with scientists at the Pontificia Universidad Católica del Ecuador (PUCE) (correspondence with Montúfar-Galárraga). Seeking greater ties between some of Ecuador's leading earth scientists and indigenous communities, Sarayaku's leaders wanted to measure climate change "on the ground" to improve the Kichwa peoples' environmental stewardship and ensure their adaptability. The reliance on a scientific explanation rooted in a Western perspective of the environment was a departure from traditional cultural explanations for environmental change previously promoted by indigenous groups. A separate seventeen-year struggle against Argentine oil interests by the same Sarayaku Kichwas also relied on scientific knowledge and resulted in a July 2012 Inter-American Court of Human Rights (IACHR) ruling that the Kichwas and other indigenous groups must be consulted before outsiders encroach upon their government-designated lands.

Reserves have been located in some areas along the Pastaza River Basin, further south, but drilling has not commenced, as social mobilization kept three separate companies from drilling in Block 24. The people of this region strive to make their living off ecotourism and seek also to develop solar

---

1. The two authors took the "toxic tour" in 2014 and again in 2017 and noted, through participant observation, the worst contamination either of them had ever seen by far. Eisenstadt remembered the 1970s Santa Barbara, California, oil spill, which he experienced as a child who had to constantly remove tar from his bare feet with paint thinner after walking on the beach. A class action suit by oil spill victims against Chevron, which has been in domestic and international courts for years, continued in 2018.

energy–powered motorboats. They have more environment to protect than do the people of the northern Amazon Basin, near Lago Agrio, which has been heavily degraded, and even the central Napo River area, where attitudes regarding environmental conservation are mixed. In this southern zone of Morona Santiago, people had a stronger attitude toward the environment, as shown in chapter 2. Portions of this region are experiencing social conflict as several dozen people have been expelled from a mining area, but the tensions have been mostly contained since 2017, after a few skirmishes with casualties. Having disconfirmed postmaterialist arguments for environmental activism in favor of our vulnerability argument in chapter 2, this chapter bridges the analysis of individuals as survey respondents and the analysis of groups, aggregating the attitudes of the most vulnerable subsistence dwellers, as channeled through their leaders, into group interests and outcomes. The rainforest peoples may be those most directly involved in experiencing the impacts of the "environment vs. development" debate. They must decide whether to accept the economic gains from development, seek state-defined environmental protection, or take the "third position" delineated in chapter 1, a more environmentally pure position to protect nature in as pristine a condition as possible, consistent with *sumak kawsay* (the Kichwa cosmovision). We build on the argument in chapter 3, that in concrete situations—such as those presented by prior consultation and, as elaborated here, the negotiation of drilling rights—citizen self-interest, manifested as vulnerability, predominates over more abstract concerns such as post-materialism or indigenous cosmovision beliefs. In chapter 5 we show that more abstract cosmovision beliefs are statistically significant when viewed as causes of abstract environmental beliefs, such as in climate change. But here, with regard to attitudes relating to the environment as a concrete setting for their daily lives, respondents do seem to link this strongly with their cosmovisions.

We further aggregate our unit of analysis in this chapter, focusing on indigenous groups within the extractive frontier of the Amazon region, rather than on the individuals surveyed, although we start with positions aggregated from the survey. Using a comparison of survey results from the north, central, and southern "extractive frontiers," we show that environmental attitudes are driven by the geopolitics of negotiating oil contracts. For example, as evidenced in Table 4.1, indigenous respondents from the Amazon areas where oil drilling has occurred (North) are much more likely to support acts of protest than the general population (or even than other indigenous respondents). Those negotiations are conducted by the Ecuadorian state with international companies. However, provincial and municipal governments, and indigenous leaders who hold lands sought

Table 4.1 APPROVAL OF PARTICIPATION IN DEMONSTRATIONS AMONG
INDIGENOUS GROUPS

	"Do you approve of people participating in legal demonstrations?" PROT1.		"Do you approve of people blocking highways as a form of protest?" PROT4.		"Do you approve of people organizing to block mining and oil companies from entering the community?" PROT8.	
	Agree	Disagree	Agree	Disagree	Agree	Disagree
Andean Indigenous*	197	78	41	259	230	60
Percent	62.3	24.7	12.9	81.9	72.8	18.9
Northern Amazon Indigenous**	54	8	11	51	42	8
Percent	85.7	12.7	17.5	80.9	66.7	12.7
Central Amazon Indigenous***	144	32	39	138	140	36
Percent	75	16.7	20.3	71.9	72.9	18.8
Southern Amazon Indigenous****	360	67	99	344	312	93
Percent	78.2	14.6	21.5	74.8	67.8	20.22
Self-Identify as Indigenous (National Sample)	558	107	149	533	494	137
Percent	78	14.9	20.8	74.5	69.1	19.1
Overall National Sample	1322	371	303	1379	991	546
Percent	74.2	20.83	17	77.4	55.6	30.7

Note: Based on responses to the statement: "For the following questions, please tell me if you are in agreement or disagreement with . . ."
Percentages do not add up to 100 because some respondents did not reply, or responded "Do not know."
* Self-identify as indigenous and as Saraguros, Salasacas, Chibuelos, Cachas, Coltas, Otavalos, and Kichwa from the Andes.
** Self-identify as indigenous and live in area where oil has been drilled (Northern).
*** Self-identify as indigenous and live in area where oil debate is occurring (Central).
**** Self-identify as indigenous and live in area where oil has not been drilled and there is no present oil debate (South).

for oil extraction, also negotiate public programs such as new clinics, scholarships for children, and infrastructure (such as housing with electricity and internet access). We discuss case studies of extraction in each of the three sections of the Amazon (already exploited and polluted, in process of extraction, and "pristine" and undrilled rainforest), comparing, where possible, the positions of survey respondents with those of group leaders. We show that whether a group's oil has already been removed—and whether this process was done in an environmentally responsible manner—greatly affects respondent attitudes. Before elaborating the "within Amazon region" comparison, we start with a brief discussion of the different evolutions of state-society relations among the Andean Kichwa peoples and those of people in the Amazon region in general.

The Andean indigenous peoples primarily pertain to the Kichwa group, which is millions strong and includes economic and political leaders integrated heavily into the power structure of Ecuador's population center. That group has been the historic base of both the indigenous political party, Pachakutik, and the indigenous social movement, the Confederation of Indigenous Nationalities of Ecuador (CONAIE). The Andean Kichwa peoples have sometimes been co-opted via individual clientelism and group corporatism, depending on the administration. They were, under Correa, the beneficiaries of policies such as recognition of the Rights of Nature and other symbolic political acts. President Moreno seems to rely less on the populism of such symbolic acts.

The Andean groups have demonstrated strength through numbers. The Amazon indigenous communities, fragmented among small, isolated, and distant linguistic groups, have traditionally held much less authority. While the Sarayaku people did undertake a national march in the 1990s, most of the Amazon peoples' advancement of group causes has been through international lawsuits and work with national and international scientists promoting rainforest conservation through the United Nations Programme to Reduce Emissions From Deforestation and Forest Degradation in developing countries (REDD+) and other programs.

While the Andean peoples have mobilized through strength in numbers, the Amazon peoples have had to rely on knowledge-driven movements using technical approaches—such as scientific measurement of conditions and legal expertise—to file cases before national and international judicial institutions. Such cases met with success in the Sarayaku vs. Ecuador case, while the Chevron vs. Ecuador case drags on in international courts. By contrast, the Monte Bello Dam case won victories based on the failure by the Brazilian state to undertake prior consultation as specified in national law, but the Brazilian government ignored the verdict and built the dam anyway. Power was the currency in the Brazilian case, whereas in Ecuador the international verdicts (in the Inter-American Human Rights Commission on both occasions) of knowledge-driven movements were respected. In Ecuador too, the national government has often tried to force communities to take positions through populist appeals, and through old-school state corporatism, to be discussed later in the chapter.

If the movements in Ecuador were driven by multicultural identities, as prior research suggests, this would imply that some ethnic groups succeed whereas others fail to stop oil drilling, or at least manage to gain economic windfalls from it. This argument was a staple of past claims, which often characterized the Waorani, Achuar, and Shuar, who killed invaders of their lands in the past, as "savages" (Newcomb, cited in Kimerling 2013, 49). Indeed, movement observers (Tumink, Aragón, Tibán interviews) argue, with reason, that the Ecuadorian state "divides and conquers" indigenous groups, having "initially offered the Waorani money [to drill oil on their lands] and now not offering them money and saying they have to work for the money, and furthermore, that they have to be professionals [oil engineers, for example] in order to work" (Tumink interview). The Waorani, known in the past for "spearing oil workers, missionaries, and *cohouri* [or *cowode*] (non-Waorani) in general" (Holt 2005, 200), would not seem the most permissive of oil drilling under identity-based arguments. Furthermore, divisions within the Waorani were evidenced directly by the authors, who heard National Vice President Alicia Cahauigia argue for further oil drilling (with indemnities to the people), while, at the very same interview in the same room, National President Moi Enomenga argued against Waorani support for further oil drilling (interviews). Regarding oil drilling, communities like the Kichwa, Secoyas, Shuar, and Waorani divided, while others, like the Cofán and the Achuar, seemed to unite despite Ecuadorian government efforts to divide them too.

Power-driven movements, those based on numbers, were successful in the Andes at the turn of the twenty-first century but seem to have diminished in effectiveness even as they have increased in frequency. Andean-led movements, headed by long-standing indigenous groups like the CONAIE, helped to topple presidents Abdalá Bucaram Ortiz in 1997 and Jamil Mahuad in 2000. In the Amazon region, small groups, such as the Waorani and the Shuar, did in the twentieth century perpetrate violence as a show of power to keep outsiders away from their lands, but without a commitment to sustain these practices, great divisions over whether to perpetrate them, and strong international reprisals, violence was mostly abandoned. In the sections that follow, we discuss the differential rise of Andean and Amazonian indigenous communities. We then partly refute identity-based strategies by demonstrating that Andean and Amazonian respondents answered questions about indigenous mobilization very differently (even if attitudinal differences among Amazonian linguistic groups were less pronounced). Next, we inventory approaches by ethnic groups to negotiating with the state and private companies over extraction in the post-extractive north, the extractive central basin, and the pre-extractive south. Upon demonstrating that the Ecuadorian state sought to manipulate groups through corporatist means to obtain permission for oil drilling, we conclude that new forms of state-society relations, beyond multicultural rights recognition, are needed.

DIFFERENCES IN ETHNICITY OR HISTORIES OF MOBILIZATION AND LEVELS OF VULNERABILITY?

According to Ecuadorian scholars, the modern indigenous movement was solidified in the 1970s, when Ecuador began its transition to social democracy (Guerrero 1991; Barrera Guarderas 2001). However, the stage was set for the movement's formation long before that time. The very formation of politicized indigenous identities began with colonization, whose inherited social structure persisted for twenty-six years after the independence of the Republic of Ecuador (Guerrero 1991). The organizing principle of colonial society was the legal-political classification of inhabitants into two groups: the *indios*, who were forced to pay taxes and work in *concertaje*[2], and the "whites," who were exempt from tax contribution (Barrera Guarderas 2001, 85). With the withdrawal of the colonial tax in 1857, ethnic classifications in Ecuador were formally extinguished and, at least in theory, the principle of citizenship equality was extended to all Ecuadorians. The colonization focused almost entirely in the Andean region, as the Amazon was not entirely colonized until the mid-twentieth century.

In practice, the formal termination of ethnic classifications created an "ambiguous space" in much of the Andes for the indigenous in terms of their role in society and their legal rights according to the state (Barrera Guarderas 2001, 85). Indigenous communities maintained their own authorities, institutions of government, rituals, and beliefs, but their autonomy was never legalized or legitimized. And because Spanish was the formal language of the state, *indios* were excluded from many state services for not being Spanish-speakers; they could not vote in formal elections or be elected into office, and with the Law of 1868, the ethnic territories they possessed were legally recognized as "barren lands of the community" (Guerrero 1991). Thus, with the end of the tax, there was no explicit or

---

2. *Concertaje* is a "contract" in which the indigenous are obliged to do agricultural work without pay, or with only minimal pay, due to supposed inherited debts that they owe large landowners.

identifiable institutional relationship between the state and indigenous communities.

The history of the indigenous movement in the Andes takes a very different shape than does its development in the Amazon. In the Andes, there arose an informal, territorially situated administration of *indios*, a form of power relations that "mixed the public and the private" (Barrera Guarderas 2001, 86). In particular, the indigenous were dominated by three central political actors: "the *hacendados* and land owners, responsible for the economic exploitation of 'their *indios*'; the conservative Catholic Church, that in addition to continuing to collect tithes and *primicias* from the indigenous, were considered intermediaries . . . that presided over the cultural-ritual domain of the tribes; and, the white people of the towns, that benefited economically from these links of unequal reciprocity" (Guerrero 1991). The landlord, the priest, and the political official formed the dominant trilogy of power that endured as natural and little problematized for almost a century (Barrera Guarderas 2001, 85).

It was not until the reforms of the 1960s and 1970s, with the creation of the corporatist state under military rule, that this informal power relationship in the Andes began to deteriorate. The greater presence of the central state—the expedition of agrarian reform and the resulting parcellation of the *haciendas* of the church and the state, the extension of basic education, and state and international assistance to the farmer—began to chip away at the bases of ethnic administration (Barrera Guarderas 2001). In particular, the 1964 and 1973 land reforms were crucial in establishing the corporatist regime (Yashar 2005). These reforms first eradicated the semi-feudal *hacienda* systems of *concertaje* and *huasipungueros*,[3] providing the indigenous with certain civil rights, and then initiated programs of more serious land redistribution and rural development (Yashar 2005). The indigenous took the reforms one step further, utilizing the 1937 Ley de Organización y Régimen de las Comunas (Law of the Organization and System of Communities) to create their own legally recognized autonomous communities, governed by their own locally elected councils, and serving as a protected space for indigenous cultural practices (Pallares 2002). Together, these reforms granted indigenous communities with "social and civil rights that had not existed previously" (Yashar 2005, 97).

These reforms also set the stage for the first steps in the organization of indigenous communities in the Andes. With the eradication of the *hacienda*

---

3. *Huasipungueros* were indigenous families that worked the land of large haciendas and in exchange were permitted to live on the land, use its water, and keep a small share of the crops for themselves.

system, the reforms de-privatized agrarian conflict, which until then had been trapped in the confines of local power (Barrera Guarderas 2001). This aperture allowed Communist party militants and then the progressive Vatican II Catholic Church to form social ties with indigenous groups, providing them with both symbolic and material resources that assisted in their mobilization. Indeed, from the 1920s until the 1970s, the Communist party maintained the Ecuadorian Federation of Indians (Federación Ecuatoriana de Indios, FEI), which claimed to "manage and represent" indigenous peoples, mostly located in the Andes. And although the indigenous communities were not officially at the helm of FEI, the creation of the organization initiated a process labeled by the indigenous themselves as the construction of their own representation (Barrera Guarderas 2001).

Despite the landmark autonomy granted to indigenous peoples by the corporatist regime, inequalities persisted; the indigenous communities continued to have unequal access to social programs and the state and faced open discrimination within the public sector (in schools, hospitals, workplaces, markets, and state offices) (Pallares 2002). The indigenous peoples thus utilized mobilization networks initiated by the Communist Party, labor unions, and especially the Catholic Church, to form their first regional organization. In June 1972, the Highland Kichwa founded Ecuador Runacunapac Riccharimui (Awakening of the Ecuadorian Indian, Ecuarunari). A good part of the organizational support was reinforced by the Catholic Church, committed to "the indigenous cause" as part of their program of social action against inequality (Barrera Guarderas 2001). Indigenous leaders and Catholic officials alike agree that the church was crucial in providing networks for the indigenous to organize beyond the community level, and was thus key in the formation of the regional Ecuarunari (Yashar 2005, 105), the most prominent political group to date representing Andean Kichwa interests.

The process of indigenous mobilization occurred somewhat differently in the Amazon. There, the indigenous groups wanted to maintain de facto control over land that the state had historically ignored, but had grown interested in with the advance of neoliberal policies (and the discovery of oil). The state had little control within the Amazon region until the 1960s, when it encouraged colonization of the region via the first land reform, and when oil was discovered in the area in 1967. Before this, the indigenous people lived in relative autonomy on vast stretches of ancestral lands (Yashar 2005). When this autonomy was threatened, Amazonians utilized the educational skills and social networks that had been created again by the Catholic Church, as well as by evangelical missionaries who had entered the area in the 1950s under the auspices of the US-based Summer Institute of Linguistics (SIL). From these networks of schools and churches came the formation of local town centers (*centros*) and the motivation for the indigenous to organize along community and ethnic lines. Assisted by church officials, the Amazonian indigenous peoples initially founded several local federations, including the Federación de Centros Shuar, Federación de Organizaciónes Indígenas del Napo (FOIN), and Organización de Pueblos Indígenas de Pastaza (OPIP). Spurred by the pro-Indian rhetoric of the new democratic regime created in 1979, these Amazonian organizations (along with several others) came together in 1980 to form the Confederation of the Ecuadorian Amazon's Indigenous Nationalities (Confederación de Nacionalidades Indígenas de la Amazonía Ecuatoriana, CONFENIAE) (Yashar 2005), the region's aggregate interest group representing the Amazon peoples to this day.

In the Andean and Amazon regions, the construction of these new forms of representation did not occur without conflict. Throughout the 1970s and 1980s, these federations survived successive crises of organizational and political unity. Various decisive debates on the future of the indigenous movement occurred throughout this time. At the heart of this debate was the contradiction between a classist vision of indigenous politics, one that privileged the rural-peasant dimension and drove the alliance with the workers' movement, and another specifically focused on indigenous identity, whose central demand emphasized the ethno-cultural dimension and required construction of indigenous representation (Barrera Guarderos 2001). This ethno-specific current, which forged the nationwide umbrella interest group, the CONAIE, questioned even the tutelage of external agents, including the very church that had supported their formation, and adhered to a thesis of absolute autonomy and independence (CONAIE 1989). In this debate were forged some of the most important elements of the discourse of indigenous leadership, such as that of "look with two eyes, as poor and as *indios*, as exploited peasants and as an oppressed culture and race" (Macas 2001). The national indigenous "lobby" vowed to fight for ethno-specific representation and to end all forms of dependence on outside groups. These debates continue to be reflected in indigenous politics today as ethnic identity tends to supersede the left-right political divide as a cleavage.

Historically, Andean and Amazonian indigenous peoples have struggled to maintain strong inter-regional alliances. As per chapter 1, Andean Kichwa insurgents, under the banner of CONAIE (which they dominated over the Amazonian groups until a leadership rotation between the two regions emerged over the last few decades), overturned presidents around the turn of the twenty-first century. The Andean Kichwas (of the *sierra* or mountains) have had a great influence on national politics in Quito due to their great numbers, economic power, and demographic concentration in the country's densely populated and well-traveled Andean highlands. With a national population share of 4.8 percent, the Kichwa peoples of the Andes have been able to express themselves much more visibly politically than the Amazonian indigenous groups, which combined represent well below 2 percent of the population, or fewer than some 300,000 people (79,709 Shuar, 7,865 Achuar, 1,485 Cofan, 2,416 Waorani) (Instituto Nacional de Estadística y Censos 2010). In addition, the state had not entered the eastern portion of the Amazon before the 1990s and much of the "colonization" of the sometimes antagonistic Waorani, Shuar, and Achuar communities was undertaken by religious groups, such as the many Catholic missionaries, who first arrived in colonial times, and the Protestant Summer Institute of Linguistics (Kane 1995), which arrived in earnest by the middle of the twentieth century to translate the Bible into indigenous languages and convert indigenous citizens to evangelical Christianity.

In the 1990s the Andean indigenous communities undertook extensive social mobilizations, using tactics that few in the Amazon—such as the Sarayaku Kichwa people, who marched to Quito seeking land reform and autonomy—ever attempted. Some of the smaller Amazonian groups, still mostly isolated and without permeation by the Ecuadorian state, tried to stave off encroachment by outsiders through violence, attacking those who entered. However, as the state's presence grew more extensive and permanent, and the zone grew increasingly militarized as international investments were made and protected, many in the Amazon adopted nonviolent approaches to confrontation. When the Sarayaku Kichwas succeeded through a legal strategy with domestic and international allies to prevent oil drilling in their territory, other indigenous communities took notice. Amazonian leaders joined, and sometimes even led, international movements, as evidenced by the CONAIE presidencies of Amazon-based Shuar leader Miguel Tankamash, CONAIE's first president in 1986, Amazonian Kichwa leader Valerio Grefa in the 1990s, and Marlon Santi of Sarayaku in 2008.

While the indigenous groups of the Amazon and Andes have traditionally had different political interests based on their geographical, demographic, and economic differences, their platforms have converged as both sought to speak for nature against the Ecuadorian government's extractivist policies. "There is an agreement between the Andes and Amazon regarding extractivism," said Carlos Pérez, president of ECUARUNARI in 2014, still the most powerful regional group representing Andean interests (interview). "They are against petroleum and we are against mining, but it is more or less the same. In the Amazon, leaders are more vulnerable to cooptation by multinationals and the government. . . . It happens here [in the Andes] too, but less." Pérez observed that in the Amazon, emblematic struggles in Sarayaku, in Lago Agrio with Texaco/Chevron, and in the anti-mining movement in the south had elevated the struggle in the Amazon. But for him, in the Andes, "the struggle is constant. Demographics, population and geography make the difference, with the Andean region being more powerful" (interview).

The CONAIE, the national federation consisting of the leadership of ECUARUNARI and the CONFENIAE (the Amazon umbrella group) and indigenous people from the coast, has in recent years been headed by an Amazonian leader. And as stated by Franco Viteri, a recent CONFENIAE president (interview), tactics of peaceful mobilization are increasingly fruitful. "We combine the strength of our companions, the technology of our allies, and the spirituality of the people. We could have tried the strategy of arming ourselves but we would have lost. In this framework we understand the importance of presenting documents and videos on websites with our friends around the world, and using peaceful language. The state wants to provoke internal conflicts to incite the situation to justify sending in the police and the army to pacify us and protect the oil wells." The Sarayaku people have not ceded to the temptation of violent language and have led the pacifist resistance, even as the Waorani and Achuar have occasionally resorted to kidnapping and violence.

THE HISTORIC RELATIONSHIP BETWEEN INDIGENOUS ORGANIZATIONS AND OIL

Because land was the dominant interest shaping early indigenous uprisings, even in the early stages of the indigenous rights movement, control over natural resources was critical. For example, as part of the uprising in 1990, CONAIE submitted sixteen points—or demands—to the government. Contained within these demands were requests to resolve "water and irrigation needs" of indigenous communities, as well as revisions to how the government granted land titles, conducted land reform, collected land taxes, and distributed funds to indigenous nationalities (Pallares 2002). Although oil and minerals were not explicitly mentioned in the list of demands, control over indigenous lands implied that the indigenous communities would have a say in how their lands were utilized by the state and other potential extractive interests.

Although explicit demands regarding rights to oil were not included in the sixteen points submitted in 1990, CONAIE was becoming recognized as an important political actor with respect to oil production (Inter-American Development Bank 2004). Because oil was located primarily under the soil of indigenous lands, CONAIE had strong interests in what the government identified as "strategic areas," such as the *zonas petroleras* (IADB 2004, 9). Furthermore, funds from oil extraction were viewed as a primary means for development, yet were being funneled away from indigenous communities. As a result, indigenous organizations bypassed the Ecuadorian government completely by composing a letter to the World Bank asking for a loan to *expand* the oil industry (Martínez 1995, 190). At this time, some indigenous groups viewed extraction as a potential source of development funds—a vision that continues to divide indigenous communities today. The starkness of this divide is evident in nearly all contemporary indigenous communities where oil drilling is underway or being considered.

Oil extraction continued in the 1990s without the involvement of indigenous organizations, and was expanded into previously untouched areas of the Amazon, as indigenous groups grew weary of the unmitigated environmental impacts of drilling. These concerns reached a climax in July 1992, when a large oil spill in the Napo River at the Sacha Norte Uno Station near Limoncocha prompted a movement by two indigenous organizations—the CONFENIAE and the Federation of Communes "Union of the Natives of the Ecuadorian Amazon" (Federación de Comunas "Unión de Nativos de la Amazonia Ecuatoriana," FCUNAE). These groups gathered in August to draft and ratify an analysis of the implications of the oil spill. Also in 1992, indigenous organizations gathered in Coca to participate in the international conference titled "Alliance and Strategies on the Petroleum Problem in the Ecuadorian Amazon." During this meeting, indigenous organizations resolved to implement an independent and permanent system of environmental monitoring and vigilance (Martínez 1995). Furthermore, they encouraged the creation of vigilance committees not just at the organizational level, but within the communities as well.

With the oil spill, indigenous communities that had been previously unaffected by oil extraction grew savvy to the negative environmental costs of the activity. A year later, in 1993, CONFENIAE held another assembly to reinforce their resolve to create a vigilance team that would monitor extractive activity (Martínez 1995). At the same time, the Organization of the People of Pastaza (Organización de los Pueblos de Pastaza, OPIP) insisted on participating in management plans for oil drilling in their province. The culmination of all of this activity was that both indigenous groups and environmentalists came together to contest the Law of Hydrocarbons, which was proposed in 1993. Following these demands, the government sanctioned the creation of a technical team that would monitor oil activity in the Amazon. However, indigenous representatives were not incorporated into the team, and indigenous groups continued to feel excluded from an activity that was impacting their livelihoods, and for which they received no financial benefit.

By 1994, when the Ecuadorian government initiated the Seventh Round of auctions of oil blocks, indigenous organizations in the Amazon were sufficiently concerned with how extraction was affecting their communities and were capably organized enough to express their demands. Together, indigenous groups and environmentalists protested the opening of the round in June, during the inauguration of the Congress on Petroleum and the Environment. One of their major demands was again formal state recognition of an independent monitoring team, but this time one that comprised indigenous organizations and environmentalists. Indigenous communities had achieved little in the way of environmental protection until this moment, and intensified their organizational efforts to strengthen their social movement aggregation and, within a few years, the creation of political parties as a complement to these social movements.

Concretely, CONAIE protested the 1994 Agrarian Development Law being considered by the national legislature, including demands regarding natural resources. The Agrarian Development Law directly threatened indigenous autonomy by ceasing land redistribution, privatizing water rights, and allowing the sale of previously protected indigenous lands. In addition to insisting on the withdrawal of the agrarian reform bill, CONAIE requested government funding to resolve existing land disputes and reconstruct villages damaged by national disasters (Yashar 2005, 148). Importantly, CONAIE also suggested that *1 percent of oil revenues be channeled through the organization* for indigenous development purposes (Yashar 2005, 148; emphasis ours). The government responded by creating a commission to address the demands, in which 50 percent of the participation came from indigenous leaders. The result of the negotiations produced a law that differed significantly from the original proposition and included "credit for small farmers who produce for the local market, state control of water resources, continuation of land redistribution, development of indigenous agricultural knowledge, and a 2/3 majority vote required for indigenous communities to sell their community land" (Andolina 1999, 213). These two protests represented both the danger and the lure of oil presented to indigenous communities: on the one hand, the potential for environmental disaster; on the other, the influx of development funds.

Despite achieving significant political advances without the aid of electoral politics, CONAIE decided to enter the political arena in 1996 through the vehicle of the Movimiento de Unidad Plurinacional Pachakutik[4]—Nuevo País (Movement of the Awakening Plurinational Unity—New Country; Pachakutik or MUPP-NP). Scholars have identified factors that led CONAIE to enter into electoral competition. For example, electoral reforms passed in 1994 "made it much easier for the indigenous movement to gather the necessary signatures to register its own party and to form alliances that would enable it to compete in a sufficient number of districts to make an electoral project worthwhile" (Van Cott 2005, 100; see also Birnir 2004). Van Cott (2005, 122) also notes that around the same time that CONAIE was gaining power, the labor movement and other leftist organizations were struggling to define themselves in the transitioning democracy. As CONAIE became more successful, leftist party leaders began to see the political potential of the movement, and many eventually altered their discourse to join forces and/or ride the coattails of indigenous peoples' political successes.

In addition to these national-level influences, oil extraction was also part of the driving force behind Pachakutik's relatively quick entrance into national politics. At its 1993 congress, CONAIE had originally chosen to participate only in local and provincial elections (Yashar 2005, 149; 2002, 89). However, local leaders within the Amazon's CONFENIAE were eager to bring their issues—in particular, their concern about the environmental and financial repercussions of oil—onto the national political stage, and independently formed an electoral vehicle called the Movimiento Político Pachakutik (Pachakutik Political Movement) to field their own national-level candidates in 1996. At that time, Amazonian leaders—such as Kichwa leader and former president of CONAIE Valerio Grefa—formed an alliance with another new electoral project, a coalition of activists (including those advocating for the environment), labor leaders, and intellectuals—the Movimiento de Ciudadanos por un Nuevo País (Movement of Citizens for a New Country). According to Van Cott (2005, 121), leaders of Nuevo País realized that "they would need the organizational and voting support of the [entire] indigenous movement," so they also approached some CONAIE leaders. During CONAIE's thirteenth assembly (January 31–February 1, 1996), the organization voted unanimously to join the national-level alliance of the Amazonian indigenous communities and Nuevo País, and formally created the party that has come to represent the national indigenous movement, the Movimiento de Unidad Plurinacional Pachakutik—Nuevo País (MUPP-NP).

4. *Pachakutik* is a Kichwa word that can mean "awakening," "rebirth," or "a return to good times."

The early goals of Pachakutik as a political party mirrored those of the broader indigenous movement. Former CONAIE president Luis Macas (2001) defined MUPP-NP's initial objectives as twofold: 1) a historical-cultural (or ethnic) dimension, which identified struggles specific to the indigenous as a group; and 2) a struggle for the formation of an indigenous class identity, what he called the "social class struggle" of the indigenous peoples. The first objective focused on the needs of indigenous citizens that have traditionally been ignored by the state and dominant society, such as bilingual education, land reform, etc. The second is the struggle not only for the indigenous people to unite and themselves identify what it means to be indigenous, by articulating their "experiential understanding of social and political phenomena," but also to have the dominant society recognize them as an important socio-political group with a distinct outlook on politics (Macas 2001, xii). Macas (2001) argued that Pachakutik would achieve these goals primarily by operating in a way that was different from traditional parties, and through the ideological consistency of MUPP-NP parliamentary representatives. When it came to oil extraction, Pachakutik also mirrored the wishes of both CONAIE and regional organizations, such as CONFENIAE. However, as we discuss next, Pachakutik's demands with respect to oil were part of what led to their electoral decline. Macas envisioned an inclusive Pachakutik, which perhaps could embody both the class and ethnic unities discussed in chapter 2. However, in practice, such unity was impossible as one cleavage—class or ethnicity—had to take precedence.

DIFFERENTIATED IDENTITIES BETWEEN ANDEAN AND AMAZON GROUPS

Before elaborating the forms of clientelism practiced by the Ecuadorian government to divide and conquer Amazonian indigenous groups into communal assemblies that would approve extraction, it is worth reiterating that these groups spent the decade of the 1990s uniting. We also demonstrate that while indigenous groups (such as the Shuar and Waorani) often divided bitterly over whether to allow oil drilling, Amazonian communities did not fundamentally disagree on many important issues. As noted in Table 4.1, positions on political protest regarding Andean Kichwas did have great and possibly determinant differences with the Amazonian groups, but the differences among Amazonian groups were nominal. To illustrate these patterns, we explore survey responses to three relevant questions, broken down by ethnic group. First we summarize the historical difference between Andean and Amazonian groups through their own eyes.

As evidenced in Table 4.2, Andean indigenous respondents agreed that solidarity existed between Andean and Amazonian groups at about the same rate as the national average (18 percent said there was a lot of solidarity, while 60 percent said there was some). However, the Amazonian groups varied much more in their responses, depending on whether they were from areas where extraction had already occurred (North), was under debate (Central), or had yet to occur (South). The Northern and Southern Amazon respondents seemed less likely to possess solidarity, and also, looking at the rightmost column of Table 4.2, these same groups were less convinced than the overall average or than their Andean counterparts that efforts to unify the two populations (Andean and Amazon) had succeeded. These two groups' responses seem to contradict multicultural rights policy that would argue for strong solidarity between indigenous people in general.

Such multicultural affinities seem to exist more among the Central Amazon peoples with other indigenous groups. Respondents from the Central Amazon region, where oil is under debate, and where the Sarayakus have averted oil extraction and the home of a disproportionate number of national indigenous leaders, convey greater enthusiasm about solidarity between groups and also of efforts to unify. Note that formally politically active indigenous groups (those identifying with Pachakutik) offered more-optimistic views of the unity of indigenous groups and the solidarity between them than the more philosophically indigenous respondents (those sharing the indigenous cosmovision).

With regard to protest, only 17 percent of our survey sample agreed to blocking freeways and transit as part of protests (PRO 4), whereas fully 55 percent agreed that this tactic was okay with regard to blocking entrances to oil facilities. As expected, a higher percentage of those identifying as indigenous agreed with transit-blocking protests (20.8 percent) as compared to non-indigenous respondents (14.3 percent). However, fully 69.1 percent of those identifying as indigenous agreed with blocking mining and oil companies from entering communities, whereas the rate for non-indigenous respondents was 46.7 percent. This finding would likely be attributed to the fact that the majority of respondents in areas where extractive companies had entered communities identified as indigenous. In fact, according to our survey, 53 percent of respondents that claimed to be directly harmed by extractive activities also self-identified as indigenous.

And, as demonstrated further in the section that follows, the Andean indigenous communities were more amenable to cooperative solutions than to confrontational ones, which were favored by the Amazon groups.

Table 4.2 COOPERATION BETWEEN AMAZON AND ANDEAN
INDIGENOUS GROUPS

	"Do the indigenous groups from the Andes and the Amazon have solidarity between them?" ID16.			"Have efforts to unify Andean and Amazonian indigenous groups been successful?" ID17.	
	No	Some	A Lot	Yes	No
Andean Indigenous*	68	176	52	122	155
Percent	19.7	59.5	17.8	44	56
North Amazon Indigenous**	11	39	3	22	29
Percent	20.7	73.6	5.7	43.1	56.9
Central Amazon Indigenous***	18	128	41	92	77
Percent	9.6	68.4	21.9	54.5	45.5
Southern Amazon Indigenous****	1	101	10	32	64
Percent	0.9	90.2	8.9	33.3	66.6
Pro-Cosmovision (From Entire Sample)	148	748	205	452	515
Percent	13.4	67.9	18.6	46.7	53.2
Identify With Pachakutik (From Entire Sample)	6	88	26	58	51
Percent	5	73.3	21.7	53.2	46.8
Self-Identified as Indigenous (From Entire Sample)	98	444	106	268	325
Percent	15.1	68.5	16.3	45.2	54.8
Overall National Sample	229	1024	271	579	774
Percent	15	67.2	17.8	42.8	57.2

Note: Percentages do not add up to 100 because many respondents did not reply, or responded "Do not know."
* Self-identify as indigenous and as Saraguros, Salasacas, Chibuelos, Cachas, Coltas, Otavalos, and Kichwa from the Andes.
** Self-identify as indigenous and live in area where oil has been drilled (Northern).
*** Self-identify as indigenous and live in area where oil debate is occurring (Central).
**** Self-identify as indigenous and live in area where oil has not been drilled and there is no present oil debate (South).

The Andean indigenous people had a 65.9 percent rate of agreement with blocking extractivists, whereas among the Amazonian groups the Waorani had an 82.5 percent rate of acceptance, the Shuar responded with a 77.2 percent rate of acceptance, the Achuar had a 75.5 percent rate of acceptance for extractive blockades, and the Amazon Kichwa respondents were in agreement 67.7 percent of the time.[5] The Amazon communities were much more accepting of these tactics, probably due to their history of more-radical mobilizations, the fact that the environmental degradation from oil drilling affected their backyards, and the fact that contrary to the Andean peoples, whose histories were interwoven with those of the state, the Amazonian people acted independently of the state. The integration of Andean interests with those of that state as longtime participants in government and civic life, and the efforts to coopt these Andean Kichwa communities, through corporatism and clientelism, when the state's interests were at odds, explain this trend. The Amazon peoples were historically much less integrated into the nation-state and even now seem to regard their own group identities as higher than those of the nation-state.

With regard to whether the indigenous communities of the Andes and those of the Amazon have achieved solidarity between them, Amazonian groups have distinct perspectives. The majority of Achuar (64.2 percent) and Shuar (66.6 percent) believe that there is *little* solidarity between Amazon and Andean groups. The Waorani respondents in our survey tended to have more favorable views of solidarity between Andean and Amazonian groups, with 53.8 percent saying there was *some* solidarity between the two (rather than just a little). Amazonian Kichwas were very divided on their perspectives on Andes-Amazon solidarity, with 38.7 percent saying there was *some* solidarity, 30.2 percent saying there was *little* solidarity, and the remaining divided between believing there is *no* solidarity (11.2 percent) and *strong* solidarity (19.7 percent). Furthermore, 61.7 percent of Andean Kichwa respondents believed that there is only little solidarity between Amazon and Andean groups, though in Kichwa pueblos (such as Otavalo and Salasaca) with strong indigenous identities, that percentage does decrease to 39 and 38.7 percent respectively. Overall, however, there are relatively few who believe that there is strong solidarity between Andean and Amazonian indigenous. Among the Andean Kichwa, only around 11 percent agreed that there was a strong sense of solidarity across the regional divides. Multiculturalism does not seem to generate the ties that bind.

Given this relatively pessimistic view of solidarity between Amazonian and Andean indigenous groups, it is perhaps not surprising that they are also divided on their perspectives of who is qualified to speak for nature Table 4.3. We asked survey participants which group is more connected

5. The number of people in each sample were as follows: Andean indigenous (Kichwa) 263, Amazon Kichwa 103, Waorani 33, Shuar 61, and Achuar 34. The non-indigenous sample for that question was 497.

Table 4.3 WHETHER INDIGENOUS "SPEAK FOR NATURE" BY TRIBAL GROUP
(AMAZON DISAGGREGATED)

Indigenous Self-Identification	Agree	Disagree	Depends/Maybe	Total
Achuar	40	3	1	44
Percent	90.9	6.8	2.3	100
Waorani	24	15	1	40
Percent	60	37.5	2.5	100
Shuar	69	7	1	77
Percent	89.6	9.1	1.3	100
Kichwa Amazon	165	40	1	206
Percent	80.1	19.4	0.5	100
Andean Indigenous	264	69	4	337
Percent	78.3	20.5	1.2	100

Note: Survey question was: "Do you agree or disagree with the following statement: 'Indigenous people are closer to nature and Mother Earth or Pacha Mama than non-indigenous people.'" Percentages do not add up to 100 because many respondents did not reply, or responded "Do not know." Andean category is those who self-identify as indigenous and as Saraguros, Salasacas, Chibuelos, Cachas, Coltas, Otavalos, and Kichwa from the Andes. Andean indigenous peoples were those who self-identify as indigenous and do not live in Orellana, Napo, Pastaza, Sucumbios, or Morona Santiago (Amazon provinces), although 16 Shura residents of Zamora Chinchipe were the only residents of non-Amazon provinces coded as Amazon indigenous respondents.

to nature: those from the Andes, those from the Amazon, or both. Among the Amazonian indigenous respondents, sentiments were very strong that only Amazon peoples were close to nature. In a related question (discussed in chapter 1), we asked whether the indigenous were equipped to speak for nature, and here the Waorani were the outliers. Around 91 percent of Achuar, 90 percent of Shuar, and 80 percent of Amazonian Kichwa believed that Amazon communities were closest to nature. The Waorani were less certain, with only 60 percent believing the indigenous people are closer to nature. As noted in Table 1.1, 80 percent of the national survey sample believed that the indigenous speak for nature, meaning that the Waorani and Andean indigenous communities, largely believed to have been assimilated, and with great disruption to their social fabric in the case of the Waorani, have weaker beliefs in the indigenous as stewards of Mother Earth than the overall national population. Viewed through our regional lens, this finding is not surprising, as the Waorani, from the northern Amazon region, are the group from those listed whose environment has suffered the most destruction due to extraction.

When asked whether they felt Mother Earth deals directly with problems like food and water scarcity, 57 percent of the overall population agreed, but among indigenous groups, the percentage was higher, except among

Table 4.4 WHETHER MOTHER NATURE HELPS OVERCOME SCARCITIES
BY TRIBAL GROUP (AMAZON DISAGGREGATED)

Indigenous Self-Identification	Agree	Disagree	Depends/Maybe	Total
Achuar	29	6	5	45
	64.4	13.3	11.1	100
Waorani	31	9	0	40
	77.5	22.5	0	100
Shuar	37	9	28	79
	46.8	11.4	35.4	100
Kichwa Amazon	173	24	6	207
	83.57	11.59	2.9	100
Andean Indigenous	237	86	7	344
	68.9	25	2	100

Note: Survey question was: "'Do you agree or disagree with the following statement: 'Mother Earth (the Pacha Mama) takes care of issues like scarcity of food and water.'" Percentages do not add up to 100 because many respondents did not reply, or responded "Do not know." Andean category is those who self-identify as indigenous and as Saraguros, Salasacas, Chibuelos, Cachas, Coltas, Otavalos, and Kichwa from the Andes. Andean category is those who self-identify as indigenous and as Saraguros, Salasacas, Chibuelos, Cachas, Coltas, Otavalos, and Kichwa from the Andes. Andean indigenous peoples were those who self-identify as indigenous and do not live in Orellana, Napo, Pastaza, Sucumbios, or Morona Santiago (Amazon provinces), although 16 Shura residents of Zamora Chinchipe were the only residents of non-Amazon provinces coded as Amazon indigenous respondents.

the Shuar, where only 47 percent agreed (as per Table 4.4): It may be that the Shuar, who in some regions face more scarcity than in others (and they are known for their internal migration around Ecuador), believe there is more scarcity and thus may have uncertainty about who resolves it, or that it has been resolved.

Taken together, these descriptive data depict a difference between the Andean indigenous communities, who are much more integrated into Ecuadorian society, and the Amazonian groups, whose positions do vary by linguistic/ethnic group. A strong correlation exists, as will be seen below, among the Waorani and the Northern Amazon extractive area (drilled for oil in the 1970s and 1980s with tremendous damage to the environment), the Central Amazon and the Amazon Kichwa population (where oil drilling has started more recently with less damage and is under debate), with the Sarayaku Kichwas (resisting drilling through legal means), and the Shuar and Achuar communities of the Southern Amazon. We next present these differences and their origins. Overall, these differences argue against strong multicultural solidarity based solely on ethnic backgrounds and in favor of environmental vulnerability as the central determinant of attitudes about inter-ethnic solidarity, how far communities will go to oppose extraction, and the role of nature as a protector of their environments. We now summarize differences in patterns of resource extraction and indigenous responses that account for these group differences.

OIL DRILLING AND RAINFOREST CONTAMINATION IN THE POST-EXTRACTIVE NORTH

Oil was discovered in the Lago Agrio region in 1967, prompting the construction of a 300-mile pipeline from that area to the Pacific coast. Oil quickly became the nation's most important product, generating half the nation's export earnings within a few years. The parastatal company PetroOriente (later PetroAmazonas) owned a majority stake in drilling by the late 1970s, although Texaco led the operations. Oil roads were constructed and "Ecuadorian policymakers had little intention of entrusting the valuable petroleum region to the Siona-Secoya, Cofanes, or Huaorani [sic], native peoples whose national allegiance they did not trust" (Sabin 1998, 150). Vast environmental damage was left by the extraction. Then, the Ecuadorian government in the late 1970s adopted a policy that claimants of land had to put it to use (i.e., clear-cut and put to agricultural use), and conflicts emerged among the indigenous communities, the state, and the companies—national and international—that sought to exploit Amazon resources, such as timber and soil fertile for palm oil plantations.

As explained by Kimerling (2013, 48), the Ecuadorian government's treatment of the Waorani (and other indigenous peoples) was based on a doctrine of *terra nullius*, "a legal fiction that treats lands that were claimed by discovering European states as uninhabited—and thus belonging to no one—despite the presence of Indigenous peoples." An effort by Summer Institute of Linguistics/Wycliff Bible Translators (SIL/WBT) in the late 1960s and early 1970s to "colonize" the Waorani, who were sometimes violent to outsiders, was abetted by Texaco, which provided the aircraft used by the missionaries when they dropped gifts and called out to Waorani people over radio. Hundreds of Waorani were pressured into leaving their lands. One set of family groups, the Tagaeri-Taromenane, resisted contact and remained in isolation, as they have into the twenty-first century. These groups are known now as the Uncontacted Peoples who inhabit the so-called Intangible Zone bordering the Yasuní National Park.

SIL/WBT missionaries regarded Waorani assimilation as one of their most important missions ever, and the interests of the oil extractors was also evidenced in one account, in which a missionary (cited in Kimerling

54) recalled why the "oil people" freely lent their helicopters to the cause of taming Waoranis (also known by the Kichwa word "Auca"):

> The thing costs $200–$300 an hour to run; and it was a three-hour operation—besides the four high-priced employees! The oil people, in turn, are more than willing to do what they can for our operation, since we have almost cleared their whole concession of Aucas. They assure us that they aren't just being generous!

Indeed, Waorani elder Tipaa Quimontari Waewa remembered being scared to death by this effort. She was orphaned when her family was enslaved and sent to Brazil, according to her personal account, although they returned years later to reunite with her. She said that household items like pots and machetes were airlifted and dropped, and that the Waorani, who fought extensively among themselves at that time, thought the products had been brought by evil spirits (Quimontari Waewa interview).

By the late 1970s, even the recalcitrant Waorani people had assumed an ambivalent relationship with the Ecuadorian state and its extractivist allies. While they had blocked entry of oil drillers to their lands, including with violence, fully 60 percent of the Waorani depended on economically oil-related jobs like clearing the forest for seismic tests (Sabin 1998, 152). Internal conflicts emerged between the Waorani and the regional indigenous federation Confederation of the Ecuadorian Amazon's Indigenous Nationalities (CONFENIAE), which also represented the large Kichwa presence and the Shuar settlers who had come to the northeast from their native lands in the south to farm and ranch on land claims. The Waorani occupied an Esso Company oil well in 1988, seeking an extension of their airstrip so that larger planes could land and connect remote Waorani outposts to regional markets. The Kichwa and Shuar of the CONFENIAE wanted any social spending by the oil company to go through them for distribution, whereas the Waorani wanted to be direct recipients. The Waorani forced the CONFENIAE away from the negotiating table at spear point.

As the indigenous groups argued about who officially represented them, the Ecuadorian state did little to represent their interests with multinational oil companies. Texaco spilled nearly twice as much oil in Ecuador just from its main Amazon-to-Pacific pipeline as that spilled from the *Exxon Valdez*, and without any unique circumstances (such as the drunkenness of an oil tanker captain) to blame. Ecuadorian officials, such as former Petroecuador manager Rene Vargas Pazzos, said of the relationship between the parastatal regulator and the multinational: "We thought Texaco used the best methods. . . . We did not interfere in technical decisions because that was

Texaco's responsibility. That is what we paid them for. . . . We controlled only the production rates, the payment of taxes [and things like that]" (Kimerling 59). Ecuadorian officials seemed to shrug their shoulders about the environmental degradation, which apparently raised cancer rates to nearly four times beyond normal (San Sebastián et al. 2001), polluted local drinking water, endangered wildlife that indigenous communities relied upon for their livelihoods, and jeopardized their lands (see Red Amazónica Jurídica 2013 and Yanza 2014 for documentation).

In 1993, a class action lawsuit was filed in New York, the site of Texaco's corporate headquarters in White Plains, against the company by indigenous people and others affected by Texaco (which in 2001 merged with Chevron). After roughly a decade, the case was dismissed in favor of litigation in Ecuador, where a 2003 complaint was filed in Lago Agrio (named after an early Texaco gusher in Sour Lake, Texas) by four indigenous groups (the Waorani, Cofan, Secoya, and Siona), colonists, and members of the Kichwa peoples. That lawsuit resulted in a 2011 verdict that Chevron was responsible for cleanup of the toxic waste Texaco workers left behind when their contract expired, and for continuing threats against the environment, health, and indigenous culture. The $19 billion award in punitive damages (including $1.7 billion to the Frente de Defensa de Amazonía, the NGO that brought the suit) was appealed, and the Ecuador Supreme Court ruled in the plaintiffs' favor, although Ecuador has no Chevron assets and, despite a supportive ruling by the Inter-American Human Rights Commission (IAHRC) in 2013, the US case was dismissed on technicalities. Plaintiffs were left hoping that Chevron subsidiaries in third-party countries (such as Argentina and Canada) could be held responsible, but the Ecuadorian villagers have yet to find victory in the courts of either country, with the case dismissed in Argentina in 2017, and an appellate court decision in favor of Chevron in Canada in 2018.

The Waorani were given trinkets[6] and relocated, but they were not accorded the dignity of a sovereign people and allowed to make their own choices. Even in 2011, Kimerling (2013, 103) reports attending a meeting with Waorani leaders regarding the future of the Yasuní Biosphere Park, of central importance to that group, located on traditional Waorani lands

---

6. Indeed, the CONAIE showed in 2001 that some Waorani representatives had agreed to let the Italian oil company AGIP extract oil in exchange for the following: one bag each of rice and sugar, fifteen plates, two spoons, a bucket of lard, one pack of noodles, two frying pans, two packs of salt, two soccer balls, a stopwatch, and a referee whistle (Saavedra).

and juxtaposed with the Intangible Zone where Waorani families continue to live. At the meeting, the Ministry of Environment official who managed Yasuní told those assembled he had organized a management plan, but that the Waorani did not need to know the contents of the plan as "it is not pertinent." The official, Santiago Bonilla, told Kimerling that UN agencies would manage relations with the Waorani (who were present at the meeting) by asking "'extremely simple questions' in order to facilitate 'comprehension of the problem' and 'it would be harmful to the Huaorani [*sic*] people' if the author [Kimerling] spoke 'since they [the Waorani] have never been taken into account'" (Kimerling 104). The degradation of the Lago Agrio area and patronizing treatment of the Waorani and other groups in the northeast generated largely negative attitudes relating to oil extraction. In the central eastern Amazon (the Napo Basin), an important lawsuit was also lodged by indigenous people, the Kichwa of Sarayaku, but with strongly positive results, yielding a different sort of environmental attitudes.

While other northern groups like the Cofanes retained greater autonomy than the Waorani, some anthropologists have argued that the Waorani are unique, given their "late" contact with Western colonists and their individual- and family-based units of organization (compared to the community- and group-based identities of most other groups), according to anthropologists (Lara interview). "When the oil boom started, the Ecuadorian state had no presence in the Amazon. . . . The organizations representing the Waorani are a construction of the state which was reached to legitimize their agreements with oil companies" (Lara interview). Waorani leader Tega Baihua (interview) said the Waorani had no choice but to make agreements in order to receive "a few cents" from oil extraction on their lands. "They gave us paper and said 'sign this' and then gave us twenty rights for twenty years even though we didn't know what twenty years was. Our parents and forebears did not know how to read." Whatever the disagreement over which group was at fault for the pollution of Waorani areas, and that group's cultural division and disarticulation, indigenous groups to the south did try to avoid the adverse results of that group's dealings with oil companies and the Ecuadorian government.

THE BATTLE OVER SUSTAINABLE DEVELOPMENT OF OIL RESOURCES IN THE CENTRAL RAINFOREST

Former CONFENAIE president Franco Viteri (interview) argued for multicultural rights, but he agreed that groups use these rights in extremely differentiated ways. He said that indigenous rights are treated differently in the northeast, where rights now center on indigenous citizens' rights to work, whereas in the center and south these rights focus mostly on preserving nature. The Waorani are a case study of allowing people to dominate nature, as opposed to adapting to nature. As Viteri argues (interview):

> Oil companies threw crackers and tuna from helicopters and took away the Waoranis' autonomy. To live in cities they [the Waorani] need money and they like computers and iPhone 6s. . . . The rapid contact [with outsiders] disarticulated them and confused them. Forty years of contact is few. The Waorani in the prior generation took up spears and spoke of killing to solve problems. This generation talks about diplomacy, but how can we make the Waorani take up diplomacy so quickly? This is a long process of cultural adaptation. That is why they sometimes kidnap oil workers.

The Kichwa and Shuar have been exposed to Western colonizers for one hundred years, according to Viteri, allowing them to take more assimilated positions, even though the Shuar too are being manipulated, according to Viteri (interview), as northern oil extraction takes extensive technology. Yet the Shuar can mine gold and have strived to do so, even though the government has outlawed "artisan gold panning." Equity could be achieved through the establishment of a Kichwa-Shuar oil company, Viteri said, but this runs counter to his insistence that the oil should stay in the ground. Indeed, Viteri (interview) argues that education is the only real answer, as "a people that manages information technology and diplomacy and influences public policy is a strong people." On the other hand, he argues strenuously for the primacy of nature and the hubris of humanity in trying to affect nature.

Just as divisions between the Waorani and other indigenous groups (represented within the CONFENIAE) occurred in the northeast, divisions among indigenous political organizations occurred in the east central Amazon region too, offering additional evidence to favor polycentric pluralism rather than pure multicultural arguments. In the early 1980s an evangelical group in Pastaza, the Asociación de Indígenas Evangélicos de Pastaza y la Región Amazónica (AIEPRA), broke away from the secular Organization of Indigenous People of Pastaza (OPIP) to negotiate social projects (schools, water pumps, and a landing strip) with Atlantic-Richfield, and to seek to "protect the valued rivers and forests against the hazards revealed previously in the northeastern petroleum zone" (Sabin 1998, 154). Thousands of Shuar settlers from the southeast moved north at this time, as "using the land" was a prerequisite for claiming it until Ecuador affirmed in a 1997 submission to the IAHRC that it had ended the practice of requiring Amazon land tracts be cleared and planted (or ranched) to be claimed by colonists.

The most organized of the Kichwa groups in the central Amazon, OPIP, received a land concession in 1992 from the national government to manage and develop. In 1989, the people of Sarayaku (one of OPIP's largest settlements) had held hostage representatives of the land reform agency, the state oil company, and the president's office. These threats of violence eventually gave way to efforts of passive resistance, although Viteri (interview), who is from Sarayaku, said that some community activists continue to push for violence. In 1989, the government promised to stop seismic work until the indigenous communities had secure land titles, and additionally, the Sarayaku people demanded compensation for the wood cutting, explosives detonation, and trail-making that had been part of the oil companies' "footprint" to that point (Sabin 1998, 161). The Sarayaku Kichwa's landmark achievement, perhaps the truest success to date of any Amazon region lawsuit, was the judgment it received in the June 2012 Inter-American Court of Human Rights (IACHR) case *Kichwa Indigenous People of Sarayaku v. Ecuador*.

That case, yielding a US $1.25 million settlement for the people of Sarayaku, was based, in part, on the failure of the Argentine Compañía General de Combustibles (CGC) and Petrolera Argentina San Jorge to get permission of the people of Sarayaku before undertaking seismic tests. According to the judgment, CGC expressed interest in exploring for oil in Block 23 (Sarayaku's location) starting in the late 1990s, and in May 2000 the company's lawyer visited Sarayaku and "offered US $60,000 for development projects and 500 jobs for the men of the community" (IACHR 2012, 21). While the Sarayaku community rejected this offer, neighboring communities accepted it, and in 2001, CGC hired Dyam Service, sociologists and anthropologists who specialized in community relations. "According to Sarayaku members, its strategy consisted of dividing the communities, manipulating the leaders, and carrying out defamation campaigns to discredit the leaders and organizations" (IACHR 2012, 22).

Sarayaku community members argued that the seismic survey was proceeding without community permission. CGC convened a community hearing to seek such permission; no one attended from Sarayaku, but CGC officials insisted the meeting had occurred, even though they could not produce any transcript of said meeting (IACHR 2012, 24). Members of the Sarayaku community, aided by Quito lawyer Mario Melo, who was working with the Ecuador office of the California-based Pachamama Foundation, filed the legal complaint to the IACHR. But in the meantime, tensions escalated as in 2003 several Sarayaku citizens were detained by CGC personnel and the Ecuadorian armed forces. CGC continued executing its seismic survey, laying down seismic lines, setting up seven heliports, and destroying caves and water sources needed by the community (IACHR 2012, 27). Additionally, some 120 members of the Sarayaku community were allegedly attacked by people from neighboring Canelos, who had staked their community's economic development on the extraction.

After nearly a decade in the courts, the indemnity was used to launch a fund for the community that purchased a tractor, truck, and airplane, as well as a fund with scholarships and a micro-lending bank for development projects. "The fund is so that we can stop depending on NGOs," Viteri said (interview). Much of the mobilization, including marches from Puyo to Quito in the late 1980s and other "power" movements, were efforts to secure property rights, according to Santi (interview). The future will be one of knowledge-based movements, he said, adding that the community hopes that scholarships established in the indemnity will go to environmental engineers and scientists, pilots, and lawyers, arguing that combining indigenous cosmovision-based knowledge with Western knowledge should yield the best results: "Humanity should move forward with tools from wherever we can find them" (Santi interview). Echoing tenets of polycentric pluralism, the Sarayaku leaders said that their community would need strong national and international allies in order to move forward in protecting the environment.

Sarayaku activists concur with the survey results conveying stronger environmental attitudes in the Napo River area and the central Amazon Basin than in the North. "In the North all that remains is misery and poverty, and even Chevron recognizes this," said Santi. "But in Sarayaku the forest has not been destroyed. It is going to be in 100 years as it is now; we will not negotiate oil." Critics of the Sarayakus abound. Representatives of other Pastaza groups, such as the Andwa and the Sápara, argue that "while the Sarayakus win internationally, go see how they live. They go abroad to the best hotels and their people live on the floor" (Proaño interview). Others accuse them of hypocrisy in their environmentalism and reverence for the indigenous *sumak kawsay* cosmovision, as their leaders "live in Puyo with cars and enter Sarayaku when they need to manipulate people. If I wanted an alternative style of life, I would live there and protect my surroundings. But here they do not drink *chicha*; they drink beer" (Coka interview). But the group has succeeded in beating the odds and drawing extensive international attention to oil company exploitation attempts, and in demonstrating the potential of the knowledge-based approach to social movements, choosing this approach over that of violent confrontation, as was practiced in the past.

Just to the north of Sarayaku, on the outskirts of the largest cities of Tena and Misahuallí in the Napo province, groups have not been successful at remaining unified in the face of government pressure to allow for extraction. Oil was expanded into the Napo province relatively early with the concession of Block 7 to British Petroleum in 1985 (Environmental Justice Atlas 2016). However, extractive activity in the province greatly accelerated at the turn of the millennium, particularly with the government's concessions of Blocks 20 and 29 in Napo in the Ninth Round in 2000. At the time, the Napo Kichwa were relatively unified under a central provincial organization, then known as the Federación de Organizaciones Indígenas de Napo (Federation of Indigenous Organizations of Napo, FOIN), but which changed its name in 2000 to the Coordinadora de la Nacionalidad Kichwa de Napo (Coordinator of the Kichwa Nationality of Napo, CONAKIN). CONAKIN continued the status of FOIN as the primary vehicle for the province's indigenous movement and the Napo indigenous population's direct connection to the regional CONFENIAE and then the national CONAIE indigenous organization. Founded in 1969, FOIN (CONAKIN) represents over 180 indigenous communities across the Napo province, who, as their name indicates, are predominantly Kichwa.

In 2003, the Ecuadorian government through the Salesian Polytechnic University carried out prior consultation for Oil Blocks 20 and 29. During the process, local resistance within the indigenous communities emerged and was linked to local environmental organizations opposed to oil activity (Environmental Justice Atlas 2014). Despite this, CONAKIN came to an agreement that would permit extraction on their lands. Conflict resulted; the communities that formed the bases of CONAKIN argued that the organization's leaders ignored their wishes and were manipulated by the state and the oil companies to allow drilling. In 2004, with the support of environmental and human rights NGOs, several communities filed suit over the legality of the consultation. Oil exploration in the region came to a halt. The indigenous communities of Napo fragmented, and CONAKIN disbanded. As a result, Napo province's indigenous movement decided to return to their roots and reinstated the name of their original organization, FOIN.

In 2008, Correa reinvigorated the expansion of oil in Napo by giving concessions for Block 20 to Ivanhoe Energy—this time without any prior consultation (Environmental Justice Atlas 2014). Indigenous groups scrambled to respond. FOIN, trying to regain credibility within the national indigenous movement, revoked its pro-extractivist position when (as CONAKIN) it had made the controversial decision in 2003 to strike a deal with the government. By 2014, FOIN had taken a staunch anti-Correa response and had disavowed support for extraction that ignored consultation of the communities. As the president of FOIN Marco Aurelio Licuy explained, the goal of the organization is to "care for and maintain our ancestral territories, the environment, and nature, and to recover our culture" (Licuy interview). To do so, they have remained "vigilant that the government comply with the rights of *pachamama* established in the constitution" (Licuy interview). Because the government was not engaging in extraction "with environmental control," and because the state was not providing any funds to affected communities ("even 0.001 percent would be acceptable"), FOIN was against all government-sponsored extraction in Napo (Licuy interview).

However, the divisions that emerged following the failed 2003 prior consultation in Napo deepened once oil exploration and extraction were resumed under Correa in 2008. As FOIN president Licuy explained, "the social situation here in Napo is chaotic" (interview). Because FOIN made it clear that, like CONAIE, they were unwilling to work with Correa, communities that wanted to make deals with the state over oil created alternative federations to represent their interests. One such organization is the Amazonian Federation of Indigenous Organizations of Napo (Federación Amazónica de Organizaciones Indígenas de Napo, FAOICIN). As FAOICIN president Cristina Shiguango explained, the thirty-three communities included in her federation "don't work with FOIN and CONAIE" because their "rights are not respected" under these umbrella organizations (interview).

Shiguango listed the concerns she associated with extraction. "Before, we lived healthy lives. We ate natural food. Now, we have illnesses, our chicken and meat are contaminated, our water is contaminated, people have cancer and burned skin. The companies are not vigilant" (Shiguango interview). However, for Shiguango, extraction "is different with the state, we have more control. We can hold prior consultations and we can protect the environment" (Shiguango interview). The implication is that foreign companies are the problem as they contaminate the environment, whereas the state oil company will not, and will better work with indigenous communities conducting "technical studies of oil production" to ensure that they can "live healthily" (Shiguango interview). As a result, Shiguango was a staunch supporter of Correa and his expansion of state-regulated extraction, arguing that (in spite of all of her environmental concerns), she was in favor of expanding oil into Napo—and even into Yasuní—because the state will ensure that it will benefit the communities. Her position was one that sought pragmatically to utilize support from the Ecuadorian state to provide for her community.

Two other indigenous federations in Napo had also broken with FOIN (and CONAIE) and mirrored the perspective of FAOICIN and Shiguango. The Federation of Peasant and Indigenous Organizations of Napo (Federación de Organizaciones Campesinos y Indígenas de Napo, FOCIN) and the Evangelical Federation of the Kichwa Nationality of Napo (Federación de Evangélicos de la Nacionalidad Kichwa de Napo, FENAKIN) both worked with Correa's government to allow oil drilling in their communities. As President of FOCIN Guido Grefa Chongo put it, "Because the president is an environmentalist, he cares for the environment" (interview). "There is no contamination in our zone because we have local technicians of environmental control. We worked with Correa to develop a program of environmental regulation that combines ancestral knowledge and Amazonian wisdom with scientific instruments" (Chongo interview).

The implications are, of course, that the government is reimbursing these communities in one form or another. Although Chongo acknowledged that the state had provided education for local members of his organization, he would not admit to any monetary benefits that his organization or the thirty-three communities associated with his federation received in return for the expansion of oil. However, the president of FENAKIN, Lenin Alfredo Grefa, was a bit more forthcoming. "We have to benefit from *pachamama*," he explained (Grefa interview). "Many of the communities don't want to be limited by CONAIE . . . They require more resources, they want [oil] concessions" (Grefa interview). For Grefa, allowing oil extraction that has "minimal impact" is a boon to the communities, especially when the government signs "an agreement with the nationalities" that ensures that they receive benefits (interview). By his pragmatism, alliances with environmentalists, even outside of indigenous communities, would help advance the common interest.

The divisions in Napo reinforce our findings in chapter 2 surrounding how difficult it can be to determine who speaks for nature in areas where oil is being debated, as it is in Napo. Community splits around the issue of extraction parallel those that often occur in the southern Amazon region, where, as described in the sections that follow, the central government has actively divided indigenous communities to gain community support for oil drilling. Even within organizations whose leaders worked with Correa, as FAOCIN's president Shiguango did, communities are divided. As Shiguango put it, "We go around socializing with community leaders, talking about our work with the president, but some communities are corrupt and don't let me enter" (interview). These "corrupt" communities are those like that of Teodoro Rivadeneyra, president of the Shiripuno Community, whose livelihood depends on "community tourism," a brand of ecotourism that allows foreigners to experience indigenous lifestyles. For him, oil extraction would never be worth the costs to his community. "We replant the forest, we cultivate manioc. The company interrupts our way of life, destroys our livelihood" (interview). Even if, as Shiguango argued, Correa's brand of extractivism was better—more regulated and less harmful for the environment—there are some communities for which the costs remain too high. Indeed, both the pro-extractivists and the anti-extractivists in the Napo area were more than willing to find allies inside their multicultural blocks, but were also glad to go outside of these.

ECONOMIC DEVELOPMENT AND HUMAN RIGHTS VERSUS CONSERVATION IN THE SOUTHERN AMAZON

In the southern Amazon Basin, the Achuar people share the view of the Sarayaku Kichwas about not drilling and have successfully mobilized against oil drilling. The Federation of Shuar People (FIPSE) persuaded Ecuador's Constitutional Court that ARCO was trying in 1999 to splinter the group, and that anti-extraction perspectives needed to be respected. Community pressures kept ARCO and its successor, Burlington Oil, from drilling before the Ecuadorian government annulled their contract in 2005 and Conoco Phillips purchased the Block 24 lease under question, but then withdrew from Ecuador (Amazon Watch 2010) under pressure. The upshot is that drilling has for the most part not yet commenced in the southern expanse of Ecuador's Amazon rainforest.

The Shuar and Achuar have refused to allow drilling in even the region's proven reserves such as Block 24, although here too ambiguity exists, as leaders want their next generation trained as petroleum engineers and interlocutors between their indigenous cosmovision and Western technologies. Achuar economic development director Pasqual Callera observed that the Ecuadorian government offers "crumbs"[7] and that self-sufficiency will depend on ecotourism, such as the Hotel Kapawi rainforest lodge they have operated for over a decade, with support also from a European hotel operator. The Achuar, who separated officially from the Shuar people in 1991, forming their own national group even though they do speak the same language, seem more united than the Shuar, who are deeply divided on the critical issue of whether to allow oil drilling. Achuar

---

7. Diego Callera (interview) disparaged the approach of the Waorani, who he said "could be bought" for $5,000 or less and that communities could be placated for oil drilling through the granting of a boat motor or even bags of rice (interview).

leaders said that international allies were central to their mission of eco-tourism and sustainable development, but not to be fully trusted, as they had different interests from those of the Achuar.[8]

Achuar leader Pasqual Callera was readily willing to disparage the economic strategies of other Amazon indigenous groups. To Callera (interview), the Waorani and Kichwa were willing to "sell out" the rainforest for oil money, while the Shuar were so divided their platform was impossible to tell. "But our plan," he declared, "is to develop alternative technologies which do not pollute, to show it can be done that way." However, concluding more tenuously, he added that: "We are not completely against extractivism" (Pasqual Callera interview). The tensions were sharply drawn on these issues between these groups, which share the same national multicultural rights and, by the presumption of many, would share interests and positions.

One important Shuar group, the Federación Interprovincial de Centros Shuar (Interprovincial Federation of Shuar Centers, FICSH), opposes oil drilling, insisting it will always fight against oil extraction and mining, but at the same time says there will be a moratorium on drilling in their lands for twenty years while they "prepare our children to be part of the business" (Wachapa Atsau interview). The group also claims that a dialogue can proceed when both sides [the Shuar and the Ecuadorian state and multinational oil companies] are willing to compromise, "but not now." Other observers (Entza and Laurini interviews) indicate that this apparent contradiction in position exists because the Shuar themselves are internally embattled, like the Waorani, and while the FICSH opposes extraction, the regional Shuar organizations of Pastaza and Morona Santiago are not so certain. Indeed, just as FICSH rejects oil drilling (but with some exceptions, it turns out), the Morona Santiago–based Shuar Organization of Ecuador (OSHE) claims that "We have never said 'no' to extraction. If we were to say no, I would have to take off my shoes and my shirt and mobile phone, the chip for which comes from mining" (Pidru interview).

Contrary to the numerous and divided Shuar factions, the Achuar Nation of Ecuador, a much smaller group, seems more united in its determination to find economic development alternatives to extractivism, even

---

8. In fact, Roberto Paes, national vice president of the NAE, demonstrated this to us by insisting that we would "get rich" from interviews and research conducted on their lands, and should thus pay $800 to interview him. While we refused to pay outright bribes, we did have a grant budget line for a translator/guide on Achuar lands and we did agree to pay $230 for this service, with a portion going directly to the community we visited and a portion going to him and his office (Paes interview and participant observation).

if, rhetorically, they tend to leave all options open. "We don't accept extraction under the terms suggested, but we do have alternatives. . . . The people speak of *sumak kawsay* but we want to ground that term in practice" (Callera interview). Indeed, one author found Callera in the antechamber of the Prefect of Macas, where he was seeking to pitch the idea of launching a solar-powered boat. The project was funded by the Embassy of Finland with a grant and by the Inter-American Development Bank with a loan, and Callera and international NGO activist Oliver Utne (a US national working for the NGO Aldea) sought to enlist support from the provincial government of Macas for that project and for renovations to the Kapawi Lodge, the Achuar's ecotourism enterprise. Callera had gathered baseline data to make his argument more precise, justifying the pilot boat's $285,000 cost. His rational and knowledge-informed approach was strongly suggestive of the approaches by other Amazon-based indigenous activists. Callera was seeking to use polycentric entries into the solar energy business as a means of bypassing the debate over extractionism entirely. While it was a clever idea, the purchase of one solar-powered boat seemed only to be the beginning to the diversification of Achuar economic development.

THE ECUADORIAN GOVERNMENT'S "CRUDE" POPULISM: SPEAKING FOR NATURE, BUT WITH A SHRILL VOICE

In chapter 1 we defined populism, in general terms, as leaders' actions to place short-term political imperatives ahead of longer-term national interests. The application of "extractive populism" to Ecuador's petroleum-financed development (the petro-state) referenced efforts to finance an extensive increase in development programs by speculating on oil futures (selling pledges of future oil production to China at below-market prices in exchange for short-term liquidity). Here we define a complementary strategy, corporatism, and discuss its use by the Ecuadorian government to favor factions of the Sápara and Achuar populations who supported oil extraction. Corporatism is "a general system of interest representation in which specified groups are awarded monopoly status with regard to their clientele and, in one form or another, brought into official recognition as the central bases for decision-making" (Chalmers 1977, 34). Corporatism is not always anti-democratic but has tended to develop this way in Latin America. Corporatism, where peak associations are officially recognized by the government to represent the interests of groups like labor and business, contrasts with pluralism (as exemplified by Dahl's 1979 rendering of the United States, for example), under which all groups are said—at least hypothetically—to have equal status, or at least equal access. The battle for prior consultation—and approval—by indigenous communities in the Ecuadorian rainforests offers examples of contemporary manifestations of corporatism.

The Sápara people are a tiny group, numbering only a few hundred in Ecuador and Peru, but their extensive rainforest landholdings, reminiscent of a pre-colonial population of over 100,000, include large portions of Oil Blocks 79 and 83, which were contracted in 2015 for exploration and exploitation, to the China National Petroleum Corporation (CNPC) and China Petrochemical Corporation (SINOPEC). Early in 2012, as the Eleventh Round of oil solicitations was getting underway, a majority of Sápara communities, constituted as the Sápara Nation of Ecuador (NASE in Spanish), assembled and voted to continue resisting oil extraction on their territory. However, the president of NASE, Bacilio Mucushigua, one month later signed another document advocating for oil exploitation that he had negotiated, apparently without the knowledge of the Sápara Government Council. In August 2012, Mucushigua was voted out of office with anti-extractivist replacements elected. Lacking internal support, Mucushigua convoked an assembly, but of Achuar and other migrants to the area; was proclaimed president of the NASE (despite the existence of another, legitimate president); and was promptly recognized by the Ecuadorian government's national secretary of political affairs to negotiate on behalf of the Sápara people (*Audiencia Temática: Derecho a la Asociación de los Pueblos Indígenas en el Ecuador*, 20–22).

Another case of corporatist support by the Ecuadorian government for an official group but which did not represent that group's majority position occurred against the Achuar Nation of Ecuador (NAE) in September 2015. The president and coordinator of the NAE were voted out of office, but in November the national secretary of political affairs insisted that the vote had not occurred and that ex-president Ruben Tsamaraint retained his position. The newly elected president, previous vice president Bolivar Wasump, was supported by a majority of voting delegates at the National Assembly. He wrote a resolution denying the Ecuadorian government's decision and took office. The conflict between the two leaders started when the CONAIE convoked the Achuar (and Ecuador's other groups) in August 2015 to participate in an indigenous protest to end large-scale mining, among other objectives. Tsamaraint unilaterally decided not to participate, according to media accounts, prompting Wasump, in his words, to follow public demands and overthrow Tsamaraint: "In our system of government, no leader can take their own decision without asking the rest of the people think. The people rose up, got angry, and asked that he leave his position" (Márquez 2015). Wasump was later summoned for a criminal trial by the state prosecutor, alongside seven other indigenous leaders, for the alleged offense of paralyzing public services as a result of their participation in the protests against extraction (Business Human Rights 2016).

Both the Sápara and Achuar people argued that the central government used distributive programs to lure Amazon indigenous community support for extraction. For example, the government agency Ecuador Estratégico had tried to co-opt people in oil-rich areas, constructing Cities of the Millennium (communal housing with electricity and sewage), clinics, and public schools with computers, in addition to bidding out development projects to local communities in highly impacted areas. In the words of Paes, of the NAE, "Around the time of the elections they [Ecuador Estratégico] were offering marvels—water and telephone hookups, housing and schools of the Millennium, electricity, everything. People fell for it like mosquitos. We reached an agreement and they explained to us where the money would be coming from. We organized a workshop and agreed to the time and place, but they never showed up" (interview). More recently, several interviewees claimed that in the Sápara dispute, the dissident pro-extractive communities were enrolled in Socio Bosque (where peasants were paid to maintain forested lands), whereas the benefits of this program were not extended to anti-extractivist members of the Sápara (Akachu, Greene, Mazabanda, Santi interviews).

CONCLUSIONS: GEOPOLITICS AND THE FAILURE OF NEGOTIATIONS UNDER EXTRACTIVE POPULISM

The Ecuadorian government's efforts to pick and choose which groups would represent indigenous communities at the table where oil drilling projects and compensations were decided is reminiscent of what may have been Latin America's most notorious corporatist system of the twentieth century, Mexico's labor unions. Official labor unions in pre-democratization Mexico participated in negotiations over minimum wages and workplace conditions, whereas independent union leaders were persecuted and even killed (Aguilar Camín et al.). Ecuador is not known for twentieth-century authoritarian corporatism to the extent of Mexico, Argentina, and Brazil, but this has changed in relation to indigenous support for extractivism. As we have seen, the Sáparas in the central Amazon active oil block, and the Achuar to the south, have received the same "divide and conquer" treatment the Waorani earlier attributed to the international oil companies and Ecuadorian state.

And while this chapter has tended to assume indigenous leaders represent their communities' wills, such leaders also benefit personally from positioning themselves. Pro-extractivism leaders are more eligible for public programs like Socio Bosque, at least in allegations by interviewees (Greene, Mazabanda, Ushigua interviews). Furthermore, they may receive kickbacks from oil companies, if any of the widespread but difficult-to-prove allegations are true (although oil companies did reward supportive communities directly through the 1990s, when the state became the intermediary between indigenous communities and the oil companies and a more active provider of services). Anti-extractivist leaders gain favor with international environmental NGOs and win credibility among their followers. In short, this chapter has demonstrated the strategic pursuit of polycentric pluralism by indigenous leaders when it suited them, but also has shown that some interests, like the state, can collude through corporatist practices with extractive companies to block the popular will when indigenous groups do not want extraction.

Many analysts noted that the oil debates affect the subsequent trajectories of indigenous leaders. Walsh extractive industries analyst Peter Ayarza (interview) said that indigenous leaders have incentives to become leaders, as these positions give them access to international NGOs, travel, and projects. His colleague Mark Thurber added that "the communities shop around for an indigenous organization that is going to give them what they need," and that these leaders, who sometimes but not always represent their communities' views, are gatekeepers to outsider biologists, religious organizations, extractive companies, and others who seek access to community lands and resources (interview 2016). Again, like state corporatism, the corruptibility of movement leaders may be a risk of polycentric pluralist approaches.

Indigenous communities do sometimes disparage the leadership of other indigenous groups, implying that oil company and government efforts to co-opt them do work. "The Waorani are like children," said Robert Paes, former vice president of the NAE (interview).[9] "We have spoken to

---

9. When the authors interviewed Paes, he sought to charge US $800 for the interview, stating that an Italian student had paid him US $1,500 to gain open access to the Shuar. Our team said we did not pay for interviews but did offer a small donation ($30) of our personal funds to the NAE, and we did pay a translator/guide (approximately $60) to accompany us to an upriver Achuar community for a day, where we also made small donations (about $100) to that community's ecotourism fund (author participant observation, June 13 and 14, 2014).

them a lot, but they do not listen. For a little [from the outsiders], they give up everything. They should have waited like we did to get much more." On the Shuar, Paes said that some of that group's leaders have been corrupted by oil money and have had to "hide" from their fellow Shuar, most of whom do oppose extraction. "The leaders say no to oil, but the people are divided in half" (interview).

Ecuador's Amazonian indigenous groups have been collaborating on a large scale with their Andean counterparts for the first time over the last few years. However, unlike the Andean strategy of wide-scale mobilization, the Amazon peoples, where successful, have undertaken knowledge-based strategies, often with international allies. The Sarayakus represent by far the most successful of the environmental movements in all of Ecuador to stop oil drilling or at least temper its pace and regulate the process. That community, which has been an important way station and transit point for Amazon travelers of many races (Lara interview), undertook politically unifying mobilizations in the 1990s, but then in the early 2000s complemented these power- and identity-based mobilizations with their knowledge-based strategy involving domestic and international legal allies.

The Waorani, late to "contact" with the West and beset by a range of violent struggles both internally and with neighboring groups, epitomize the failure of power-driven mobilizations in the region. They embody our chapter 2 finding that respondents in already-polluted areas of oil extraction are less enthusiastic about the environment, although several indigenous leaders we asked echoed the sentiment quoted more extensively in chapter 5, that the destruction of the forest literally erases their souls. Contrarily, those in the pristine rainforest have much stronger pro-environment attitudes because, as stated by Achuar national president Tentets, "If it is already contaminated, how is it [the land] recoverable? With this change [pollution], people think of ceasing to defend themselves. Those with a clean environment are going to keep defending it forever. The Achuar nation has a clean environment and will always continue to have it that way" (interview). The Achuar themselves are divided, as evidenced above by Paes's interest in oil extraction in Achuar lands, albeit under Achuar leadership, whereas Tentets, who leads the "true" assembly and had to regroup after the national government recognized the specious one, insists that the Achuar will not allow oil drilling and that the NAE communities have come back to that point of agreement since the government's efforts to divide them through corporatist strategies (interview).

Despite the Ecuadorian government's manipulation of consent to achieve its revenues from oil royalties, most respondents (regardless of ethnic origin) regarded international mining and oil companies as greater

Table 4.5 INTERNATIONAL THREATS AS PERCEIVED BY INDIGENOUS GROUPS

	Chinese Mining and Oil Companies		US Mining and Oil Companies		Other Indigenous Communities		PETROECUA-DOR		Other Ecuadorean Mining and Oil Companies	
	Yes	No	Yes	No	Yes	No	Yes	No	Yes	No
Andean Indigenous	327	42	313	58	119	247	156	190	216	140
Percent	81.9	10.5	78.4	14.5	29.8	61.9	39.1	47.6	54.1	35.1
Amazon Indigenous	270	25	263	27	138	154	154	107	160	99
Percent	85.4	7.9	83.2	8.5	43.7	48.7	48.7	33.9	50.6	31.3
Pro-Cosmovision (From Entire Sample)	1,031	103	1024	128	399	739	547	511	630	434
Percent	81.5	8.1	80.9	10.1	31.5	58.4	43.2	40.4	49.8	34.3
Identify as Indigenous (From Entire Sample)	600	57	575	78	234	420	342	263	409	206
Percent	83.9	7.8	80.4	10.9	32.7	58.7	47.8	36.7	57.2	28.8
Overall National Sample	1430	157	1427	184	649	948	814	683	918	584
Percent	80.3	8.8	80.1	10.3	36.4	53.2	45.7	38.3	51.5	32.8

Note: Based on responses to the survey question: "Speaking of the Amazon region, do you believe that the following are threats to the indigenous communities there, or not?"
Percentages do not add up to 100 because many respondents did not reply, or responded "Do not know."

threats than Petroecuador and other Ecuadorian mining and oil interests. The entire population viewed both Chinese- and US-based companies as highly threatening, with over 80 percent of respondents perceiving multinational companies from these countries as threats, while fewer than half as many viewed Petroecuador and "other Ecuadorian mining and oil companies" as threats (see Table 4.5).

Chapter 6 introduces more explicitly the role of international actors, but these play a role also in chapter 5. Power-driven mobilizing is a long-standing tradition among the Andean indigenous communities, and it has also been practiced by Amazonian groups and relied upon by most other non-elite citizens around the world who perceive that "strength in numbers" is their only chance. In the next chapter, we consider knowledge-driven sources of mobilization (awareness of climate change), rather than power-driven mobilizations and corporatism.

The case studies presented in this chapter confirm findings in chapters 1 and 2, that oil spills and other forms of degradation in the northern rainforest have conditioned attitudes at the group level (among the Waorani in particular) as well as at the individual level. The failed Texaco/ Chevron cleanup, leaving hundreds of small, open oil pits throughout the rainforest, has been a source of domestic and international consternation since the 1980s (Red Amazonica Juridica 2013; Yanza 2014). In the central Amazon (the Napo and Pastaza), where oil drilling is still under discussion, the livelihoods of rural people are in jeopardy, and the Kichwa and Shuar are more divided both in whether extraction should occur, and how the environment should best be used. In the south, the Achuar in particular have a more unified anti-extractivist view, and a stronger pro-environment position. The geographic relativity of community positions was summarized by a Sápara leader: "Those whose lands have been polluted are in favor [of more extraction]. They live in that reality. Those who are opposed are those of us whose lands have not yet been contaminated, and above all, those of us who do not live near a paved highway" (Ushigua interview 2014).

CHAPTER 5

༓

How Science, Religion, and Politics
Influence Indigenous Attitudes
on Climate Change in Ecuador

Across the globe, indigenous communities have been particularly vocal about climate change as a threat to their traditional ways of life represented in their cosmovision—or traditional worldview—resulting in demands for protection of the earth as part of their core beliefs.[1] Is this because indigenous peoples "living off the land" are the most vulnerable, and feel the impact of climate change more directly? Or is it because of the centrality of the earth and its climate patterns to their traditional beliefs? This chapter makes a significant contribution to our understanding of how indigenous beliefs contribute to the climate change debate in Ecuador and beyond. Most statistical analyses of public opinion have ignored those of the world's indigenous people, an increasingly salient set of voices in the debate over climate change. Using our nationwide survey of citizens in Ecuador, we find respondents who adhere to indigenous cosmovision are more likely to acknowledge the threats posed by climate change, confirming that traditional belief systems in the developing world can strongly support worldwide mitigation efforts toward climate change. Furthermore, we find that these traditional views complement—rather than conflict with—Western science.

---

1. We adopt the definition of cosmovision as a "worldview [that] consists of the suppositions, premises, and ideologies of a socio-cultural group which determines how they perceive the world." (See Sánchez 2010, 79.)

(146)

Both scientific knowledge and religiosity help determine belief in climate change in Ecuador. Climate change is one of the most important public issues in the world, yet little is known about what shapes public belief systems regarding this global phenomenon. In some countries—like the United States—there remains a substantial proportion of citizens who deny the existence of anthropogenic climate change (IPSOS Mori 2014). However, in many other countries, climate change is recognized as man-made and is considered a serious problem. Pathbreaking studies on aggregate opinions of climate change around the world have attributed cross-national differences to climate vulnerability (Brechin 2010). Yet few studies have examined what determines attitudes toward climate change *within* countries, which is arguably where variation in vulnerability to climate change is highest. Most within-country studies of climate change beliefs have focused on public opinion in the United States, where political factors, such as partisanship (McCright and Dunlap 2011a), and social factors, such as religious attendance (McCright and Dunlap 2011b) and religious beliefs (Kilburn 2014), provide powerful explanations. However, given the idiosyncratic nature of the American two-party system, and the fact that America is known to be "distinctively religious compared to its peers" (Kilburn 2014, 474), what explains citizen beliefs in the United States may not translate worldwide. Indeed, in the developing world, where global North-South equity questions dominate the discussion at international fora (see, for example, Jinnah 2014 and Andresen and Agrawala 2002), it might be expected that politicians arguing for economic development over stringent climate change rules impact domestic opinion, rather than scientific experts or religious leaders. However, that is not the case.

Because religion has proven to be an obstacle to acceptance of science-based evidence of climate change in the United States, it is important to assess the extent of the influence of these factors elsewhere in the world, and particularly in countries of the global South who are subject to climate negotiations dominated by the North. Indeed, by some estimate, around 30 percent of the US population denies the phenomenon of climate change, making the US home to possibly the largest proportion of climate change skeptics when compared to other countries in the world. In contrast, indigenous people across the globe have been particularly vocal about climate change as a threat to their traditional ways of life represented in their cosmovisions—or traditional worldviews—resulting in demands for protection of the earth as part of their core beliefs. As advocates for climate change policies, indigenous Ecuadorians offer a "hard case" for assessing how religiosity affects belief in climate change, serving as an important counter to US Tea Party climate change opponents. The indigenous acknowledge the threats posed by climate change, showing that poor and highly vulnerable citizens in the developing world can strongly support worldwide mitigation efforts. In the survey of Ecuadorians as well as in one-on-one interviews, indigenous respondents convey to us that religion need not detract from citizen views of climate change.

To assess the influence of science and religion on climate change, we analyze our national survey focused on climate change in Ecuador and find that with regard to climate change specifically, while indigenous identity does not matter, religiosity and indigenous religious beliefs do impact respondents' belief in climate change. And contrary to much of the US-centered literature on religious beliefs and climate change in the West, religiosity and cosmovision have positive effects on climate change beliefs. Recognizing that possession of an indigenous cosmovision and a Catholic or Protestant religious identity are not incompatible, we also consider how these traits interact to affect belief in climate change. In addition to being influenced by both science and religion, we found further that respondents adjust their beliefs in climate change depending on whether they were located on the nation's extractive frontier. These findings duplicate results from Eisenstadt and West (2017), as discussed in chapter 2 relating to the determinants of broader environmental attitudes. Therefore—in terms of climate change—science, religion, and a history of extractivism all appear to have an impact on citizen beliefs in developing areas.

We also analyze the extent to which climate vulnerability shapes beliefs surrounding climate change, as recent studies indicate (Kim and Wolinsky-Nahmias 2014). We introduce proximity to extractive industries as an additional measure of vulnerability and find that respondents adjust their belief in climate change depending on whether they are located on the nation's extractive frontier. Together, these findings challenge post-materialism as a significant cause of broader environmental concern, confirming the trend of global environmentalism that others have discovered (Dunlap and York, in Steinberg and VanDeveer Eds., 2012). In addition, the current study answers a recent call (Purdon 2015) to utilize comparative political science to gain further understanding of the politics surrounding climate change. In particular, by analyzing public opinion in a developing country, this chapter extends our understanding of climate change "beyond institutions and better address[es] interests and ideas at the . . . state and subnational levels," a key message that has emerged in the literature on climate change (Purdon 2015, 3).

In addition, this chapter contributes to the mounting evidence that vulnerability matters more than post-materialism in shaping attitudes toward the environment. With regard to our other overarching thesis in this book, that polycentric pluralism is likely better suited than multiculturalism to help groups convey their interests regarding extractive conflict, this chapter offers further evidence of the complexities of attitudes within groups. We demonstrate that peoples' religious convictions strongly impact their belief in climate change. In other words, just as we have sought to debunk in the last three chapters the simplistic multiculturalist stereotype in which indigenous communities possess a singular view on the environment and extraction, we here show that this division extends also to attitudes on climate change. Indigenous and non-indigenous practitioners of Catholicism and a Kichwa indigenous religious worldview are much more apt to believe strongly that climate change should be addressed as a major issue than evangelical (Protestant) strong believers, who made up a minority of our survey sample but were sufficiently numerous to allow us to draw strong and indisputable conclusions. Also in the climate change issue area, inter-ethnic groups—here joined by religious beliefs—possess much greater solidarity than mere ethnic identity.

After briefly reviewing the literature on climate change attitudes in other countries, with particular attention to Latin America and Ecuador, we develop hypotheses regarding how beliefs consistent with Kichwa cosmovision and Western science affect one's understanding of climate change. We also reintroduce the vulnerability argument, operationalized as the effects of living proximate to extractive industries, for understanding climate change. After a discussion of our survey and the variables that we generate from survey responses, we present the findings of our statistical analysis. Consistent with our evidence summarized in earlier chapters, we find that cosmovision and living with extraction are the most powerful determinants of belief in climate change in Ecuador, and we conclude with a discussion of the relevance of our results for policies surrounding global climate change.

EQUITY AND CLIMATE CHANGE ATTITUDES: VARIATION ACROSS COUNTRIES AND WITHIN ECUADOR

Very little systematic and comparative work exists on climate change issues in general (Giddens 2011; Harrison and Sunstrom 2010; and Eisenstadt, Fiorino, and Stevens 2018 are exceptions). Even less has been done in comparing public opinion in one country over time (Brulle et al. 2012 and Ansolabehere and Konisky 2014 are exceptions), or even a cross-section of nations (Kvaloy, Finseraas, and Listhaug 2012 and

Kim and Wolinksy-Nahmias 2014 are among the only examples). Hence we know little about how attitudes toward climate change play out in the global South.

What we do know is that the North-South debate has been firmly manifested with regard to climate change. As stated by Najam: "Developing countries have consistently contextualized environmental issues as part of the larger complex of North-South concerns, particularly concerns about an iniquitous international order and their desire to bring about structure change in that order. This has become more poignant in recent years as environmental negotiations on issues such as climate change have become increasingly focused on trade and economic aspects" (Najam, in Axelrod and VanDeveer 2014, 220–21). Indeed, the question has been framed succinctly by Shue (2014, 183) as one of inequality:

> Unilateral initiatives by the so-called developed countries (DCs) have made them rich, while leaving the less developed countries (LDCs) poor. In the process the industrial activities and accompanying lifestyles of the DCs have inflicted major global damage upon the earth's atmosphere. Both kinds of damage are harmful to those who did not benefit from Northern industrialization as well as to those who did. Those societies whose activities have damaged the atmosphere ought . . . to bear sufficiently unequal burdens henceforth to correct the inequality that they have imposed.

Shue's position is controversial, to be sure, as nations of the industrial North argue that when they were industrializing the enduring dangers of coal pollution to the atmosphere were not known, but that Southern polluters must constrain industrialization—and the great economic gains from that process—because those dangers are now known. This breach in views has possibly been the leading cause of international negotiation failures to reach a United Nations agreement regarding carbon dioxide emissions (for a recent policy review, see Klinsky et al. 2014).

A regional version of this equity argument has played out in indigenous Latin America, where it has been argued at least since the era of Chico Mendes (see Mendes with Gross 1989) that indigenous stewards of the rainforest merited preferential treatment with regard to their ancestral lands because they developed forest commons much more sustainably than others. This debate is exemplified in the controversy over the Programme of the United Nations for Reducing Emissions From Deforestation and Degradation (REDD), which compensates rural dwellers for preserving stands of trees intact, rather than cutting for crops and ranching, in order for the forests to serve in carbon dioxide sequestration. The program has been both praised and criticized, with the indigenous represented on both sides of the issue (REDD-Monitor 2015, 364–67).

In Ecuador, the REDD debate has occurred (Seiwald 2012; Hall 2012) alongside a range of other climate change–related controversies. As a result, Ecuador is one of the most relevant developing countries for study, as the public generally has views on a range of climate-related issues. For example, left-leaning President Rafael Correa made inequality in the international environmental realm one of his signature policies. After ratifying the first constitution in the world giving Mother Nature (in Kichwa,[2] the "Pachamama") "human" rights (Gudynas 2009; Acosta and Martínez 2009), Correa sought to protect the biodiverse rainforest of Yasuní National Park from imminent oil drilling, but did so by asking international donors to pay Ecuador to offset the oil revenues the nation would forgo by leaving the oil in the ground (Martin 2011; Narváez 2009). After collecting a few million US dollars—only a fraction of the funds sought—the Correa administration decided in the summer of 2013 to discontinue the campaign and drill for oil in the national park.[3] While less directly tied to climate change prevention than the conservation of carbon-absorbing forests like those in Yasuní, environmental degradation in the form of mineral tailings spillage and related water pollution (Chicaiza 2014) and oil spills in the jungle have also been heavily publicized in Ecuador. In particular, the failed Texaco/Chevron cleanup, which left hundreds of small, open oil pits throughout the rainforest, has been a source of domestic and international consternation since the 1980s (Red Jurídica Amazónica 2013; Yanza 2014). Amid these controversies, citizens have developed strong views on environmental degradation, including that which could impact climate change.

Furthermore, indigenous culture has played an important role in climate change advocacy in Latin America. In both Ecuador (Acosta 2012; Acosta and Martínez Eds. 2009; Acción Ecológica 2012; Fernández et al. 2014; Recasens 2014) and Bolivia (Fabricant 2013), leftist presidents have adopted indigenous cosmovision rhetoric to legitimize climate change and other environmental policies. Some consider this strategy as mere "political marketing" (Fernández et al. 2014, 105) and others argue even more forcefully that politicians' "timeless vision of indigeneity, particularly using . . . pre-Columbian land-holding patterns as solutions to climate

2. Kichwa, also known as Quichua, is the eponymous language spoken by the largest indigenous group in Ecuador.

3. The decision was particularly controversial because the Ecuadorian government pledged to return funds only for large pledges, meaning that the tiny donations by schoolchildren who had sent money to "save jaguars and freshwater dolphins" were not returned (Larea interview).

crisis, poses dangers" (Fabricant 2013, 159). However, most indigenous leaders and politicians have found references to *sumak kawsay* (recall that this is a "harmonic life," or "living close to nature" in Kichwa) a legitimizing, authentic, nationalist, and profoundly resonant cloak within which to wrap their policies. Former President Correa, for example, utilized the concept dozens of times, particularly in the lead-up to the passage of Ecuador's new constitution. We next elaborate on how citizen polarization on these issues in rural Ecuador, as well as how popular renderings of *sumak kawsay* and other formulations of indigenous religion, may impact respondent views on climate change.

"HARMONIC LIFE" IN THE AMAZON: FROM INDIGENOUS COSMOVISION TO STATE POLICY

Unlike Western religious traditions, which have sometimes been found at odds with believing in climate change and other scientific findings (see Evans and Feng 2013), we argue that *sumak kawsay* advocacy actually reinforces beliefs in the agency of nature, even at the expense of humanity. In other words, this is a religious belief that reinforces climate change advocacy rather than undermining it. Upon better defining the term, we consider its integration into the Ecuadorian public discourse, and then address its several practical applications in the continuum between more primordial versions of the concept, and versions which seek to integrate the term with a globally competitive approach seeking syncretism between the best of indigenous cosmovisions with Western science.

What is *sumak kawsay*? Is it a religion or a marketing strategy? In Ecuador, this Kichwa term for "harmonic life" has emerged over the last decade as a central pillar of the public discourse, and hence is a concept familiar to many respondents. As interpreted by Seiwald (2012, 22), it is a fluid and relational concept, establishing a constantly adapting bond among humanity, nature, and spirituality, and a responsibility for maintaining this bond for future generations. Indeed, interpreters of the concept, as well as some of its originators (such as Acosta 2012; Acosta and Martínez Eds. 2009) in the Andes are not so removed from priorities named by other scholars of indigenous religion elsewhere, such as Vine Deloria, Jr., in the United States. To Deloria, time was a question more of space than temporality, geographic entities were known for the stories they inspired and the proximity to nature, and indigenous people placed an emphasis on collective identities (which often included nature and other natural beings) rather than individuals (Deloria 2003). In this context, *sumak kawsay* in Ecuador assumes a role in opposition to developmentalism, which emphasizes wealth, poverty, and hierarchical location of individuals and their economies with respect to global centers of production. "Harmonic life" prioritizes non-material benefits: a pervasive sense of place and fit with nature and among other people and a sense of well-being derived relationally from one's historic place (Recasens 2014, 55–72). The Kichwa communities of Ecuador argue that they speak for nature, and in a manner conveying harmonic life. We show in this chapter, as we did in chapter 2, that these citizens are in fact more enthusiastic stewards of nature than other groups.

A complication in the debate between *sumak kawsay* and Western science is that the term has become a banner of Ecuadorian state environmental policy. As mentioned in chapter 1, *sumak kawsay* (*"buen vivir"*) was synonymous with the 2008 Ecuador Constitution and with some of the early cornerstone policies of President Correa, such as the debate over whether to drill oil in Yasuní National Park, which was reviewed in chapter 4. However, as the Correa government grew increasingly dependent on extractivism for public revenues, the government began to devote more attention to placating citizens on the extractive frontier. Funds focused on compensating citizens near Amazon drilling sites and on national-level redistributive programs offering pensions to senior citizens and scholarships to college students, and improving basic infrastructure (like health care) and transportation. In other words, the concepts included in this indigenous cosmovision, as adopted in central government rhetoric, ran counter to the state's developmentalist policy. An internal contradiction emerged, which had implications for the government's climate change position that had begun as one of the more advanced in the developing world.[4]

Overall, four main positions emerged in the standoff between science and traditional indigenous cosmovision over how to handle the environment, ranging from primordialist views of *sumak kawsay* to a strong acceptance of Western science while rejecting the cosmovision perspective. Primordialist advocates on the side of holistic harmonization with the *pachamama* ("Mother Earth") argue strenuously that the needs of indigenous peoples, the original inhabitants and best protectors of the rainforest, precede those of others, and that the obligation of government should be to fund the development of native technologies and the restoration of the lost harmony between people and the land (Chimbo, Tumink interviews 2014).

---

4. The Correa government claimed to be the first in Latin America to have a sub-secretary for climate change in the Ministry of the Environment.

In the middle are the utilitarian position and the developmentalist position. Even indigenous activists like Carlos Pérez, the head of the powerful national Andean indigenous movement Confederation of the Peoples
of Kichwa Nationality of Ecuador (ECUARUNARI by its Kichwa acronym),
claim the utilitarian position, at least when asked to defend Western science. Said Pérez, in a private interview, "Western science is an important
tool which should not be dismissed, but all its data justify the Andean peoples who say we should not rebel against nature; we should not rebel but
nature is our mother who deserves all of our protection" (interview). To
these advocates, the Andean peoples' protection of nature is still the objective, but they acknowledge Western science as an important means to
achieving this end. Another statement of this philosophy was by Shuar
leader Gonzalo Tibi, who said that *sumak kawsay* involved being one with
nature, but that this did not preclude Western material development as long
as "development is always consistent with our culture" (interview 2014).

Developmentalists shift the ultimate objective of their efforts; to them
the central goal is to sustain humans and help them make progress, rather
than to ensure the maximum expression of nature, with humans playing
just a small part. "The national government meets with China and Canada
and multinational companies and speaks of responsible extraction," according to one social movement coordinator. "But they are exploiting
people as well as Mother Earth and this creates inequality. The fundamental
problem is inequality and we have to focus more on that" (Arpe interview
2014). Similarly, Achuar leaders like Pasqual Callera (interview 2014) argue
that the environmental degradation of drilling for oil in their pristine lands
carries too high a price, but that the only way to improve the position of his
community is to find alternative development projects and to train young
people to be the engineers and geologists of the future.

At the other extreme, perhaps, are the Western positivists. While
this group often includes indigenous leaders, they fear that regardless of
whether science or the indigenous cosmovision is more consistent with
reality, science trumps indigenous cosmovision. Though some leaders believe this to be innately true, others believe that indigenous communities
cannot afford to be "left behind" by using only ancestral knowledge when,
in order to compete globally, every advantage must be used. Mestizo
leaders like Provincial Governor Denise Coka (interview 2014) readily crit-
icize the *sumak kawsay* promoters as hypocritical for "telling us we have to
live free in the forest and then coming to demand all kinds of services and
infrastructure," but do also insist on finding appropriate technology and
developing in accordance with Ecuador's needs, rather than those of the
international community. For example, although controversial, one Shuar

leader argued that "we cannot eat leaves" and Shuar and Achuar leaders claim that if these tribes decide to forbid oil production on their land, it should be for a limited time until the tribe could train its own people to benefit from the exploitation (Pidru and Paes interviews 2014). Kichwa and Waorani leaders in the Napo province, where oil drilling is already underway, recognize the importance of Western science as a way to advocate for themselves against the state and oil companies, requesting that scientific techniques be used to assess environmental quality (Granja and Portilla interviews 2014). Thus, for many Amazonian indigenous, the scientific foundation behind climate change is a primary way to advocate for themselves amid the advancing extractive frontier.

FACTORS EXPLAINING CLIMATE CHANGE BELIEF IN LATIN AMERICA

A small but influential group of indigenous leaders from the Amazon, where international carbon dioxide "sink" efforts to mitigate global CO_2 pollution have been focused, seek to negotiate development projects involving the protection of forests under the UN REDD framework. These activists, including groups from nine nations in a Coordinating Body for the Indigenous Peoples' Organizations of the Amazon Basin (COICA), acknowledge the centrality of Western science in quantifying and mitigating climate change, but also insist that their traditional cosmovision (and, consequently, a lighter human presence in areas where they live) has in fact made some indigenous communities ideal stewards. COICA has sought to add an Amazon indigenous element to REDD by ensuring that beyond just offsetting carbon pollution in other parts of the world, "what we want is integral conservation of the forest including biodiversity, environmental services, ecosystem and cultural services" (Katan interview). COICA seeks international development assistance to promote integral rainforest conservation, and also has joined private efforts to set standards for extractive industry clean-ups in the rainforest. This collaboration is embodied, for example, by the EO100 Standard for Responsible Energy, a set of rigorous performance standards for energy development projects, developed through extensive consultation with the energy industry, leading international NGOs focused on energy, and indigenous communities affected by development projects (Equitable Origin 2018).

Indigenous leaders like Callera and Paes have called for application of indigenous knowledge to tackle climate change, and the Ecuador-based COICA, in its mission statement, captured the sentiment: "Our accumulated knowledge about the ecology of our home, our models for living with the peculiarities of the Amazon Biosphere, our reverence and respect for the tropical forest and its other inhabitants . . . are the keys to guaranteeing the future of the Amazon Basin . . . for all of humanity" (COICA 2014, 316). Given that the backdrop to the Ecuadorian policy debate prominently features the indigenous cosmovision and discussions of relations among indigenous communities, nature, and the earth, our first hypothesis focuses on these relationships. We argue that rather than diminishing respondent belief in climate change, religiosity and support for indigenous cosmovisions actually increase such beliefs. Public opinion on the use of indigenous versus Western knowledge to address environmental issues is divided, consistent with our thesis, but indigenous leaders, like non-indigenous leaders at the highest levels, have found the *sumak kawsay* banner to be a unifying one, and one that stirs international support as well, as discussed in chapter 6. Below, we address the hypotheses tested here:

Hypothesis 1—Cosmovision Religiosity Hypothesis: Support for indigenous religious cosmovision is expected to increase respondents' propensity to believe in climate change.

This hypothesis has important expressions in other religious belief systems as well. The underlying debate, as conveyed by Arbuckle and Konisky (n.d., 3–4), is whether religions depict the relationship between humans and nature as one of dominion (fundamentalists in the Judeo-Christian tradition, especially those expressing a literal belief in the Bible) or stewardship (usually less literal interpreters of the Bible, and other more communitarian religions, epitomized by the indigenous cosmovision believers described above). In the sections below we consider not only indigenous cosmovision, but also Catholic (the majority religion, covering a wide spectrum of "literalism" in interpretation), and evangelical Protestants, found by Smith and Leiserowitz (2013) to be less likely than non-evangelical Protestants to believe that climate change is happening and by anthropogenic causes. We therefore expect differences in whether Catholics and evangelicals believe in climate change, and argue that those differences are contingent upon religiosity (Eckberg and Blocker 1996). Specifically, we expect that evangelicals are less likely to believe in climate change as their religious intensity increases.

However, we also expect that Catholic and evangelical religious identities are compatible with and mitigated by adherence to indigenous cosmovision. Both Western-based religions have been adopted by indigenous communities in Ecuador as a result of a variety of strategies pursued by missionaries as well as community leaders (see Andrade 1999). Syncretism, or the combination of different belief systems, has occurred between Western organized religions and indigenous culture across Latin America, leading to religious reinterpretations of the Bible as well as ancient indigenous myths and beliefs about mountains and "enchantments." These reinterpretations are also at play in how Catholic or evangelical citizens understand nature and the phenomena of climate change. We therefore expect that the influence of a respondent's Catholic or evangelical beliefs will be conditioned by their sympathy with cosmovision, such that cosmovision will make it more likely that citizens identifying with Western religions will believe in climate change.

In the United States, the popular debate over whether climate change exists and, secondarily, whether its causes are anthropogenic, is framed according to ideology. Climate change communicators have framed the debate thusly in the popular media, although it is more nuanced in the academic literature on political psychology. In that literature, some, like Kahan et al. (2012), argue that climate change believers tend to be more hierarchical and individual in their beliefs (as opposed to egalitarian and communitarian), others claim that partisanship (Democrats versus Republicans) drives the difference, and still others claim that how strongly a citizen believes in science dictates whether they believe in climate change (Gauchat 2012). While translation of Kahan et al.'s (2012) dichotomy to Western cultures has proven to be complex, our main concern is to juxtapose the religious cosmovision of indigenous peoples with other religious views and Western science. Like Gauchat (2012), we argue that believers in science are more likely to also believe in climate change. The caveat is that, as pointed out by Bolsen, Druckman, and Cook (2015), greater scientific knowledge does not necessarily translate into greater acceptance of the consensus belief in climate change. Peoples' acceptance of particular scientific phenomena depends on the values, context, ideology, and personal experience at their starting points. Nevertheless, to contrast with the religious perspectives, we hypothesize the following parsimonious relationship between science beliefs and climate change.

Hypothesis 2—Western Science Hypothesis: Strong support for Western scientific positivism is expected to increase respondents' propensity to believe in climate change.

Finally, we also expect the political and environmental context of citizens' livelihoods should prime their beliefs in climate change. Extensive oil production has been found to hinder nations' environmental performance, probably due to the expectations such oil production brings for economic development and how that production gets distributed (Eisenstadt, Fiorino, and Stevens n.d.). Additionally, in the Andean region, "the negative environmental and social externalities brought about by the boom in the exploration and development of hydrocarbons reserves, and the impact these have had on local communities, constitute the main trigger of local conflicts today" (Vásquez 2014, 5). In addition to triggering actual conflicts, we believe that a history of hydrocarbon production—with all of the attendant environmental, political, social, and economic implications this may bring—becomes a focal point in communities that firmly places environmental issues like climate change on the agenda.

Hypothesis 3—History of Extraction Hypothesis: Respondents in localities where there is a history of oil extraction are more likely to believe in climate change.

DATA AND VARIABLES

To test the above hypotheses, we once again use the results of our nationwide survey of Ecuadorians to capture citizens' belief in climate change, as well as the extent of their religiosity, their religious beliefs, and whether their localities have experienced oil extraction. In this section, we describe the measures of our dependent variables and key independent variables that we use to evaluate our hypotheses.

To test our hypotheses, it is necessary to conceptualize citizens' belief in climate change (the dependent variable). We rely on a single measure that we developed based on citizen responses during focus groups and extensive field tests of the survey instrument. The question simply asked respondents if they believe that climate change exists. An overwhelming majority of our sample (91.8 percent) said "yes." (See Table A1 in appendix A for a description of the survey items, question wording, and coding of this and all other variables included in the analysis. Appendix B also provides a thorough description of the sampling methodology used in the nationwide survey.)

Several elements of the survey instrument allow us to develop measures of how identity, attitudes, and behaviors related to religion affect belief and concern over climate change. The first variable that we include in our analysis is *Religiosity*, which measures the extent to which an individual views religion as important in their life, ranked on a scale of 0 ("not at all important") to 3 ("very important"), with a mean of 2.5 (between "not very important" and "somewhat important"). Around 60.5 percent of our sample said that religion was "very important" in their lives. We also asked individuals what their religion is (if they practice one) and coded individuals based on whether they claim to be *Evangelical* (1 if yes, 0 otherwise) and *Catholic* (1 if yes, 0 otherwise), the two largest religious affiliations in our sample (14.7 percent of our sample is evangelical and 75.7 percent are Catholic). We argue that the effects of religious affiliation on the belief in climate change will be conditional upon religiosity, so we also include interaction terms between religious affiliation and religiosity (expressed in the results table as *Catholic*Religiosity* and *Evangelical*Religiosity*).

Our survey included a series of questions that also allow us to measure the extent to which individuals share in the perspective of indigenous cosmovision. The first question asks whether an individual agrees with the statement that "Mother Earth (*Pacha Mama*) deals with problems such as shortages in water and food," and is coded a 1 if the respondent agrees, and 0 otherwise. Around 61.5 percent of the sample agrees with that statement. The second question asks whether an individual agrees that cosmovision and spirituality are more important than science (1 if agree, 0 otherwise), and 55.2 percent of the sample does. The third question asks whether respondents agree that the indigenous are more connected with Mother Earth than non-indigenous (1 if agree, 0 otherwise). Around 71 percent of respondents agree that the indigenous are more connected. We used these three measures to construct a *Cosmovision Index* by deriving the first component in a factor analysis. These measures loaded together fairly well, with a Chronbach's alpha of 0.45. We expect that higher values on the *Cosmovision Index* should correspond with an increased likelihood in believing that climate change exists. We also interact this index with *Catholic* and *Evangelical* to assess whether the effects of religious affiliation are mitigated by a belief in cosmovision.

For comparison, we also created a *Christianity Index*, which measures the extent to which individuals agree with a system of values perpetuated by Western Christianity. This index is comprised of four survey instruments, asking whether respondents agree or disagree with the following statements: 1) When there is conflict between science and religion, religion is always right; 2) All religions should be taught in our public schools; 3) Many of the problems in the world today can be attributed to the Apocalypse (End of Days/Judgment Day) predicted by the Bible; 4) We depend too much on science and not enough on Faith. Together, these questions have a Chronbach's alpha of 0.45.

In order to test our hypothesis about how views of Western science affect belief in climate change, we create a *Science Index* that includes five survey items. For each of the following statements, we asked our sample whether they agreed (coded 1) or disagreed/were neutral (coded 0) with: 1) Science and technology are making our lives healthier; 2) Science and technology are making our lives more comfortable; 3) Because of science and technology, the next generation will have more opportunities; 4) The agricultural techniques taught by scientists are better than traditional ones; 5) Indigenous groups should work with national and/or foreign scientists to resolve local problems. Together, these questions have a Chronbach's alpha of 0.71.

We tested the History of Extraction Hypothesis by constructing an indicator variable for the *parroquia* (or locality) in which respondents live. The *History of Oil Extraction* variable is coded 1 for areas where oil is being actively extracted. About 6.58 percent of our sample lives in areas of active oil extraction, which was coded based on information from government oil block maps given by the Ecuadorian Secretary of Hydrocarbons (Secretaría de Hidrocarburos de Ecuador, SHE) (n.d.). We also created an indicator variable for whether respondents lived in the *Amazon* region of Ecuador (1 if yes, 0 otherwise).[5] Around 23.6 percent of our sample resides in the Amazon region.

We also include a number of control variables in our analysis. The literature on political ecology argues that vulnerability to climate change may also impact an individual's likelihood to believe it exists, as well as be concerned about its effects. To measure vulnerability, we coded the variable *Rain/River Water*, which indicates whether respondents get the water they consume in their home from the rain or a river (1 if yes, 0 otherwise). About 18.1 percent of the sample claims to depend upon rain and river water for their homes. We also expect individuals who have a stake in the health of the environment to be more likely to believe in climate change and be concerned about its effects, so we include a variable that indicates whether the respondent directly benefits from ecotourism in their community (1 if yes, 0 otherwise). About 13.5 percent of respondents stated that they directly benefit from ecotourism.

Because climate change is often viewed as a political issue in Western societies, we include two measures related to political attitudes in Ecuador. The first variable—*Leftist Ideology*—is based on a question that

---

5. The Amazon region includes parts or all of the provinces of Morona Santiago, Napo, Orellana, Pastaza, Sucumbios, and Zamora Chinchipe.

asked respondents about the role of the state in solving social problems. Specifically, the question stated: "It's said that the national government can resolve problems in our society because it has the means to do so. Would you say that it can resolve 1) no problems; 2) a few problems; 3) enough problems; 4) the majority of problems; 5) all problems." The mean response was 2.71, between a few and enough problems. The second variable is whether an individual identifies with the Pachakutik party—an indigenous political party that has been active in its opposition to the government, generally because they view the Correa presidency as having been too conservative and/or neoliberal (1 if identifies with party, 0 otherwise). About 7.2 percent of our sample identifies with the Pachakutik (leftist/opposition) party.

Finally, we control for *Media* access (coded as 1 for never having access to any media outlet, and 5 as daily access to media outlets) and *Popular Knowledge* (an index created by asking respondents if they have ever heard of a list of 14 different phenomena prevalent in the media). Average media access is 4.2, and popular knowledge ranges from 16.8 percent familiarity (respondents who had heard of the 169th Convention of the International Labor Organization) to 81.5 percent familiarity (respondents who had heard of the Confederation of Indigenous Nationalities of Ecuador [CONAIE]). We also controlled for several demographic factors, such as *Indigenous* ethnicity (1 if respondent self-identified as indigenous, 0 otherwise, with 40.2 percent of sample identifying as indigenous); *Education* (ordinal variable where 1 is no education and 8 is postgraduate education, with a mean of 4.21, where a 4 corresponds to incomplete secondary education); and *Age* (continuous variable ranging from 16 to 85, mean of 37.56). The *Income* variable is an ordinal variable that indicates an individual's self-reported monthly income level (0 represents no income, 5 represents US $301 to US $500, and 10 represents an income of over US $2,000 per month, with a mean of 4.67).

RESULTS AND DISCUSSION

In order to analyze the relationship between our multi-level independent variables and our dependent variable of belief in climate change, we used logit with standard errors clustered around the locality in which respondents live. We did this because our *History of Extraction* variable is coded at the level of locality and therefore the observations at that level are not independent. Our results largely support our conjecture that religiosity does not conflict with a belief in climate change in developing countries like Ecuador. Instead, we find substantial support for our hypotheses about the importance of religion, cosmovision, Western science, and extractivism for belief in climate change. In this section, we briefly review and discuss the results of our analyses.

The results of our analysis are presented in Tables 5.1 and 5.2. In a simple model that does not include interaction terms (Table 5.1), we again find that post-materialist values hold no influence over environmental attitudes such as a belief in climate change, consistent with findings from previous chapters. Turning to Table 5.2, we find that there are six variables that have significant effects on the likelihood that an individual believes in climate change. The first is *Religiosity*, which has a positive effect on belief in climate change (Model 1). In addition, we find support for our hypotheses that indigenous cosmovision (*Cosmovision Index*) and support for Western science (*Science Index*) also increase the probability that an individual will believe in climate change. Living in a locality with a history of oil extraction is another significant, and substantively strong, predictor that an individual will believe in climate change. And finally, knowledge and education also positively affect whether respondents in Ecuador stated that they believe in climate change. Interestingly, we find no support for the expectation that more-vulnerable populations—such as those who rely upon rain and river water for home consumption—are more likely to believe in climate change. Furthermore, political ideology and party identification also do not matter for predicting an individual's climate change belief.

We also utilize interaction terms between *Religiosity* and the two major religious affiliations in Ecuador: Catholic and evangelical to assess the relationship between religion and belief in climate change. See Model 2 in Table 5.2. The results of this analysis demonstrate that individuals of different religious backgrounds hold distinct perspectives on climate change—but these positions are mitigated by an individual's religiosity, as indicated by the significance of the coefficients on the interaction terms. In order to more adequately interpret these interactions, we plotted the marginal effects that the two religious affiliations have on the likelihood of believing in climate change across levels of religiosity.

Figure 5.1 illustrates how being Catholic affects climate change belief for our respondents. Catholics who are not at all religious (*Religiosity* = 0) have a negative probability that they will believe in climate change. However, as *Religiosity* increases, so too does the probability that a Catholic will believe in climate change. Yet at the highest levels of *Religiosity* (= 3), being Catholic does not have a significant effect on belief in climate change (indicated by the fact that the levels of significance straddle the zero line in the

Table 5.1 LOGIT REGRESSION RESULTS OF FACTORS INFLUENCING BELIEF THAT CLIMATE CHANGE EXISTS

Post-Materialism

Human Rights	−0.632
	(0.654)
Promote Modernity	0.304
	(0.382)
Indigenous Leader	−0.077
	(0.340)
Democracy Over Development	0.405
	(0.293)
Social Media	0.932**
	(0.366)

International Networks

International Networks	0.608**
	(0.266)

Vulnerability

Rain/River Water Source	−0.617
	(0.459)
Energy Scarcity	−0.634
	(1.080)
Climate Change Concern	0.835***
	(0.218)
Food Security	1.171
	(0.763)
Ecotourism	0.611
	(0.608)

Political Orientations

Pachakutik Affiliate	−0.619
	(0.607)
PAIS Affiliate	−0.720
	(0.522)
Trust in Indigenous Movement	0.194
	(0.203)
Leftist Ideology	−0.004
	(0.219)

Extraction

Mining	−0.711**
	(0.329)
Oil Debate	−0.278
	(0.441)

(*continued*)

Table 5.1 CONTINUED

Cosmovision

Indigenous Closer to Nature	0.520
	(0.359)
Mother Earth Has Rights	1.326***
	(0.339)
Indigenous ID	−0.682
	(0.493)
Mother Earth and Scarcity	0.366
	(0.301)

Religion

Religiosity	0.504***
	(0.184)
Apocalypse	−0.683*
	(0.356)
Science vs. Faith	0.143
	(0.360)
Evangelical	−0.380
	(1.236)
Catholic	−1.482
	(1.171)

Science

Western Science Index	0.306***
	(0.117)

Controls

Income	−0.163
	(0.171)
Media Access	−0.173
	(0.163)
Knowledge Index	0.302**
	(0.118)
Education	0.250*
	(0.147)
Age	−0.006
	(0.010)
Constant	0.282
	(1.656)
N	1,123

Note: * $p < 0.1$; ** $p < 0.05$; *** $p < 0.01$; standard errors are in parentheses.

Table 5.2 LOGIT REGRESSION RESULTS OF INTERACTIONS INFLUENCING BELIEF THAT CLIMATE CHANGE EXISTS

	1	2	3	4	5
Religiosity	0.456**	0.529***	−0.598	0.435**	0.473**
	(0.182)	(0.181)	(0.612)	(0.179)	(0.191)
Cosmovision Index	0.462***	0.462***	0.488***	0.419***	0.774
	(0.152)	(0.153)	(0.154)	(0.140)	(0.475)
Christianity Index	−0.073	−0.092	−0.084	−0.106	−0.116
	(0.151)	(0.157)	(0.163)	(0.159)	(0.158)
Evangelical		39.213***		1.132	
		(1.471)		(0.866)	
Evangelical*Religiosity		−12.999***			
		(0.559)			
Catholic			−4.325**		−1.362*
			(1.817)		(0.720)
Catholic*Religiosity			1.275**		
			(0.619)		
Evangelical*Cosmo Index				0.499	
				(0.517)	
Catholic*Cosmo Index					−0.335
					(0.457)
Western Science Index	0.301***	0.313***	0.307***	0.307***	0.318***
	(0.113)	(0.118)	(0.117)	(0.116)	(0.117)
Rain/River Water	−0.545	−0.573	−0.601	−0.574	−0.563
	(0.434)	(0.449)	(0.451)	(0.449)	(0.451)
Ecotourism	0.672	0.717	0.708	0.697	0.670
	(0.509)	(0.508)	(0.510)	(0.510)	(0.517)
History of Oil Extraction	1.853*	1.884*	1.947**	1.865*	1.924*
	(1.015)	(0.984)	(0.925)	(0.994)	(0.990)
Amazon	−0.518	−0.558	−0.500	−0.504	−0.492
	(0.471)	(0.478)	(0.490)	(0.483)	(0.498)
Leftist Ideology	0.063	0.072	0.020	0.044	0.011
	(0.179)	(0.185)	(0.196)	(0.185)	(0.190)
Pachakutik ID	−0.506	−0.470	−0.424	−0.453	−0.417
	(0.458)	(0.471)	(0.461)	(0.462)	(0.459)
Indigenous	0.421	0.426	0.449	0.367	0.367
	(0.480)	(0.492)	(0.496)	(0.484)	(0.486)
Income	−0.077	−0.073	−0.084	−0.072	−0.071
	(0.148)	(0.151)	(0.160)	(0.151)	(0.153)
Media	0.019	0.009	0.068	0.020	0.036
	(0.126)	(0.128)	(0.131)	(0.126)	(0.126)

(*continued*)

Table 5.2 CONTINUED

	1	2	3	4	5
Popular Knowledge	0.354***	0.355***	0.354***	0.355***	0.361***
	(0.118)	(0.120)	(0.119)	(0.120)	(0.119)
Education	0.364**	0.358**	0.379**	0.359**	0.351**
	(0.149)	(0.148)	(0.165)	(0.149)	(0.150)
Age	−0.004	−0.004	−0.003	−0.002	−0.003
	(0.008)	(0.009)	(0.009)	(0.009)	(0.008)
_cons	1.077	0.879	4.555**	1.015	2.262
	(1.270)	(1.334)	(2.246)	(1.262)	(1.488)
	1,167	1,167	1,167	1,167	1,167

Note: * $p < 0.1$; ** $p < 0.05$; *** $p < 0.01$; standard errors are in parentheses.

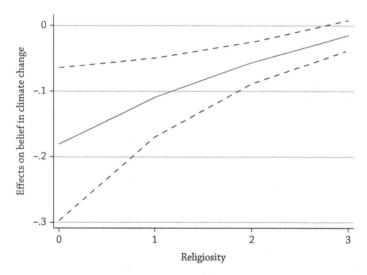

Figure 5.1 The Marginal Effect of Being Catholic on the Likelihood of Believing in Climate Change Across Religiosity

figure). In sum, being Catholic makes it less likely that individuals believe in climate change, but only for those people that are not very religious. Highly religious Catholics are no more or less likely to believe in climate change than others.

The interaction between *Religiosity* and evangelical is also significant but illustrates a very different dynamic, as shown in Figure 5.2. Being evangelical makes an individual 15 percent more likely to believe in climate change—*but only for evangelicals who state that religion is not at all important to them.* As *Religiosity* increases, the probability that evangelicals believe in

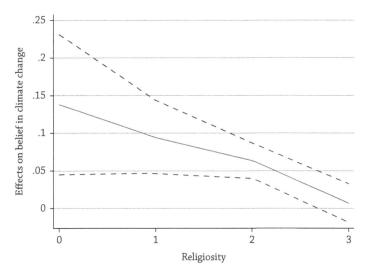

Figure 5.2 The Marginal Effect of Being Evangelical on the Likelihood of Believing in Climate Change Across Religiosity

climate change goes in the opposite direction from Catholics—it *decreases*. Evangelicals who are more religious have a lower likelihood of believing in climate change, until again we reach the highest level of *Religiosity*, in which being an evangelical is not significant for belief in climate change.

In Models 4 and 5 in Table 5.2, we include interactions between evangelical identity, Catholic identity, and cosmovision in our analyses. We argue that sympathy toward indigenous cosmovision should decrease the effects that religious identity has on belief in climate change. Our results suggest that this could be the case, although further investigation is needed. In both models, the interaction terms are not significant; therefore, we plot the marginal effects of the variables to interpret their influence over belief in climate change. In Figure 5.3, we see that, like religiosity, sympathy toward indigenous cosmovision makes individuals that identify as Catholic more likely to believe in climate change, though the effects are small. By contrast, in Figure 5.4, we see a slightly different effect. For respondents who identified as evangelical, adhering to indigenous cosmovision has no effect on whether they believe in climate change, until very high values of the Cosmovision Index. At that point, sympathy with cosmovision has a positive impact on whether individuals believe in climate change.

Together, these results suggest several trends. First, Catholics are less likely overall to believe in climate change. However, for Catholics, increased religiosity and adherence to indigenous cosmovision both make it more likely for Catholics to believe in climate change. Second, evangelicals are

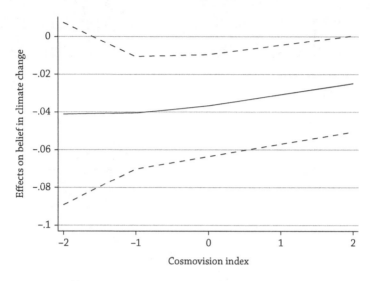

Figure 5.3 The Marginal Effect of Being Catholic on the Likelihood of Believing in Climate Change Across Values of Cosmovision Index

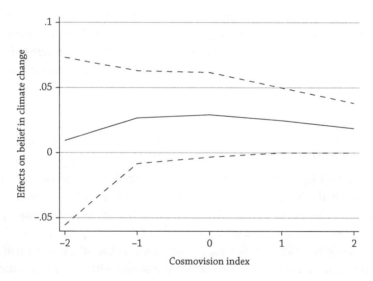

Figure 5.4 The Marginal Effect of Being Evangelical on the Likelihood of Believing in Climate Change Across Values of Cosmovision Index

actually more likely to believe in climate change overall, but religiosity has the *opposite* effect for them—evangelicals who are *more* religious are less likely to believe in climate change. Finally, cosmovision does mitigate the effects that religious affiliation has on climate change belief, making both Catholics and evangelicals who are very strong supporters of cosmovision more likely to believe that climate change exists. Rather than being in contradiction, beliefs based in traditional organized religions are compatible with cosmovision, working together to increase belief in climate change in Ecuador.

SPECIFYING THE CATHOLIC-EVANGELICAL CLEAVAGE AND KICHWA COSMOVISION

Why are Catholic believers more likely to have strong beliefs in climate change than Protestant or evangelical believers? To answer this question, we must explore the differentiated history of religious politics in the region. As elaborated in chapter 4, land reform in the 1960s and 1970s opened the way for progressive actors in the Catholic Church, bolstered in the early 1970s by the Vatican II move toward liberation theology, to fight inequality. That move inspired a generation of new indigenous pastors, but also created a tension between those who lived in villages challenged by the risks of subsistence economies wishing to resolve problems "in this world," and more traditional adherents to the notion of a prioritization of "saving souls." As stated by Luis Alberto Tuazas, a native priest in the central Andean city of Riobamba, in Chimborazo:

> The indigenous pastors have had problems with the official Catholic hierarchy, as they see us as a threat, as they are more conservative. On political issues such as the environment they always viewed us with reserve, but we ask 'does it matter to save souls via tradition if the first priority is to address the here and now?' The issue is how can we accompany indigenous organizations to solve problems of water scarcity and lack of education and health care. (interview)

Social reality may have been more important for respondents in some cases than whether they were Christian or believers in the Kichwa cosmovision. On some issues (see Table 5.3), the gap was greater within Christian groups (between Catholics and evangelicals) than between Catholics and Kichwa cosmovision adherents. The overlap of Catholic beliefs with the Kichwa cosmovision, evidenced in the survey responses, also did not surprise Tuazas: "We have to always speak of a syncretism between cosmovision and the indigenous communities and christianism, even though myths persist that these are separate" (interview).

While characterizing singular Catholic or evangelical Protestant positions is difficult, the evangelical experience has been focused to some extent since the 1950s in the Amazon area, where proselytized

Table 5.3 ATTRIBUTION OF WORLD PROBLEMS TO BIBLICAL JUDGMENT DAY

	"Do you agree that many of the problems in today's world are due to the fact that we are entering the apocalypse (End of Days/ Judgment Day) as predicted by the Bible?" REL5.		
	Agree	Disagree	Depends
Has No Plumbing	137	144	15
Percent	46.3	48.7	5.1
Oil Debated or Drilled	168	160	18
Percent	48.5	46.2	5.2
Mining Debated or Underway	96	97	76
Percent	35.7	36.1	28.2
Indigenous Self-Identification	273	268	91
Percent	43.2	42.4	14.4
Identifies With Pachakutik	28	44	32
Percent	26.9	42.3	30.8
Catholic	509	538	145
Percent	42.7	45.1	12.2
Protestant (Including Evangelical and Pentecostal)	195	89	16
Percent	65	29.7	5.3
All Other Religions(Residual for others who are not the 2 above)	57	40	6
Percent	55.3	38.8	5.8
Pro-Science*	602	535	133
Percent	47.4	42.1	10.5
Pro-Nature**	488	337	109
Percent	52.2	36.1	11.7
Pro-Cosmovision***	601	397	135
Percent	53.1	35	11.9
Overall National Sample	761	667	167
Percent	47.7	41.8	10.5

* From those who agree that "Science and technology are making our lives more comfortable."
** From those who agree that "Mother Earth deals with problems like food and water scarcity."
*** From those who agree that "Indigenous people are closer to Mother Earth or Pacha Mama than non-indigenous people."

communities have retained stronger separate identities. As mentioned in chapter 4, the state had little control within the Amazon until the 1960s, when it encouraged colonization of the region via the first land reform, and when oil was discovered in the area in 1967. Before this, the indigenous lived in isolation on ancestral lands and confronted Westerners, including

Catholic and evangelical missionaries, who tried to enter their lands. While religious leaders sometimes claim there exists no tension between Catholic and evangelical communities, they have sprung up separately, and in the Amazon, where the state did not penetrate enough to provide social services until the oil extraction infrastructure was put in place in the 1970s, the Catholic and evangelical churches in fact competed for corporatist control. Indeed, as indicated through the construction of extensive competing assemblies among the Achuar (as discussed in chapter 4) to obtain permission for oil extraction, the Shuar people were divided into a Catholic assembly and an evangelical one in the 1970s.

The Protestant Summer Institute of Linguistics, which also sent missionaries to other Latin American countries including Colombia and Mexico, established a presence in Ecuador's Amazon region in the early 1950s. The SIL was in fact formally granted control of the protectorate of the Waorani people in 1953 by President José María Velasco Ibarra. Early efforts to reform the indigenous community failed, as five missionaries were speared to death in 1956 and "attacks on oil, timber and other workers failed" (Gerlach 2003, 52); in 1987 a bishop and a nun were "pinned to the forest floor with twenty-one Huarani [sic] spears as a warning to others to stay out of their territory." The Protestant missionaries moved the Waorani into several communities, faced a nationalist backlash, and then were forced to leave the country in 1981 (Gerlach 2003, 51–53).

The legacy of the SIL and that era may remain in terms of interpretive literalism of the Bible. Indeed, as per Table 5.3 presenting results from our survey sample, some 42 percent of Catholics agree that many problems, presumably including environmental degradation, are due to the fact that the world is entering the apocalypse "end of days" predicted by the Bible, whereas over two-thirds of the Protestant evangelical sample believed in this prophecy as a cause of world problems.

Are indigenous people better guardians against climate change than their non-indigenous counterparts? José Gualinga, a leader of the Sarayaku people who has represented them at United Nations climate change meetings such as the historic Paris Agreement meeting in December 2015, has argued for a syncretism of indigenous and Western views of climate change, and of environmental conservation more broadly. Gualinga (interview) said that conservation makes even more sense in the context of climate change, as:

> All of the pueblos [indigenous communities] have contact with the earth and believe that the earth itself is alive. But many of us have lost touch with this connection to the earth, as have many Westerners. Sarayaku seeks that this project

of a living rainforest (*selva vivente*) is transformed without borders so that the whole world can unite behind this proposal. I went to Paris to the COP [UN Conference of Parties] 21 with a 400-kilogram canoe.

In the lens of polycentrism, syncretism implies taking the most useful logic from the Kichwa cosmovision myth (with attention to how well it motivates its adherents and inspires others) and combining this with resources and knowledge from the outside. The Sarayaku people, while outwardly multiculturalist, convey a strong message of pragmatic syncretism, which is essential to polycentrism.

As also seen in chapter 4, the Amazonian indigenous people overall are viewed as better stewards of the rights of nature than their Andean counterparts, perhaps because they are perceived to rely more directly on nature for their livelihoods than their more urbanized Andean counterparts. The Amazon peoples may have also been less influenced by the state, which is viewed as having "divided and conquered" the Andean Kichwa peoples and assimilating them into Ecuadorian national life for hundreds of years rather than just a few decades.

But the political and religious views vary extensively among Amazon people, based partly on their environmental vulnerability and religious cosmovisions. Additionally, as evidenced in chapter 4, the Ecuadorian state has had difficulty co-opting Amazon peoples, even with corporatist practices, while at least some Andean peoples have traditionally been integrated directly into the government structure. Chapter 6 further discusses the independent rise and subsequent state assimilation of Ecuadorian indigenous groups and interests, but in conjunction also with non-indigenous groups, both national and international. While these interest groups still define indigenous political participation in much of Ecuador, there is a compelling argument for keeping Amazonian political participation decentralized and local.

FITTING CLIMATE CHANGE INTO THE POLICY SPACE ON ECUADOR'S EXTRACTIVE FRONTIER

Former President Correa's stance on climate change was a strong one, and followed his anti-imperialist bent. At the climate change summit in Paris in 2015, Correa spoke about controlling climate change by creating an international court that would regulate country participation in curbing the production of greenhouse gases. This call hearkened to Correa's sense of justice about who is more responsible for climate change—the rich countries—and who is suffering as a result—the developing countries, like Ecuador. While no such international court has yet been created, non-governmental groups in an international "rights of nature" movement, headed by Acosta and other Ecuadorians, as well as scholars and practitioners from several other nations, including the United States and New Zealand, started taking form several years before that fateful Paris meeting (Kauffman and Martin 2017). While the scope of this international action was much broader than climate change, including a range of cases that included the violation of the rights of animals and damages from oil spills, it also addressed climate change.

Consistent with the national government's position, Ecuador's new generation of Amazon indigenous leaders grew up reconciling abstract Kichwa cosmovision imperatives to speak for nature with community economic imperatives to help humans develop sustainable economies in the forest. Tuntiak Katan, former climate change project coordinator for the nine-nation COICA, strived to split the difference, but views extraction as a foregone conclusion, economically necessary, and a central part of the national government's agenda, even if rainforest protection programs like Reducing Emissions From Deforestation and Forest Degradation (REDD) are also essential for mitigating climate change. Said Katan (interview):

> There is a national context for extracting resources and an international context for generating [carbon sink] projects. Indigenous communities feel pressured on the one hand, but on the other hand do have real needs. There are two groups, those who are far from the pueblos [indigenous communities] and those who are close to these. The young people (in both groups) want to educate themselves. . . . The socio-economic and ecological realities vary from community to community. . . . The truth is that extraction will happen with community approval or without community approval. The communities have to participate in a manner that ensures the creation of ecological standards.

Katan and an increasing number of other millennial indigenous leaders are becoming involved in "ecological services" provision as well as the extractive economy. They seek greater Ecuadorian participation in the worldwide move toward rainforest protection as a means of offsetting carbon dioxide emissions but have reservations about REDD.

In general, REDD is controversial for several reasons. First, it has been argued that creating carbon trading markets to give value to protecting forests would not itself reduce emissions (as would, for example, mandating carbon scrubbers for smokestack factories), but rather only "treat the symptom." Second, it is not clear who would fund REDD projects, as no multilateral donor like the World Bank has offered ongoing funds. Third, carbon is stored in trees only temporarily, and it is difficult to measure how much additional carbon would be in the atmosphere if not sequestered in trees. The small Ecuadorian program within the Ministry of Environment that paid peasants and indigenous communities to preserve communal and private rainforests, Socio Bosque, confronted these issues as well as others, such as allegations that it was used for political ends (see Sápara case referenced in chapter 4). Additionally, the notion existed early in the Correa administration, when Socio Bosque was launched, that the initiative would be part of a vigorous participation by Ecuador in the international environmental movement, as the government seemed to view the Ecuadorian rainforest as a central and irreplaceable international resource. Former director Max Lascano said the awarding of new REDD funds in Ecuador was put on hold in 2015 because the program needed to be accorded higher priority as a permanent budget line rather than a temporal and discretionary project (interview). As of 2018, funds had been frozen for nearly two years, meaning that payments were no longer being made.

The initiation of the stranded oil movement by fundraising internationally to "keep the oil in the soil" under the lush Yasuní National Park rainforest (considered further in chapter 6) was viewed as a centerpiece of the Correa-era *sumak-kawsay*-goes-international policy. But environmental activists also expected Ecuador to become an active participant in the international "carbon offset" markets supported largely by European donors. That never happened, however, perhaps in part because of the Ecuadorian government's expulsion of international lenders like the World Bank and foreign assistance agencies like the United States Agency for International Development, and the shutdown of non-governmental organizations such as Acción Ecológica and the Pachamama Foundation.

COICA activists sought Ecuadorian participation in REDD, but in an indigenous form that measured success not in the cubic tons of carbon dioxide emissions offset by the maintenance of carbon-absorbing forests, but in the square hectares of forests maintained. Furthermore, Katan argued (interview) that international donors should pay to conserve all rainforest, rather than just areas at risk, and that a more comprehensive view of conservation is required. "We want to conserve the forest in an integral way which includes biodiversity, environmental services, and cultural services, rather than just be a carbon sink" (Katan interview). Socio Bosque's former director acknowledged that the Ecuadorian government hoped to participate in an international carbon trade market, but because the nation did not have access to those markets, the nation was in 2014 (before Socio Bosque shut down in 2016) selling carbon credits based on forests conserved to program donors Germany and Norway (Lascano interview). Indeed, Ecuador's international projection as a progressive climate change actor started with great fanfare after Correa's 2006 election and solicitation of pledges at the 2009 Copenhagen UN Climate Change Summit to preserve Yasuní. But as the nation's economy grew increasingly dependent on extraction to finance the citizenry's increasingly insatiable demand for social programs, Ecuador backpedaled on its carbon emissions–reducing heroics. The public opinion effects of this positioning of the public sector version of *sumak kawsay* are considered in chapter 6.

The community of Ecuadorian ecologists working in Quito struggled to negotiate environmental activism under Correa's administration and have found more space under Moreno's presidency. These organizations recognize the importance of indigenous communities for conservation projects, and not just because the indigenous share in a cosmovision that promotes harmony with nature. As Víctor López of the NGO EcoCiencia described, Amazon indigenous organizations are crucial for promoting an agenda of conservation to reduce climate change for pragmatic reasons. EcoCiencia relies on social and institutional actors like indigenous groups to "manage cartography, develop new conservation methods, and serve as water laboratories" for assessing contamination (López interview). Working with indigenous communities in this way allows NGOs access on the ground to promote the sustainable use of biodiversity, what López summarizes as the main focus of his organization (interview). For him, mineral and oil extraction are not sustainable, and it's the responsibility of the government to reduce their impact (interview). However, given the central government's extractivist agenda, López recognizes the obstacle in achieving climate-friendly policies at the national level. Therefore, local governments—known as Decentralized Autonomous Governments (Gobiernos Autónomos Descentralizados, GADs)—and indigenous communities play key roles for NGOs trying to do conservation work. López describes "strengthening GADs" as a strategy for combating climate change, because enacting change at the local level is not only more feasible, but also because it can have the greatest impact (interview). Furthermore, combining indigenous local knowledge with more advanced scientific methodologies is, for López, one of the benefits of working against climate change at the local level (interview). Perspectives like those of López demonstrate not only the coordination that is possible between indigenous cosmovision and science, but also the difficulty that environmental activists faced in Correa's Ecuador.

CONCLUSIONS

Some of the indicators assessed in this chapter, mainly those indicating vulnerability, significant in chapter 2 when we used "concern for the environment" as our dependent variable, were not statistically significant in this analysis, even if they were referenced consistently during interviews. Perhaps part of the reason for this apparent inconsistency with our overall argument is that climate change is much less immediately tangible than other forms of environmental degradation, such as deforestation, water shortages, and contamination from fertilizers. The abstract nature of climate change does however lend it to more abstract consideration as an issue for values, ideology, personal experience, and religion. And focusing on the last of these, this study offers several findings of great relevance to the growing literature on the relationship between science and religion. More specifically, the relationship between religion and a belief in climate change, posited as mostly negative in the United States, need not always be so. Indigenous cosmovision believers shared environmentalists' "stewardship" approach as opposed to the belief in domination favored mostly by evangelical Protestants and other biblical literalists. Furthermore, belief in climate change is not always challenged by increased enthusiasm for religion. For Catholics, the more religious they considered themselves to be, the more likely they were to believe in climate change. The interaction between indigenous beliefs and evangelical Protestants confirms many of the long-standing claims by indigenous leaders: that no matter what religious identity they adhere to, they have internalized their stewardship role with nature, and thus can make credible claims to being the best guardians of rainforests and other natural lands. It is important to note that our survey was conducted in early 2014, prior to Pope Francis's encyclical about the importance of climate change as an issue relevant to the Catholic Church, and prior to his visits to Ecuador. Perhaps the Pope's vocal support of climate change would alter the effect that Catholic identity has on belief in climate change, as demonstrated here.

Recall this book's main findings, that environmental vulnerability trumps post-materialism as a cause of concern about the environment, and that polycentric pluralism is a more viable means through which citizens can articulate their positions to the political system than multiculturalism. We showed in chapter 2 that concrete measures of vulnerability drove concern for the environment, and we also showed, in chapters 3 and 4, that in addressing concrete issues such as prior consultations on extractivism (chapter 3) and whether indigenous groups should negotiate community benefits from oil extraction on indigenous communal lands (chapter 4), these concrete issues do lead to stronger citizen participation than is conveyed in relation to abstract issues like post-materialism. We also showed in all of the earlier chapters that multiculturalism is a stereotype more than an empirical phenomenon, as differences pervade intraethnic dealings on a range of issues, from concern about the environment, to modalities of consultation over extraction, to whether and how to negotiate the entrance of government and oil companies.

We have argued for polycentric pluralism and might go so far as to claim in fact that has been the *de facto* form interest articulation has largely taken, even as indigenous leaders (who disagree vehemently and even publicly) claim to speak for the indigenous perspective and government leaders co-opt *sumak kawsay* as legitimizing rhetoric for oil drilling and its economic benefits. This chapter has demonstrated that abstract reasoning about peoples' spiritual relationship with nature, as manifested in religious views—including the Kichwa cosmovision—and how strongly people follow them, plays a strong part in determining respondents' beliefs in climate change as a scientific phenomenon. Our broader claim is that peoples' religious cosmovision is one important component of their attitudes toward the environment. Vulnerability is of course another. And the implications of this chapter's claims for polycentric pluralism are more direct. Climate change is a more abstract and less contentious environmental concept than extraction, and as such has received widespread support—in the abstract—from policymakers at all levels, from the most local to the most international. While former President Correa's Yasuní conservation plans did not receive the international funding he anticipated, his polycentric appeals to *sumak kawsay* clearly convey that mestizos could legitimize themselves with multicultural myths just as indigenous leaders could. In chapter 6 we turn back to more concrete questions than climate change and religion, but with an international dimension, to show that here too, concrete expressions of self-interest, those of vulnerability and polycentric pluralism, offer more resonant appeals to survey respondents than more abstract values.

Reconciling respondents' inward-looking need to address vulnerability to environmental changes that could worsen poverty with an outward-looking effort to insert their communities into regional, national, and global debates about climate change and the equities related to this may be the attitude-defining debate of the next two decades in much of the world. Even the poorest and most remote Ecuadorians have positions on these issues, and their perceptions of the urgency of these matters may in the future offer even further evidence of the need to bring vulnerability theory and polycentric pluralism into the realm of political science explanations. Indeed, participant observation at the United Nations Framework Convention on Climate Change 2014 meeting in Peru revealed that the developing world is a macrocosm of the Ecuador rainforest peoples. Their positions regarding climate change policy are dictated in large part by how vulnerable they are to environmental changes exogenous to their national spheres of influence, where they are located (at least metaphorically) on the carbon emissions "frontier," and what domestic actors have to gain or lose from engaging in the international debate.[6] Changes in the political importance of environmental issues are not just changes in esoteric values, but stem from peoples' rational dependence on the environment for day-to-day survival and the extent to which they feel that environmental change may be outside their direct control.

Protection of Ecuador's rainforest carbon sink may seem like a domestic issue, but as explored further in chapter 6, the international diplomatic implications have been profound. And perhaps even more important than Ecuador's role in "green diplomacy" worldwide is the scope of the ownership and management of indigenous communal lands. According to recent World Resources Institute (WRI) data,[7] one-half of the world's lands supporting a third of the planet's population is under indigenous communal land control, even though only 10 percent of this land is legally titled. The WRI estimated that 24 percent of the carbon stored above ground in tropical forests worldwide is attributable to these indigenous land holdings, giving the carbon sink potential of Ecuador's rainforests economic potential. We turn now to the dichotomy between this domestic struggle for Ecuador's rainforests undermined by the negotiation of oil drilling leases, to the triumphant international projection of Ecuadorian environmentalism.

6. Eisenstadt observed the Lima, Peru, meeting from December 8 through 13, 2014.
7. See http://www.wri.org/blog/2017/03/numbers-indigenous-and-community-land-rights?utm_campaign=wridigest&utm_source=wridigest-2017-03-21&utm_medium=email&utm_content=learnmore.

CHAPTER 6

❧

Exploring the Contradiction of Extractive Populism Between Domestic and International Politics in Ecuador

Even before launching and stewarding the first constitution in the world to guarantee the rights of nature, President Rafael Correa (2007–2017) was establishing his green credentials by making the highly public and unprecedented pledge to "leave the oil in the soil" at Yasuní National Park. Yasuní is one of the world's most pristine and biodiverse rainforests and home to several hundred uncontacted peoples who have, to date, hunted and gathered within that vast rainforest without much interaction with the outside world. The pledge galvanized many around the world and at home, prompting the United Nations in 2009 to announce that it would administer the Correa-inspired Yasuní fund. Schoolchildren from all over Ecuador contributed coins from savings jars to protect jaguars and river dolphins. In chapter 1 we briefly described the course of Correa's environmental policies, but here we focus on the internal contradiction of Correa's policies, and the reasons why that contradiction did not threaten Correa politically. While President Lenin Moreno (2017–) has taken much less outspoken—and more conciliatory—positions on saving Ecuador's rainforest environment, his hands were largely tied by Correa's literal mortgaging of the country's future through the extensive sale of Ecuadorian oil to Chinese parastatal buyers to generate revenue for his extractive populism.

Correa's idea of linking the government to environmental protection originally came not from the indigenous cosmovision but from then-Minister of Energy Alberto Acosta. As discussed in chapter 3, some, but not all, indigenous communities do view the world and the relationship between humans and nature more holistically, which served as Acosta's inspiration. According to Carlos Larrea, the Correa administration's first technical director of the Yasuní-Ishpingo-Tambococha-Tiputini (ITT) Initiative, from 2007 to 2011: "Correa accepted it [the Yasuní-ITT Initiative] in good faith at the beginning, although he never really seemed to support the premises of the initiative. He never had much sensitivity regarding the environment, but it was a huge hit, Correa understood this support, and he got lots of international support" (interview).

As part of his anti-imperialist policies, Correa ran nonprofit international lenders like the World Bank out of Ecuador in 2008, leaving his government with a liquidity shortfall to finance the government's extractive populism. By 2013, China was offering tenfold the financing of other international lenders like the Inter-American Development Bank (IADB). Other donors, like the United States Agency for International Development (USAID) and the German Konrad Adenauer Foundation, also ceased to offer programming in 2014, partly as a protest against the Correa government's closure of non-government agencies that these donors worked with. This increasingly left the Chinese government as the only source for government liquidity, with its insatiable appetite for Ecuador's low-quality crude at ridiculously low prices for volume purchases. Said Larrea, about planning the Yasuní-ITT initiative, "The whole time the president was speaking of oil extraction as his Plan B. The case of Yasuní is a clear example of the inconsistency of foreign policy and environmental policy. Extractivism was the model of ALBA" the left-leaning Bolivarian Alliance for the Peoples of Our America, where Correa held great cachet, and was inspired by the extractive populism and anti-imperialist rhetoric of Venezuela and Bolivia.

As per chapter 3, tensions emerged between the environmental side of the Correa administration, which we show in this chapter was really for international consumption, and the "extractive populist" side, which represented Correa's true policies, and the ones he needed to execute in order to get funds for development projects. This tension is ongoing, as human rights lawyers seemed to have lost with the commencement of drilling on Yasuní starting in 2016. But the issue has now been reopened with the passage of Moreno's referendum on restricting drilling in Yasuní in February 2018. While drilling near Yasuní rather than right in the park would make a negligible difference in domestic oil production, the symbolic impact on international allies and their domestic constituencies in Ecuador would be substantial, especially given the Correa regime's shutdown of work in Ecuador by international agencies like the World Bank and USAID, and closure of central non-governmental environmental actors, such as Acción Ecológica and the Pachamama Foundation. President Moreno appears to be transitioning away from these more authoritarian tendencies exhibited by Correa, but only time will tell how effective Moreno's permissiveness will extend (de la Torre 2018).

The first several chapters of this book explained that contrary to post-materialist views, Ecuador's citizens, and especially those on the front lines of environmental change, are more likely to care about the environment as a result of their vulnerability and proximity to extraction. Here, we address empirical demonstrations that in practical terms, vulnerable citizens—those with material needs on the front lines of the battle against environmental degradation—are the ones fighting against the encroachment of extractive populism. More specifically, in this chapter we argue that, as per the contradiction Larrea identifies, former President Correa did, at the domestic level, prioritize extraction, while seemingly prioritizing the environment in international fora. Concretely, we consider public attitudes against extraction in the Yasuní Reserve and whether Ecuador has partial responsibility for climate change, and demonstrate how group coalitions within Ecuador bolstered Correa's international positions.

This chapter partly leaves aside the importance of vulnerability as a cause of views about the environment—so important earlier in the book, and strongly affirmed in chapters 2 through 5—to focus more on polycentric pluralism, mostly at the international and national levels, and in contrast with chapter 4, which addressed this issue locally. As we demonstrate, Ecuadorians hold uniformly nationalistic positions on the benefits of oil drilling, regarding protecting Yasuní National Park specifically, and largely agree that foreigners—such as those from China and the United States—pose threats to protecting the Amazon. However, this uniformity of position—belying multiculturalism, which would predict differences between ethnic and non-ethnic respondents—does not hold when respondents are asked about whether Ecuadorian interests also pose threats to the Amazon rainforest. Here Pachakutik supporters envision a strong threat, while PAIS supporters do not. Given the constituency of the Pachakutik party in our survey, this also confirms our argument about the failure of multiculturalism. In particular, only 15.10 percent of self-identified indigenous respondents in our sample identify with Pachakutik. Further, 7.55 percent of self-identified indigenous respondents identified with PAIS, while the remaining self-identified indigenous did not affiliate with any party (72.31 percent) and a small percentage identified with other parties (about 5.04 percent). Rather than the indigenous being a unified block in favor of Pachakutik, they spread their votes across parties and lack strong party affiliation in general. The indication that Pachakutik supporters view extraction as a threat illustrates that extractivism has become a political and economic issue, not a cultural one.

After briefly introducing the theoretical rationale behind the interaction between international and domestic policy positions, we provide descriptive statistics that show how extraction is perceived in Ecuador. We show that while there was consensus among Ecuadorians that foreign extractive interests are threats to the Amazon, Ecuadorians were starkly divided along party lines in how they viewed Correa's pursuit of extraction, illustrating the political—rather than cultural—nature of the extractive debate in Ecuador. Next, we summarize the government's dependence on oil extraction and how this bound Correa's hands regarding any wishes for the progressive environmental policies that first launched his presidential campaign over a decade ago. We then further elaborate on the nation's outward representation, as mentioned above by Larrea, and draw out the contradiction between this international representation and how Correa's domestic oil production commitments and price fluctuations caused that administration to extract with ever greater abandon and pass this legacy of overspending to President Moreno.

The upshot is that the Correa administration largely failed to maintain both its international and domestic image as an environmental force, while at the same time funding the process through increased oil drilling. Our survey, conducted at the height of international oil prices in 2014 before the 2016 international price collapse, underscores that even at the zenith of this policy's financial benefit, in the form of high oil revenue, it was not entirely popular. Furthermore, consistent with our argument that polycentric pluralism has been the form that interest articulation takes— even as multiculturalist rhetoric pervades indigenous assemblies and government radio shows—the variations in policy differences are more readily explained by cleavages defined by vulnerability and by political party affiliation than by ethnic identity.

THEORIES RELATING PUBLIC OPINION, DOMESTIC INTERESTS, AND INTERNATIONAL ENVIRONMENTAL POLITICS

International politics has long been characterized as a balancing act between domestic pressures and diplomatic relations (Rosenau 1969, 1973; Putnam 1988). There are a seemingly endless number of domestic constraints that political leaders face when negotiating on the international stage. Importantly, however, the relevant pressures shift depending upon the type of international policy being addressed. When it comes to global environmental issues, scholars have primarily focused on the influence of environmental movements (Kamieniecki 1993) and ecological parties (Jensen and Spoon 2011) at the domestic level. However, scholars have yet to examine the role that more-specific domestic contexts and policies— such as the dominance of extractive-led development and other relevant socio-political organizations—play in shaping countries' international positions. In this chapter, we examine the channels taken by former President Correa's domestic policy of "extractive populism." To study the international impacts of policies, we also pointedly address the evolution of positions of key domestic actors, such as the Pachakutik indigenous political party and the Confederación de Nacionalidades Indígenas del Ecuador (Confederation of Indigenous Nationalities of Ecuador, CONAIE), Ecuador's two key interest group defenders of indigenous rights, as well as environmental policies, given how the government fused them to Kichwa cosmovisions—in *buen vivir/sumak kawsay*—from the start.

Academics have paid little attention to how elected leaders construct international environmental positions to generate support for domestic policies. There is a modest amount of literature theorizing how elected leaders react to international factors strategically, as a means of shoring up political support and achieving domestic policy goals (Staiger and Tabellini 1999; Aklin and Urpelainen 2013). Much of this literature focuses on how international governance regulations or international exogenous shocks serve as constraints on the strategic behavior of leaders in domestic political arenas. We present an alternative argument—less studied but no less important—through which political leaders utilize international positions to generate domestic support. Gourevitch (1978) dubbed this strategy the "second image reversed,"[1] referring to trade protectionism during the hard times of the Great Depression in the run-up to World War II. Here, we offer this argument in relation to the rationale behind elected leaders' adoption of international positions on the environment. Political leaders can take environmental positions in the international arena to justify and generate support for their domestic policies. Rather than being constrained by their political stance at the international level, politicians can use international positions to promote domestic environmental policies. Specifically, we argue that Correa adopted environmental positions in the international arena to help legitimize his extractive policies at home.

---

1. The reference is to Kenneth Waltz's (1979) three "images" in international relations.

In addition, as we have throughout this book, we focus on the role that domestic public opinion played in influencing Correa's environmental policies. Empirical evidence of public influence on foreign policy has been reported in a large and growing body of research by students of international relations and foreign policy, specifically in the context of the United States (e.g., Hartley and Russett 1992; Holsti 1996; Nincic 1990; Russett 1990; Sobel 1993, 2001; Wittkopf 1990). However, more recent research has found that, at least in the United States, the influence of public opinion on presidential foreign policy is mediated through the pressure exerted by organized groups and experts (Jacobs and Page 2005). We argue that three organized groups should be the most relevant for Correa's environmental positions: the indigenous movement, the indigenous Pachakutik political party, and Correa's own Alianza PAIS party. We show that these organizations help shape public opinion, and in doing so, serve as potential interest groups that influence Correa's stance on environmental policies. In addition, we consider how the public most affected by Correa's "extractive populism"—those living in areas where extraction is debated or underway—also form relevant groups within the popular sector, shaping the former president's stance on the environment.

Though Correa rhetorically supported the Yasuní-ITT initiative, his "Plan B" (Larrea's quote) was always to exploit the national park for oil. During the 2013 presidential campaign, Alberto Acosta—the key former Correa ally and strategist who defected largely as a result of Correa's stance on the environment—ran for president against him in an alliance with Pachakutik. At the time, Acosta noted his view of Correa's true intentions for Yasuní. "Correa takes credit for the ITT initiative outside of Ecuador. But really he doesn't feel comfortable with it. He's preparing to blame rich nations for not giving enough to make it work" (Varas et al. 2013). Perhaps one of the most consistent strains of Correa's rhetoric was his anti-imperialist positions, blaming the United States and other rich countries for many of Ecuador's historic problems. For example, despite Correa's support for drilling in the Amazon, he consistently and publicly assumed an anti-imperialist position in supporting the case against Chevron. He claimed the primacy of Ecuadorian sovereignty and the rights of the Amazon residents without frequently mentioning the complicity of the Ecuadorian government, which failed to legislate environmental standards and to enforce the ones it had legislated. Correa won support for drilling by claiming that his form of extraction benefited Ecuador first, rather than transnational corporations and wealthy countries.

Despite the power certain groups held in shaping public opinion on environmental issues, not all groups were relevant to Correa's policymaking.

In fact, Correa was only really concerned with the opinions of groups most relevant to his political career: those of his Alianza PAIS party and the populations most affected by his extractive policies—even though indigenous organizations, whose views sometimes contradicted those of the government, had influence on public opinion. However, as we argue in this chapter, indigenous groups were not powerful enough to undermine electoral support for Correa, and as a result, they had little influence over Correa's international environmental positions. By contrast, given Ecuador's weak party system, Correa needed to maintain the support of the core members of his political party to conserve power and, eventually, pass support on to his designated successor, Lenin Moreno.[2] He also needed to ensure that his extractive policies were accomplishing their intended goals of drawing greater support for him and his administration (based on the public works generated via spending), in spite of the environmental controversies surrounding his expansion of the oil frontier. The fact that his partisan supporters and populations affected by oil extraction held opinions on environmental issues consistent with those of Correa lend support to our argument that his positions on Yasuní and climate change were indeed strategic ways to shore up support for his domestic pursuit of extractive populism. The Correa administration wound up in the ironic position of presenting a pro-indigenous international environmental position abroad, even as indigenous support for his policies quickly soured at home.

INDIGENOUS ORGANIZATIONS AND DOMESTIC OPPOSITION TO CORREA

In this section, we elaborate on the relationship between the Correa government and the indigenous movement, showing our expectation, upon commencing analysis of the survey results, that perceptions of the indigenous movement and its associated party would influence public opinion on Correa's international environmental positions. As summarized in chapter 1, the indigenous movement and its corresponding Pachakutik political party have historically been powerful political actors in Ecuador.

2. Moreno nearly lost the 2016 election, but this was attributed at least in part by political analysts like Acosta and Larrea (interviews) to Correa's loss in popularity after Correa tried to change the national constitution in 2015 to allow him to continue in power indefinitely as well as to the former president's failed environmental policies, perceptions of corruption, and mixed views of the nation's anti-imperialism and consequent increasing economic dependence on China.

Despite setbacks in the 2000s—the broken alliance with former President Gutiérrez and the fracturing of the movement around the entrance of Correa into electoral politics—it has remained relevant in Ecuadorian politics primarily because it has been among the strongest organized forms of opposition to Correa. Both the indigenous movement CONAIE (as a nongovernmental actor) and the Pachakutik party (within the national legislature and local governments) became active critics of Correa's policies. In this section, we discuss the history of indigenous groups' relations with Correa, and their carryover to the Moreno regime. We show that while indigenous organizations may not be the national force that they were in the 1990s, they did serve as the most powerful voice of political opposition to former President Correa. We argue that, as a result, attitudes toward indigenous organizations should be powerful determinants of public opinion over Correa's environmental policies such as Yasuní-ITT and climate change.

Correa's rift with the indigenous movement began when it became clear that he was primarily interested in consolidating his own power, rather than sharing it with other progressive groups—such as the indigenous movement—as he had indicated in his 2006 campaign. Once in office, Correa created social policies that at first seemed resonant with the demands of the indigenous movement, the environmental movement, and the fusion of these, which the Ecuadorian government projected internationally. For example, Correa made many moves to undermine the conservative oligarchy that had long dominated Ecuadorian politics. In July 2008 he expropriated 195 companies belonging to the Isaías Group to recover some of the assets that customers had lost when corporate corruption led to the collapse of its bank, Filanbanco, in 1998. In the process, he shifted resources to poor and marginalized sectors of society through increased spending on infrastructure and social programs. And in response to demands by CONAIE leaders, Correa passed a law in July 2010 that increased the government's share of petroleum profits from 13 to 87 percent, increasing state revenues by almost US $1 billion (Becker 2013a, 47). The result was that the Ecuadorian government had significantly more funds for development projects, including highway construction, improvements on telecommunications networks, and welfare spending. The government set about redistributing wealth in a way that had not been seen in Ecuador since its return to democracy in 1979. This redistribution was something that indigenous communities had been demanding since their rise to power in the 1990s.

Despite these gains, divisions within the indigenous movement emerged as Pachakutik prepared to enter the 2006 elections, the year that Correa first won the presidency. Initially, certain segments of Pachakutik (known also by the acronym MUPP-NP), especially militants from the Andean province of Imbabura, used the media to publicly promote the presidential candidacy of Auki Tituaña, the former mayor of Cotacachi who had received international recognition for many of his progressive policies, such as participatory budgeting (Van Cott 2008). This promotion was undertaken without the knowledge of the full MUPP-NP organization and CONAIE and resulted in confrontations among Pachakutik leaders and with CONAIE President Luis Macas (Guaman 2007). From that point on, MUPP-NP struggled to determine their electoral strategy for 2006, with many provincial level members arguing for an alliance with Rafael Correa's new PAIS party, and others arguing for Pachakutik to remain independent and promote their own presidential candidate. After a long battle, the organization voted to support Luis Macas as Pachakutik's presidential candidate, but many of the members of the party's National Executive Committee and other notable indigenous leaders failed to support his campaign (Guaman 2007). Although Macas was a strong candidate in terms of his ideological purity and support for the indigenous cause, Pachakutik leaders knew that he was unlikely to win the presidency because he was seen as a purist unwilling to form alliances or make broader appeals that would garner votes from across the Ecuadorian electorate (West n.d.). Pragmatic indigenous candidates therefore distanced themselves from the campaign of this multiculturalist, especially in the face of the widely popular polycentric pluralist candidate Correa. In the end, Macas won only 2.1 percent of the vote in the presidential race, and Pachakutik deputies earned only 6 of 137 seats in the National Congress (Tribunal Supremo Electoral, 2006), despite having won 8 seats out of 100 at their founding in 1998, and 11 seats out of 100 in 2002. Correa and PAIS were elected to the presidency in the second round of elections in November 2006.

Immediately upon election on his center-left platform paying homage to environmentalists and indigenous rights, Correa called for an Asamblea Constituyente (Constituent Assembly, AC) to rewrite the constitution. The people of Ecuador first voted on a referendum calling for the AC on April 15, 2007, which was supported by approximately 70 percent of the population. Once it was determined that the AC would occur, parties scrambled to define their goals for the new constitution and to nominate leaders who would run for positions in the AC. Indigenous groups were confronted with another decision about how they would participate in the AC—alone, or as part of a coalition with Correa's PAIS. The indigenous Pachakutik party identified three components of their ideological base: 1) the indigenous movement, which focused specifically on the cultures and struggles of indigenous peoples; 2) the New Left, which stemmed from Marxist and socialist thought, but which incorporated democratic ideals and a more open definition of class; and 3) social movements, or all movements that struggled against forms of oppression, such as Christian sectors, the feminist movement, and importantly, environmentalists, etc. (West n.d.).

The clear identification of movements outside of the immediate indigenous community was an obvious attempt to broaden Pachakutik's base of support in a polycentric direction. Indeed, for the elections on September 30, 2007, to select members of the AC, MUPP-NP allied with the socialist party, Partido Socialista—Frente Amplio (Socialist Party—Broad Front) in their nomination of national candidates. Unfortunately, the PS-FA/MUPP-NP alliance earned less than 1 percent of the vote nationwide. In total, MUPP-NP (in various provincial-level alliances) gained only 4 of the 130 seats in the AC. President Correa's Movimiento PAIS garnered the most seats by a significant margin, earning 73 seats on its own, and 6 more seats in provincial-level alliances (Tribunal Supremo Electoral 2007). In short, the president entered the Constituent Assembly process with a sizable majority, while Pachakutik remained on the fringes.

Correa had initiated his presidency in 2006 by positioning himself on the left. In correspondence with other leftist governments in Latin America, Correa pledged to create more-participatory governing structures, enabling the incorporation of groups—like the indigenous—who were traditionally excluded from formal politics (de la Torre 2010). At least initially, Correa seemed to follow through with these promises, particularly in his creation of social and economic policies. For example, Correa implemented laws that shifted resources—if not power—to poor and marginalized sectors of society. In addition to the Isaías Group expropriation, he defaulted on more than US $3 billion in foreign bonds. Although the treasury had the liquidity to make payments, not doing so was a political statement in defense of the country's sovereignty. Correa rhetorically labeled the debt that previous governments had contracted as "illegal, illegitimate, and corrupt" and designed only to benefit the upper classes (Becker 2013a). He argued that Ecuador should sacrifice debt payments rather than cut social investment. All of this garnered Correa significant acclaim among sectors of Ecuadorian voters and generated substantial party loyalty in a society that had previously been largely fragmented and generally anti-party. Although CONAIE and Pachakutik remained officially independent from Correa and his party, many indigenous leaders supported him, and they were hopeful that Correa would sincerely work toward advancing indigenous interests. At this point, Correa had commenced his anti-imperialist alienation of international capital and foreign donors, gaining him widespread support of Ecuador's domestic indigenous environmentalists.

However, oil extraction emerged early on as a key issue defining the relationship between Correa and the indigenous movement. Leading up to Correa's election in 2006, Pachakutik had developed an entire platform relating to the nationalization of the oil industry (*El Universo* February 19, 2006). The party framed their demands in terms of how oil revenues would benefit all of Ecuador, claiming that the government had traditionally concerned itself with governing only for the benefit of an economically privileged few, rather than for the country (*Bolpress* February 22, 2006). Early in his administration, Correa favored domestic interests over international ones by using oil proceeds to diminish inequality, placing the industry much more strongly in state control. He passed a law in July 2010 changing government petroleum royalties on profits from 13 to 87 percent, increasing annual government revenues dramatically. Just as importantly, Correa's government also increased its ability to collect taxes, especially from corporations—including those participating in extractivist efforts. As a result, Correa significantly added to the domestic revenue available for infrastructure investment and social spending without burdening the country with debt (Becker 2013a). The big losers were international oil companies, particularly those from the United States.

But despite the Ecuadorian government's strong gestures of support for domestic constituencies at the expense of international companies and lenders, activists complained that the president was too willing to sacrifice empowerment and broader levels of popular participation to achieve higher levels of economic performance, particularly in the extractive sectors (Becker 2013a). Indeed, Correa's prioritization of economic development— in the form of extraction as well as in terms of agrarian policies such as the 2014 Ley de Aguas, which complicated indigenous communities' access to water—made it clear that he had no interest in accommodating groups such as environmentalists and the indigenous on the traditional left. That law, discussed in chapter 5, was yet another effort of the Correa regime to use corporatist measures to try to undermine indigenous community autonomy and restrict polycentric rule-making that conflicted with Correa's pursuit of unrestricted economic development (Boelens, Hoogesteger, and Baud 2015).

As mentioned in chapter 1, Ecuador's national government had granted rights to nature in the 2008 Constitution, in a seeming nod to indigenous interests, but designed in part by non-indigenous intellectuals, including Constituent Assembly Chair Alberto Acosta. Also in 2009, Correa's administration had launched their high-profile demand at the UN Stockholm meeting for international donor funds to "keep the oil in the soil" at Yasuní, despite having refused to pay back lenders in 2008. But while the country's international image seemed strong, internal divisions between Correa and the indigenous movement were brewing. In June 2010, four indigenous leaders—then CONAIE President Marlon Santi and Vice President Pepe Acacho, then Ecuarunari President Delfín Tenesaca, and then-President Marco Guatemal of a local federation—were charged with threatening public security following their protest marches at an Alianza Bolivariana para los Pueblos de Nuestra América (Bolivarian Alliance for the Peoples of Our America, ALBA) summit in Otavalo, Ecuador. All told, by 2011, Correa's administration had charged 189 indigenous activists with sabotage and terrorism for contesting the use of their lands for extraction. Denouncing the criminal charges as a mechanism of social control, Ecuarunari President Tenesaca stated that "this government has declared war on Indian peoples" (*El Tiempo* July 19, 2011).

In response to these allegations of repression of indigenous leaders, Correa called for a referendum in 2011, which began as a single issue of modifying the penal code to extend the period of pretrial detention for criminals (Becker 2013b). Given the context of the referendum, opponents feared that Correa was using rising crime rates as an excuse to increase his executive power, especially to repress the indigenous environmentalists who had been his electoral allies and the key to his international environmental platform. The 2011 referendum would seemingly give Correa more authority to hold supposed criminals at his will—a move that would make it dangerous for indigenous groups to continue to organize as opposition to the government. The threats of repression seemed consistent with the "divide and conquer" strategy of state corporatism discussed in chapter 4 with reference to President Correa's efforts to get permission from indigenous communal landholders to drill oil on their lands.

The CONAIE spoke out against this apparent radicalization of government policies. In 2012, Humberto Cholango, then-president of CONAIE, denounced the criminalization of social protest under Correa's administration. As we show in chapter 3, prior consultation was a key policy for indigenous groups seeking to control access to their lands—a policy that the Correa administration used strategically to endorse extractivist activities, rather than to genuinely consult with indigenous communities. Cholango condemned these extractive policies that permitted transnational mining and petroleum companies to commence operations without gaining true prior consent from communities that faced the direct negative consequences of those enterprises (Becker 2013a). In contrast to Correa's rhetoric of leaving neoliberalism behind, Cholango charged that the government had fundamentally continued the economic and social policies of previous governments (CONAIE 2012). Cholango also contended that the government had failed to support issues central to indigenous movements, including a redistribution of land and water, and the creation of a multicultural plurinational state (Becker 2013a).

As the indigenous environmentalists grew increasingly marginalized from a government they had originally supported, schisms appeared within the indigenous block as well. Support for Pachakutik in Andean mining provinces was resilient, despite Pachakutik's relatively small size at the national level, Correa's attempt to silence the party, and the fact that party loyalists in stronghold provinces like Chimborazo, Orellana, and Zamora Chinchipe had a lot to gain economically from supporting extraction. The case of Guadalupe Llori, a Pachakutik militant and the former governor of the Amazonian province of Orellana, illustrates regional loyalty toward Pachakutik. Llori was first elected governor in 2004, and once in office, continued to promote multicultural issues of importance to the indigenous movement. In 2007, she sanctioned a protest in the town of Dayuma that brought oil drilling in the region to a halt (Olmos 2007). The protesters demanded that oil companies hire more locals and make income tax and royalty payments directly to local governments (Baird 2008). According to Llori, Correa sent in more than seven hundred soldiers to arrest the protesters, and later, she was arrested, charged with terrorism and sabotage, and imprisoned (Llori 2010). She was released in January 2008 after the Human Rights Foundation formally appealed to the Ecuadorian government. Despite this—or perhaps because of it—Llori was re-elected governor of Orellana twice more, in 2009 and in 2014. Llori's continued success as a Pachakutik militant and critic of Correa illustrates the relevance of the party as an instrument of opposition to the president and his administration, particularly with regard to Correa's extractive policies.

Indigenous opposition to extraction was particularly acute when it came to Yasuní National Park, which was also President Correa's international symbol of Ecuadorian environmentalism and Andean cosmovision actualization. CONAIE and Pachakutik were both consistently opposed to opening the area for drilling. Even before Correa permitted oil companies to enter Yasuní in September 2013 (with the commencement of drilling in 2016), his threats to enact this "Plan B"—oil drilling if the international community did not mobilize sufficiently for Yasuní protection—incurred criticism from indigenous leaders. Their critiques were based on Ecuador's sordid history with oil extraction, highlighted in chapter 4, and the damage done to indigenous people in the past. Franco Viteri, leader of the Confederation of the Indigenous Nationalities of the Ecuadorian

Amazon (Confederación de las Nacionalidades Indígenas de la Amazonía Ecuatoriana, CONFENIAE), warned in August 2013 against the dangers of drilling in Yasuní: "The deepening of the extractive policies of the current regime, which exceeds that of former neoliberal governments," the statement read, "has led to systematic violations of our fundamental rights and has generated a number of socio-environmental conflicts in indigenous communities throughout the Amazon region." CONFENIAE pointed to a historical pattern of the extermination of indigenous groups due to petroleum exploration, including the Tetete in northeastern Ecuador forty years earlier. "History repeats itself," the federation proclaimed. "We are on the verge of a new ethnocide" (Becker 2013b). Drilling in Yasuní was a visible point of contention between indigenous activists and the president, symbolic of years of tension between Correa's administration and the social movements he tried to silence. And the "ethnocide" label deterred international companies wary of the mounting political risk of involvement in Ecuador, where several indigenous groups had disappeared over the preceding decades, and the uncontacted peoples' futures as tribal groups—the Tagaeri and Taromenane—came into doubt (Thurber interview).

Following our logic of polycentric pluralism, other indigenous leaders were disenchanted with the prospect of drilling in Yasuní, but less for reasons related to environmental protection and indigenous sovereignty, and more for reasons surrounding the continued tension between Correa and indigenous communities. Many groups opposed the national referendum on extraction in Yasuní proposed by the environmental group YASUnidos. They preferred to negotiate directly with the government about the terms of extraction in the national reserve. As the president of the Federation of the Indigenous Organizations of Napo (FOIN), Marco Aurelio Licuy, stated regarding the referendum for drilling for oil in Yasuní: "If 'Yes' wins, we lose. If 'No' wins, we lose." He supported this argument by saying that the referendum could allow drilling "without environmental control and without oil funds being diverted directly to the affected communities even if just 0.001 percent." He conditionally supported Yasuní drilling, with the caveats that it be regulated and that revenue go directly to indigenous organizations (Licuy interview).

The stark contrast between government and indigenous environmentalist positions on Yasuní drilling does not hold regarding positions on climate change. As discussed in chapter 5, indigenous groups have been wary of international climate change programs. Beginning in 2009 under the leadership of Marlon Santi, CONAIE criticized international climate change programs such as REDD and its local complement Socio Bosque, arguing that the programs interfered with indigenous autonomy. However, this criticism does not extend to all climate change policies, and CONAIE has reiterated that they know that climate change is "the result of extraction and the burning of fossil fuels, agroindustry and deforestation, all of these dynamics that are intrinsic to the neoliberal capitalist system" (CONAIE 2011).

Within the Amazon region, indigenous communities such as the Sarayaku Kichwa community and the Achuar sought external allies to help them prevent oil drilling on their lands—an activity they knew was connected to climate change at the global level (Pachamama Alliance 2016). Given the extent to which organized indigenous groups have been active against extractive efforts and the link that the indigenous see between extraction and climate change, they are apt to believe that responsibility for climate change does not lie solely in the hands of rich countries. Instead, loyalists of CONAIE and Pachakutik are likely to view climate change as a crucial responsibility of Ecuador—its government and its citizens—as well.

All of these efforts by Pachakutik to oppose Correa in his strict adherence to oil extraction in the Amazon appear to have led the Ecuadorian public to view the platform and position of the party as pro-environment. In fact, Pachakutik is viewed by Ecuadorians as the most environmentally focused in the country by a significant margin. In our national survey of Ecuadorians, we asked whether respondents knew of a party that represented environmental issues. Only 11.4 percent (203) of our respondents said that they did know of such a party. However, among those respondents, the majority (55.2 percent) identified Pachakutik as the party that represented environmental issues. The only other parties that had more than 3 respondents identify them as environmentally focused were Correa's PAIS party, with 35 percent; the Partido Sociedad Patriótica (Patriotic Society Party, PSP), with 5.4 percent; and the AVANZA party, with 3.0 percent.

Because so few respondents identified any party as being focused on environmental issues, Pachakutik is not a dominant force in setting the environmental agenda. However, among respondents who do consider the nature of partisan competition with respect to the environment, Pachakutik is the overwhelming favorite in advancing environmental issues, which suggests that further investigation of the effects of partisanship in determining public opinion toward Correa's extractivist positions is worthwhile. Based on the history of the relationship between Correa, his PAIS party, and the indigenous movement (CONAIE) and its political party (Pachakutik), we would expect attitudes toward environmental and extractivist issues to be shaped by partisanship.

SURVEY RESPONDENTS' PERCEPTIONS OF THE DOMESTIC COSTS AND BENEFITS OF EXTRACTIVISM

To what extent did Correa's international positions on Yasuní and climate change affected how Ecuadorians view oil extraction? Framed differently, does polycentric pluralism, or the articulation of interests at these two different levels of analysis, yield strong results against extraction? We argue that Correa adopted pro-environmental and anti-imperialist international positions to divert responsibility for failed extraction away from the Ecuadorian government, and to drive up support for his use of extractive populism domestically.

Initial results from our survey seem to corroborate this argument. Correa seemingly had a powerful influence on perceptions of the Ecuadorian people regarding extraction. Our survey results show that a majority of all Ecuadorians are skeptical of foreign benefactors of extraction. In Table 6.1 we summarize responses to survey questions about the costs and benefits of extraction by foreigners and companies. When asked if communities should protect their lands from foreigners who want to benefit from natural resources, a sizable majority (69.6 percent) of our respondents agreed. When broken down by party affiliation, adherents to Pachakutik were more likely to agree that foreign interests should be prevented from entering onto community lands (78.3 percent agreed), but Correa's PAIS adherents (73.7 percent) were also more likely than other respondents who had no party affiliations or were affiliated with parties other than Pachakutik and PAIS (68.4 percent) to agree that foreigners should be prevented access

Table 6.1 PERCEPTIONS OF COSTS AND BENEFITS OF EXTRACTION BY PARTY AFFILIATION

	"The communities should protect their lands from the entrance of foreigners that want to benefit from their natural resources." ENVIRO9.		"Some say that allowing companies access to land to extract resources is beneficial for Ecuador. Do you agree?" ENVIRO8.	
	Agree	Disagree	Agree	Disagree
Pachakutik	78.2 (101)	13.1 (17)	31.7 (41)	37.9 (49)
PAIS	73.6 (126)	18.1 (31)	38.6 (66)	38.6 (66)
Other/ None	68.3 (1010)	23.9 (354)	33.1 (489)	48.1 (711)
Total	69.6 (1237)	22.6 (402)	33.5 (596)	46.4 (826)

Note: Based on responses to the statement: "For the following questions, please tell me if you are in agreement or disagreement with . . ." Percentage with *N* shown in parentheses.

to natural resources. In other words, this issue does not follow a partisan divide—the majority of all Ecuadorians, regardless of party affiliation, believe that communities should have the right to prevent foreign extractive interests from encroaching on their lands. Correa's anti-imperialist discourse appears to be supported by a majority of Ecuadorians, regardless of party affiliation. Multiculturalism (Pachakutik supporters versus those of non-ethnic parties) does not matter on this central issue.

This finding is corroborated further by responses to a question about whether extraction by companies benefits Ecuador. Returning to Table 6.1, it is important to note that we asked respondents about companies in general, and not about foreign companies specifically. This question captures public opinion primarily on private industry, which includes both foreign and domestic companies, but excludes Correa's state-run extractive industry (as we show in Table 6.3). The importance of the question is its emphasis on whether extraction benefits Ecuador specifically. As the summary in Table 6.1 shows, reactions to whether extraction is beneficial also do not appear to be motivated by partisan interests. Here too, *all* Ecuadorians appear to be divided on their views about the benefits of extraction by companies. The plurality of respondents (46.5 percent) disagree that extraction is beneficial for Ecuador, while about a third of respondents agree that it is beneficial (33.5 percent), and the remainder believe that it depends (13.9 percent), or do not know if it is beneficial for Ecuador (5.8 percent). Interestingly, Pachakutik and PAIS adherents seem to be almost equally likely to disagree that extraction is beneficial (38 percent and 38.6 percent respectively), illustrating the non-partisan nature of responses to this question.

Table 6.2 FOREIGN THREATS TO AMAZONIAN INDIGENOUS COMMUNITIES BY PARTY AFFILIATION

	Chinese Mining and Oil Companies		US Mining and Oil Companies	
	Yes	No	Yes	No
Pachakutik	92.2 (119)	2.3 (3)	86.8 (112)	6.9 (9)
PAIS	73.1 (125)	13.4 (23)	81.8 (140)	9.3 (16)
Other/None	80 (1182)	8.8 (131)	79.2 (1171)	10.7 (159)
Total	80.2 (1426)	8.8 (157)	80 (1423)	10.5 (184)

Note: Based on responses to the survey question: "Speaking of the Amazon region, do you believe that the following are threats to the indigenous communities there, or not?" *N* in parentheses.

Table 6.3 DOMESTIC THREATS TO AMAZONIAN INDIGENOUS COMMUNITIES
BY PARTY AFFILIATION

	Ecuadorian Mining and Oil Companies		Ecuadorian Government and Petroecuador	
	Yes	No	Yes	No
Pachakutik	75.1 (97)	16.2 (21)	56.5 (73)	35.6 (46)
PAIS	43.2 (74)	43.2 (74)	34.5 (59)	51.4 (88)
Other/None	50.3 (744)	33 (488)	45.9 (679)	37.1 (548)
Total	51.4 (915)	32.8 (583)	45.6 (811)	38.3 (682)

Note: Based on responses to the survey question: "Speaking of the Amazon region, do you believe that the following are threats to the indigenous communities there, or not?" *N* in parentheses.

Additional survey questions elucidate the strength of anti-imperialist sentiment when it comes to extraction in Ecuador. In Table 6.2, we summarize responses to the question, "Do you believe that the following are threats to Amazonian indigenous communities, or not?" highlighting responses related to foreign countries. Our respondents overwhelmingly believe that mining and oil companies from China (80 percent) and the United States (80.1 percent) are threats to indigenous communities in the Amazon. Interestingly, party identity *does* seem to influence perceptions of the threat that Chinese companies pose, as affiliates of Pachakutik are more likely to view China as a threat (92.3 percent) when compared to individuals who affiliate with other or no parties (80 percent). Affiliates of the PAIS party were the least likely (73.1 percent) to view Chinese companies as a threat, but still nearly three out of four PAIS affiliates in our survey agreed that the Chinese are a threat. Correa took a softer perspective on China, negotiating with Chinese companies on several development projects, and much more readily than with US-based corporations. Indeed, China had been Ecuador's largest trade partner in oil, and Correa publicly portrayed this relationship in a positive light. Perhaps this explains why his PAIS supporters are less suspicious than others of the Chinese, though the majority of PAIS supporters still believe that Chinese companies are a threat.

Returning to Table 6.2, it is apparent that there is no such divide in the perception of the United States as a threat. Across all partisan groups, a vast majority of respondents believe that US mining and oil companies pose a threat to indigenous communities in the Amazon. Consistent with responses to questions about Chinese companies, affiliates of Pachakutik are the most likely to view the United States as a threat (86.8 percent). However, in contrast to these views of the Chinese, Correa's PAIS adherents have the second largest proportion (81.9 percent) of respondents who view the United States as a threat, while 79.3 percent of respondents with no party affiliation or other party affiliation view the United States as a threat. These figures are all very similar proportions, and the divide between Pachakutik and PAIS that is quite wide in response to the Chinese (about 19 percentage points difference) narrows considerably in response to the United States (about 5 percentage points difference). Taken together, responses to questions on both China and the United States demonstrate that there appears to be widespread agreement that foreign interests pose a significant threat to indigenous communities in the Amazon.

However, this unity of opinion against international threats collapses when domestic threats are considered. Indeed, vast partisan divides emerge when we ask respondents about domestic threats to indigenous communities. In response to questions about domestic threats, perceptions appear to be largely dependent upon party identity, with an especially large gap between Pachakutik party adherents and PAIS supporters. Turning to Table 6.3, we evaluate perceptions of domestic threats to indigenous communities in the Amazon. We asked respondents whether they viewed Ecuadorian mining and oil companies and the Ecuadorian government and its state-sponsored oil company, Petroecuador, as threats. The only partisan group with a significant majority of respondents who agree Ecuadorian oil interests are a threat is the Pachakutik party, with 75.2 percent of its adherents agreeing that Ecuadorian companies and 56.6 percent agreeing that the Ecuadorian government are threats to indigenous communities. These two proportions are in stark contrast with the minority of Correa's PAIS supporters, who view Ecuadorian companies (43.3 percent) and the Ecuadorian government (34.5 percent) as threats to the Amazon's indigenous. The divide between Pachakutik and PAIS supporters is substantial, with about 32 percentage points difference in proportion of respondents who view Ecuadorian companies as a threat, and a 22-point difference in terms of respondents who view the Ecuadorian government as a threat.

Taken together, these results illustrate several important dynamics with respect to what shapes Ecuadorian public opinion surrounding oil extraction and its threat to Amazonian communities. First, Ecuadorians are largely divided about whether extraction is beneficial to Ecuador (Table 6.1). In fact, the plurality of respondents do *not* agree that extraction benefits Ecuador, making it even more important to evaluate the factors that shape public opinion surrounding extraction, especially in protected areas like the Yasuní National Park. Second, there appears to be a consensus that foreign interests are the greatest threat to indigenous communities, particularly in the Amazon. When asked generally about whether communities should be able to protect their lands from foreign interests (Table 6.1) and whether China and the United States pose threats to Amazonian communities (Table 6.2), the majority of all Ecuadorians—*regardless of party affiliation*—agree that foreign interests are threatening and should be stopped. The only partisan distinction that can be detected in these responses is with respect to the perceptions of the Chinese as a threat, in which affiliates of Correa's PAIS party are less likely to view China as a threat, whereas Pachakutik affiliates overwhelmingly view the Chinese as a threat. Given Correa's promotion of China as a development partner, this trend is not surprising, and gives credence to the idea that partisanship shapes opinion on the threats posed by extraction and certain extractivist actors.

By contrast, public opinion surrounding the threat that *domestic* interests in oil extraction pose is largely shaped by partisan identification. As we have described, the indigenous Pachakutik party has been highly critical of the Correa administration and its strict adherence to oil extraction in the Amazon at the expense of indigenous interests. This perspective is born out by the survey results, where Pachakutik affiliates are much more likely to view domestic actors—such as Ecuadorian companies and the government itself—as threats to indigenous communities in the Amazon. Affiliates of Correa's PAIS party, however, are much less likely to view Ecuadorian companies and especially the Ecuadorian government as threats to Amazon communities. Based on these descriptive statistics, a deeper investigation into the sources of public opinion surrounding Correa's international environmental policies is merited.

THE CONTRADICTION BETWEEN INTERNATIONAL DISCOURSE AND DOMESTIC POLICY

When Correa surged onto Ecuador's electoral scene in 2006, he did so as part of a new political party, created specifically for his presidential campaign. Originally called Movimiento PAIS, Correa referred to his party as a "movement" to expressly divorce himself from the traditional parties that he was running against. As part of his 2006 campaign, Correa promised to dissolve the National Congress upon election, and therefore did not run alongside any candidates for the national legislature. That did not stop local politicians from allying themselves with Correa in order to ride his momentum into office for themselves. As we describe in chapter 1, Correa originally courted the support of CONAIE and Pachakutik for his campaign, even going so far as to arrive uninvited to a CONAIE assembly. However, once elected, tensions arose between Correa and indigenous interests, and the national-level indigenous organizations largely divorced themselves from Correa and his party. Still, the pragmatism guiding the conduct of both groups is indicative more of a fluid polycentric approach than of a monolithic multiculturalist one.

Why did Correa allow the once large and powerful indigenous groups to become one of the largest sources of his opposition? This question is particularly crucial in the face of the fact that public perception on the environment and on domestic forms of extraction are divided along party lines. Given how strongly he and his PAIS party performed in elections, power-sharing was not necessary for Correa to win office or pass legislation. Beginning with the 2006 election that put him in office, Correa and PAIS won six elections in fewer than five years. Following his dominance of the constituent assembly that he called immediately after his election, almost two-thirds of the voters approved the new constitution that delegates had drafted largely under Correa's control. Ecuador's new constitution so fundamentally remapped Ecuador's political structures that it required new local, congressional, and presidential elections (Becker 2013a). Correa and his PAIS party again dominated these contests, including winning the April 2009 presidential election with 52 percent of the vote in the first round, negating the need for a second round. Then in May 2011, voters approved a referendum that concentrated additional power in the president's hands. After his initial election in 2006, Correa and his PAIS party dominated every electoral contest. There simply was no political reason for Correa to ally with the indigenous movement and its Pachakutik party at the national level.

However, the Ecuadorian government depended on a core demographic of PAIS supporters to maintain his popularity. Ecuador has a history of a weak and fragmented party system, so overall, support for political parties was low. For example, only 22.4 percent of our survey sample claimed to affiliate with a political party. However, among those who identified with a party, 43.3 percent considered themselves militants of Correa's PAIS party. The only other party that came close to that level of support was Pachakutik, with 32.7 percent of party affiliates identifying with the indigenous organization. All of the other parties have less than 7 percent support within our survey sample. And again, the vast majority of our sample (77.6 percent) did not identify with any political party, signifying the continued weakness of Ecuador's party system and also offering a partial explanation for the apparent ethnic cleavage on the domestic threats to the Amazon questions. It seems that the difference between Pachakutik and PAIS was more about whether respondents sided with the government or opposition than whether they held indigenous or non-indigenous views.

Party loyalists were an important part of Correa's presidency, and he used "extractive populism" to shore up support for himself and his party. Even as Correa's decade in office wound down, the president of the National Assembly and PAIS militant Gabriela Rivadeneira expressed her preference for amending the constitution and allowing for Correa to remain indefinitely in office (*El Tiempo* November 16, 2015). Within the Ecuadorian constituency, Correa's electoral base consisted of the unorganized and marginalized urban lower classes. He also drew in small business owners and the urban middle-class *forajido* (outlaw) movement that played a central role in the April 2005 street mobilizations that removed Gutiérrez from power (Becker 2013a). Furthermore, although Correa alienated the national indigenous organizations of CONAIE and Pachakutik, he was able to attract support of more local indigenous organizations. As we show in chapter 4, local indigenous communities splintered around the issue of extraction, for example in the Kichwa municipality of Tena and its surrounding areas in the Napo province, and among the national leaderships of the Waorani and the Shuar. Whereas some indigenous communities stood steadfast in their desire to protect their lands against extractive interests, others hoped to work with the national government and reap the developmental benefits of extraction. Correa used the divisive nature of extraction to his advantage, recognizing that even the indigenous were not a solidly united front against his extractivist policies.[3] This domestic division along partisan lines starkly contrasts to the unity in opinion against international interests. Correa's successor, President Moreno, seemed early in his term to seek to diminish these divisions and appeared to be successful in doing so.

THE SOURCES OF PUBLIC OPINION TOWARD YASUNÍ AND CLIMATE CHANGE

Thus far, we have argued that the indigenous movement CONAIE and its affiliated party Pachakutik have formed the strongest opposition to the Ecuadorian government's extractivist agenda, to the point that Pachakutik is viewed by survey respondents as the most environmentally focused political party in Ecuador. Furthermore, we have argued that Correa's stance

---

3. Among those who self-identify as indigenous in our survey, 7.6 percent state that they affiliate with Correa's PAIS party, while 15.1 percent state that they affiliate with Pachakutik.

on oil drilling, Yasuní, and climate change was always one that shifted the blame away from Ecuador and toward international actors.

In this section, we argue that the political nature of the conflict surrounding oil drilling will be the primary determinant of public opinion toward Correa's international policies—namely the exploitation of Yasuní, and the responsibility for climate change. Specifically, we expect that opinions on these two issues will be largely determined by three political factors: party affiliation, trust in the indigenous movement, and location on the extractive frontier. We expect adherents to Pachakutik and individuals who trust the indigenous movement to be critical of Correa's pursuit of oil in Yasuní. We also expect those same individuals—indigenous and non-indigenous respondents—to be critical of Correa's rigorous efforts to blame the rich countries for climate change while exculpating Ecuador of any responsibility. Buying into that rhetoric is contrary to the understanding that domestic-led efforts of extraction are just as damaging to the climate as foreign efforts would be. Indigenous activists who recognize the damaging role of Ecuador's domestic-led extraction should be less likely to blame only rich countries for climate change.

In addition, building off the other chapters in this book, we argue that an individual's location on the extractive frontier is an indicator of both vulnerability as well as political positioning in the climate of Correa's extractivist populism. As we showed in chapter 2 and again in chapter 4, living along the extractive frontier is a powerful determinant not only of an individual's environmental consciousness, but also of their political dispositions toward extraction overall. In this chapter, we argue that these political dispositions will also help determine opinions on the government's willingness to drill in Yasuní, and Correa's propensity to shirk responsibility for climate change and assign it to rich countries alone.

To assess which groups are most influential in shaping public opinion with respect to Correa's international positions, we analyze two questions from our nationwide survey of environmental dispositions in Ecuador. First, we rely upon a question that asked respondents about their attitudes toward drilling in the Yasuní National Park. Specifically, we asked, "Do you agree or disagree with the exploitation of the Yasuní National Park?" We coded those who *disagree* 1, and all others 0. The majority of our sample (52.5 percent) disagreed with the drilling in Yasuní. Second, we assess individuals' dispositions toward responsibility for climate change. For this, we create a measure from our survey question in which we asked respondents to indicate whether they agree or disagree with the following statement: "Climate change is a problem that only people living in rich countries have the luxury to worry about." We coded respondents who *disagree* with this statement—or who believe that climate change is something that everyone should worry about—a 1, and all others a 0. Again, a majority of our sample (63.4 percent) disagrees that only rich countries should worry about climate change. Note that the more environmentally conscious responses—and those that are critical of Correa's stances—are coded 1, representing opposition to drilling and recognition that climate change is a problem for everyone, respectively. When it comes to interpreting results, positive relationships between our independent variables and the dependent variables indicate increased support for more environmentally conscious perspectives on Yasuní and climate change. By contrast, negative coefficients represent greater agreement with Correa's stances favoring drilling in Yasuní and blaming rich countries for climate change.

The key independent variables of interest measure affiliation and support for the organizations that we argue shape public opinion on these two key environmental issues. Because we argue that Ecuador's indigenous movement organization—CONAIE—has taken clear stances on Yasuní and climate change, we include a measure that assesses ties to the movement. Specifically, we include a variable that measures the extent to which individuals trust the national indigenous movement organization, CONAIE. The variable is ordinal and is coded 1 for not at all trusting the movement, 2 for trusting the movement a little, 3 for trusting the movement some, and 4 for trusting the movement a lot. The average response is 2.12, between trusting the movement a little and some. About 27.5 percent of our respondents do not trust the movement at all, while 38.7 percent trust it a little, and 28.1 percent trust it some. Only 5.7 percent of our sample trusts the movement a lot. We argue further that the political branch of the indigenous movement, the Pachakutik party, also shapes public opinion toward Yasuní and climate change. We code respondents that claim to affiliate with the Pachakutik party 1, and 0 for everyone else. About 7.3 percent of our sample stated that they are affiliates of the Pachakutik party. We expect both measures—trust in CONAIE and affiliation with Pachakutik—to have positive relationships with our dependent variables. In other words, we expect CONAIE followers and Pachakutik adherents to be more likely to *disagree* with drilling in Yasuní, and more likely to *disagree* that climate change is a concern only for people living in wealthy countries.

We also include a variable that indicates whether individuals affiliate with Correa's PAIS party. This variable is coded 1 for individuals who stated they are affiliates of the PAIS party, and 0 for all others. Around 9.6 percent of our sample claimed to identify with the PAIS party. Given the political polarization surrounding views on domestic-led extraction, we expect a negative relationship between this indicator and our dependent variables.

In other words, we expect PAIS supporters to be *less* likely to *disagree* (or more likely to agree) with Correa's agenda to drill in Yasuní, and to buy into the rhetoric that only people in rich countries can afford to care about climate change.

We also argue that an individual's experience with extraction should influence their attitudes toward drilling in Yasuní and their beliefs about who is responsible for climate change. We therefore include our three measures that code for proximity to extraction: *Mining* (2 = respondent lives within approximately 30 kilometers of an active mine, 1 = respondent lives in an area where mining is debated, 0 = otherwise), *History of Oil Extraction* (respondent lives in an oil block where oil has been extracted), and *Oil Debate* (respondent lives in an oil block where oil drilling is being negotiated). As we have found elsewhere (Eisenstadt and West 2017), individuals in areas where oil has already been extracted are less likely to view the environment as the most important issue when compared to other issues. Therefore, we may expect that such individuals will also be *less* likely to disagree with drilling in Yasuní as well as *less* likely to believe that Ecuador should assume greater responsibility for climate change. In other words, we expect there to be a *negative* relationship between *History of Oil Extraction* and both our dependent variables.

By contrast, the influence of *Oil Debate* is more complicated. Many who live in areas where oil is debated are concerned about preserving their lands, so for them, drilling in Yasuní sets a dangerous precedent. Therefore, we expect there to be a *positive* relationship between living in an area where oil is debated and opposition to extraction in Yasuní. The expectation about how individuals living in oil blocks under concession view climate change is not as clear; therefore, we have no expectation about how *Oil Debate* relates to views on climate change. In addition, as we did in chapters 2 and 3, we controlled for expectations that *Extraction Benefits Ecuador*, because those attitudes may play a role in support for prior consultation.

Several elements of the survey instrument allow us to develop measures of how cosmovision, or adherence to a worldview reflected by indigenous beliefs, may affect support for prior consultation. We included *Indigenous and Nature* (respondent agrees that the indigenous are more connected with Mother Earth than non-indigenous), of which about 73.1 percent of our sample agreed (coded 1), while the remaining 26.9 percent said that they either did not agree or that it depends (coded 0). We also include the variable *Mother Earth Has Rights*, for which about 80.2 percent of our sample said that they agree (coded 1), while the remaining 19.8 percent said that they either did not agree or that it depends (coded 0). We also control for *Indigenous ID*, or respondents who self-identify as indigenous (1 if self-identified as indigenous, 0 otherwise). We expect these views on nature and identity to have positive relationships with our measure of opposition to drilling in Yasuní and more extensive responsibility for climate change.

Consistent with the analyses in this book, we control for the eight elements of the survey instrument that allow us to develop measures of what we consider to be post-materialist dispositions. Specifically, we include the variables *Human Rights* (respondent includes human rights as one of the six most important problems facing the country), *Promote Modernity* (respondent believes that promoting modernity and development are the most important characteristics of good local government), *Indigenous Leader* (respondent disagrees that the indigenous do not make good leaders), *Democracy vs. Development* (respondent believes that democracy is more important than development), *Climate Change* (respondent believes in climate change), *Social Media* use (respondent has used social media in the past week), the *Professional* variable (respondent's occupation is professional), and the *Eco Donation* variable (respondent has donated to an ecological organization). As with the previous chapters, we do not expect any of these variables measuring post-materialist dispositions to be significant determinants of attitudes toward prior consultation. Instead, we expect more concrete characteristics—such as political affiliations and vulnerability to extraction—to influence opposition to Yasuní and a broader attribution of responsibility for climate change.

We also include a variety of independent variables that we used to capture a respondent's vulnerability. Specifically, we include the variables *Rain/River Water Source* (respondent gets their water primarily from rain or the river), *Energy Scarcity* (respondent has less than twelve hours of regular access to electricity per day), *Climate Change Concern* (scale of respondents' worry over climate change), and *Ecotourism* (respondent directly benefits from ecotourism in their community). We expect these variables to have a positive relationship with opposition to drilling in Yasuní and a broader attribution of responsibility for climate change.

Finally, we include several controls: *Media Access, Knowledge Index, Religiosity, Education*, and *Income*. We have no clear expectations for how these variables relate to opposition to Yasuní, especially given that increased media access and advanced education may lead to conflicting knowledge or beliefs around drilling in the park reserve, and also because we expect these factors to be mitigated by political affiliations. We may expect *Knowledge* and *Education* to have positive relationships with a broader attribution of responsibility for climate change, though again, we expect this belief to be largely influenced by party identification.

RESULTS AND DISCUSSION

To reiterate, we expect attitudes toward Correa's international policies—specifically drilling in Yasuní and attributing responsibility for climate change to wealthy countries—to be shaped by affiliation with key organizations—specifically, party affiliation and loyalty to the indigenous movement (noting that both indigenous and non-indigenous respondents may be loyal to the indigenous movement).

For both questions, we expect affiliation with the Alianza PAIS party to make it *less* likely that individuals disagree with the exploitation of Yasuní and *less* likely to disagree that only rich countries are responsible for climate change. By contrast, we expect affiliation with indigenous organizations—such as CONAIE and Pachakutik—to make it *more* likely that individuals disagree with the violation of Yasuní and *more* likely to disagree with a limited definition of responsibility for climate change. While these would initially seem to affirm the multiculturalist argument, we note that the majority of self-identified indigenous—55.95 percent—had little to no trust in CONAIE and only 15.10 percent of self-identified indigenous considered themselves to be Pachakutik supporters. Further confirming our vulnerability hypothesis and also the polycentric pluralism emphasis on geospatial rather than ethnic interest articulation, we also expect a respondent's location on the extractive frontier to shape their attitudes toward these two issues.

Our findings provide strong support for our expectations. In fact, in analyses of both opposition to drilling in Yasuní and disagreement that climate change is only the purview of the rich, affiliation with the former president's PAIS party is both significant and negative, as we expected (see Tables 6.4 and 6.5). Surprisingly, affiliation with the Pachakutik party has no significant effect in our analyses for either Yasuní or climate change. However, trust in the indigenous movement does have the expected positive relationship with the idea that climate change is a problem for all, and not just the rich.

The other powerful predictors of attitudes toward Yasuní and climate change are respondents' locations along the extractive frontier. As we expected, based on prior work (Eisenstadt and West 2017), respondents who live with a *History of Oil* are less likely to disagree with drilling in Yasuní and are also less likely to believe that climate change is a problem for those living outside rich countries. In addition, as we expected, living in an area where oil is debated leads to more complicated relationships with these two issues. When it comes to drilling in Yasuní, *Oil Debate* has a positive and significant influence on opposition to Yasuní. Respondents living in

Table 6.4. DISAGREE WITH DRILLING IN YASUNÍ NATIONAL PARK
IN ECUADOR

Post-Materialism

Human Rights	0.018
	(0.262)
Promote Modernity	−0.243**
	(0.116)
Indigenous Leader	0.112
	(0.116)
Democracy vs. Development	0.086
	(0.124)
Social Media	0.188
	(0.130)
Professional	−0.519*
	(0.311)
Eco Donation	−0.065
	(0.303)

International Networks

International Networks	−0.076
	(0.047)

Vulnerability

Rain/River Water Source	0.177
	(0.173)
Energy Scarcity	0.376
	(0.408)
Climate Change Concern	−0.026
	(0.076)
Ecotourism	0.356
	(0.228)

Political Orientations

Pachakutik Affiliate	−0.002
	(0.244)
PAIS Affiliate	−1.066***
	(0.204)
Trust in CONAIE	0.020
	(0.069)

Extraction

Mining	−0.424***
	(0.125)

Table 6.4. CONTINUED

History of Oil Extraction	−1.230***
	(0.277)
Oil Debate	0.546***
	(0.192)
Extraction Benefits Ecuador	−0.308***
	(0.064)
Cosmovision	
Indigenous Closer to Nature	−0.184
	(0.134)
Mother Earth Has Rights	0.189
	(0.154)
Indigenous ID	0.026
	(0.143)
Controls	
Media Access	−0.003
	(0.063)
Religiosity	0.128
	(0.083)
Knowledge Index	−0.030
	(0.032)
Education	0.033
	(0.053)
Income	0.008
	(0.039)
Constant	-0.057
	(0.541)
N	1,416

* $p < 0.1$; ** $p < 0.05$; *** $p < 0.01$
Note: Dependent variable based on the question: "Do you agree or disagree with the exploitation of the Yasuní National Park?" (1= disagree, 0= all others).

areas where oil blocks have been concessioned are significantly more likely to oppose extraction in the national park. Interestingly, *Oil Debate* has the opposite relationship with the strict attribution of responsibility of climate change to the rich. Respondents living along the extractive frontier where oil drilling has the possibility of occurring share views similar to those where there is a history of oil extraction—they are less likely to disagree that only the rich are accountable for climate change. This is not really surprising given the strength of Correa's anti-imperialist rhetoric, and the

Table 6.5. DISAGREE THAT CLIMATE CHANGE IS A PROBLEM ONLY FOR RICH COUNTRIES

	1
Post-Materialism	
Human Rights	1.078***
	(0.349)
Promote Modernity	0.417***
	(0.124)
Indigenous Leader	0.064
	(0.123)
Democracy vs. Development	0.115
	(0.132)
Social Media	0.056
	(0.139)
Professional	0.168
	(0.355)
Eco Donation	0.621*
	(0.370)
International Networks	
International Networks	0.202***
	(0.056)
Vulnerability	
Rain/River Water Source	−0.109
	(0.175)
Energy Scarcity	−0.258
	(0.392)
Climate Change Concern	0.153*
	(0.080)
Ecotourism	0.090
	(0.235)
Political Orientations	
Pachakutik Affiliate	−0.329
	(0.256)
PAIS Affiliate	−0.603***
	(0.202)
Trust in CONAIE	0.158**
	(0.074)
Extraction	
Mining	0.020
	(0.131)

(continued)

Table 6.5. CONTINUED

History of Oil Extraction	−1.390***
	(0.268)
Oil Debate	−1.177***
	(0.193)
Extraction Benefits Ecuador	−0.046
	(0.068)
Cosmovision	
Indigenous Closer to Nature	0.129
	(0.140)
Mother Earth Has Rights	0.487***
	(0.159)
Indigenous ID	−0.161
	(0.150)
Controls	
Media Access	−0.088
	(0.068)
Religiosity	−0.098
	(0.091)
Knowledge Index	0.091***
	(0.034)
Education	−0.065
	(0.056)
Income	0.120***
	(0.042)
Constant	−0.095
	(0.578)
N	1,416

* $p < 0.1$; ** $p < 0.05$; *** $p < 0.01$
Note: Dependent variable based on the survey question: "Do you agree or disagree with the following statement: 'Climate change is a problem that only people living in rich countries have the luxury to worry about.'" We coded respondents who *disagree* with this statement—or that believe that climate change is something that everyone should worry about—a 1, and all others a 0.

heightened awareness of individuals in those areas about the role that international corporations have played in Ecuador's oil exploitation history.

When it comes to opposition to drilling in Yasuní, there are several other factors that are significant determinants of public opinion on this issue (see Table 6.4). For example, *Mining* (or living in areas where mining is debated or occurring) has a negative relationship with opposition to drilling, much in the same way that *History of Oil* has a negative relationship. Proximity to mining does not seem to make individuals more likely to desire to protect the environment, at least when it comes to domestic-led forms of extraction like those taking place in Yasuní. Not surprisingly, the belief that *Extraction Benefits Ecuador* also makes individuals less likely to oppose drilling in Yasuní. The only other factors that have significant relationships with attitudes toward Yasuní are two measures of post-materialist dispositions: *Promote Modernity* and *Professional*. Rather than these two factors leading to pro-environmental dispositions, as the literature on post-materialism would expect, they both have negative relationships with opposition to Yasuní, meaning that the desire for local leaders who promote modernity and respondents holding professional positions make it more likely that individuals support drilling for oil in the national park.

A variety of other factors have estimated effects on whether individuals believe that climate change is something that only people in rich countries can afford to care about, including three measures of post-materialist dispositions (see Table 6.5). For example, the belief that human rights are one of the most important issues in Ecuador, the belief that local leaders should promote modernity over traditions, and giving a donation to an ecological organization are all predictors of the attitude that more than only citizens of rich countries should care about climate change. This is an interesting finding, and hints at the more abstract nature of climate change when compared to the very concrete prospect of drilling in Yasuní. For Yasuní, it is only the very identifiable qualities of political affiliations and location on the oil frontier that determine support or opposition for drilling in Ecuador's nature reserve. However, for climate change—a much broader issue that is much more collective and dispersed in nature—more-subjective views are more closely related to determining attitudes. The influence of more-subjective views continues with the finding that a subjective view of *Climate Change Impacts* and the belief that *Mother Nature Has Rights* both also make it more likely that one holds the opinion that climate change extends beyond the purview of the rich. Finally, as we expected, increased knowledge also makes it more likely for individuals to attribute the responsibility for climate change to all people, and not just those living in wealthy nations.

CONCLUSION

Ecuador's former President Correa promoted seemingly pro-environmental international positions while at the same time supporting unbridled extraction on the ground in Ecuador. However, these two strategies were highly complementary, allowing Correa to shift the blame for extraction and its attendant consequences such as climate change to rich countries, and allowing Correa to achieve his goal of extractive populism at home. In this chapter, we argued that the strongest opposition to Correa were the indigenous organizations of Pachakutik and CONAIE, and we showed that there are, in fact, significant differences in how affiliates of Pachakutik and supporters of Correa's PAIS party viewed extraction. We also demonstrated that these cleavages had to do with partisanship rather than ethnicity, as indigenous self-identification is not significant in any of our analyses, and that a survey respondent's location on the extractive frontier (i.e., their polycentric special location) far surpassed all other explanatory factors. We then found that one of the strongest predictors of support for Correa's international positions—specifically on Yasuní and responsibility for climate change—was affiliation with his own PAIS party. This finding supported our argument that Correa's primary purpose in adopting international positions was to garner support for his domestic policies—and to garner that support primarily from sectors of the populations where he needed it most: among his fellow partisans. The multicultural rhetoric that characterized the early part of his presidency collapsed, leaving a more pragmatic polycentrism that Correa pitched to all levels and sought to have enlightened international policy cover over more self-interested domestic environmental policy.

This chapter demonstrates that a consensus existed about perceptions of high-risk international threats to Ecuador posed by extractive companies, especially from China and the United States. The chapter further demonstrates that these perceived international threats (discussed further regarding questions on Yasuní and, more directly, on which groups pose the greatest threats to Ecuador) may be distractions from the more divisive issues of partisanship, which do matter. The chapter addressed the central theme of this book, that environmental attitudes and movements may be more effectively expressed by citizens as individuals aggregating interests into "polycentric" pluralist forms of interest articulation. As we also demonstrated elsewhere in this book, a position parting from individual interests, such as vulnerability to environmental adversity or oil drilling, is more useful to indigenous communities than one relying on traditional multicultural identities. In chapter 7, we draw general conclusions, but also revisit some of the case material presented earlier as a more general argument for moving beyond multiculturalism to polycentric pluralism.

CHAPTER 7

ↂ

How to Effectively Speak for Nature?

This investigation of one of Latin America's most intractable areas of social tension—conflicts related to oil and mineral extraction—has used a national survey of Ecuador to demonstrate the factors that shape attitudes toward the environment. We have shown that respondents are likely to hold attitudes favorable to environmental protection when it comes to abstract issues, like their perception of Mother Nature's rights, conveyed in chapter 2 in response to environmental concern, and again in chapter 5 in response to climate change. However, vulnerability to extraction is the most powerful motivator for our respondents when they are speaking about concrete manifestations of how to protect the environment, such as in chapter 3 on prior consultation before extractive projects, in chapter 4 on the negotiation of oil contracts, and in chapter 6 on international projection of Ecuador's environmental policies.

Esperanza Martínez, a longtime advocate for environmental protection at the Acción Ecológica non-governmental group, which was at times threatened with closure during the Correa years, may have best summarized our survey findings, remarking on their intuitive plausibility. She agreed that in the north, groups like the Waorani have, at least to some extent, given up on protecting the environment as an integrated entity:

> One cannot see this commitment to the environment [in the North] because they have to have a strong sense of survival in the face of deforestation, pollution, and strong health concerns. . . . It is true that there are fewer mobilizations on environmental issues. Resistance to oil drilling is stronger in the south because they saw what happened in the north . . . And in the south there is more of

> a recognition of rights and the pressure by the state to control these territories falls within the context of these rights. (Martínez interview)

Martínez implied that the formal existence of rights, such as the norm of prior consultation, whereby indigenous peoples must grant permission for extractive projects, may have played a role in the south and not in the north. It may be that the rights recognized during the thirty to forty years between the drilling in the north and the debates now in the south about oil and mining were decisive as these were key decades in the development of indigenous group rights, in Ecuador and around Latin America, as evidenced in chapter 1.

This explanation—that group rights impacted individual attitudes—reopens the issue of whether group attitudes are more than the sum of their parts. A major normative question still not fully addressed is precisely how these individual attitudes may be best aggregated into group behavior. It seems fitting that we conclude this book with a discussion of the implications of how the enlightened self-interest of individual survey respondents can be aggregated more broadly into group-level interest articulation. Given the ways in which direct threats of extraction influence individual attitudes, how can we ensure that groups are best equipped to speak for nature? And to more explicitly address issues raised in chapter 1, we argue that while multiculturalism has given rights to indigenous citizens in the era of neoliberal state shrinkage (i.e., when the practical enforcement of rights of other groups were actually diminishing), we believe that polycentric pluralism will better achieve the objectives of both protecting the environment and indigenous rights.

Our primary case of Ecuador offers a cautionary tale given that the presidential administration of Rafael Correa came to power as one of the most environmentally active anywhere. Elected with strong support from the indigenous community and the environmental left more broadly, Correa set about demonstrating his "green" bona fides immediately by integrating the rights of nature into the constitution (the inspiration for the title of this book) and launching the campaign to preserve Yasuní as an extraction-free zone. However, Correa's "green" credentials clashed with his Pink Tide (socialist left) ideology, meaning that after expelling international lenders from Ecuador in 2008, Correa was left to finance his burgeoning populist social programming through oil royalties. As shown in chapter 6, Correa's environmentalism may have been more for consumption by international and domestic environmentalists than for the majority of Ecuador's citizens, as the government sought (as per discussions in chapters 3 and 4) to reconstitute indigenous representation and other groups to secure permission for extraction, rather than concerning itself with the regulation of that extraction. The form that the articulation of interests took was crucial, and part of the problem was that the Amazonian indigenous communities charged with deciding whether to allow oil drilling were small, politically weak, and divisible by offers of particularistic goods.

It is worth noting also that within our survey, respondents—including indigenous respondents—were more satisfied with the Ecuadorian government leadership than with their own indigenous community leadership (see Table 7.1). As with most comparisons drawn throughout this book, the Andean indigenous respondents mostly correspond to the overall national sample, with over 70 percent of both groups believing that the Ecuadorian government rules for the overall good rather than just for the benefit of a few. The government may have tried (and in the cases we have documented of the Waorani, Kichwa in Napo, and the Shuar, succeeded) in dividing and conquering the indigenous communities. But confirming our anti-multiculturalist conclusions, respondents in these very communities seemed to fault their own leaders rather than the government. It is as if people expected clientelism and repression from the government, but did not expect their own leaders to follow the government's framework. Before returning to our Ecuador cases for a final summation of the argument, we show that it extends to other Andean extractive-heavy economies outside the site of our survey.

POLYCENTRIC PLURALISM AND DELIBERATIVE DEMOCRACY IN THE ANDES: LESSONS FROM THE PRIOR CONSULTATION DEBATE

Part of the problem in the Andes, and in other nations with large indigenous populations, is to define who qualifies as indigenous. A fierce debate erupted in Bolivia following the 2010 census regarding who qualifies as indigenous, deferring the release of that census for several years (Moreno 2011). Mexico may have pioneered the practice of diverting indigenous citizens into the peasantry (see Otero 2007) to connect them to corporatist agrarian and social benefits networks (Rus 1994, Eisenstadt 2011) and church members (Trejo 2012) rather than leaving them to their own autonomous devices as indigenous communities. As extensively documented by Mattiace (2003), the Mexican government undertook an extensive assimilation project to make indigenous language speakers part of the ruling party–supporting "*raza cósmica*" during the middle of the twentieth century, which lasted until the state lost its

Table 7.1 WHETHER GIVEN LEADERS GOVERN FOR THE WELL-BEING OF ALL

	"Would you say that Ecuador is governed by a few powerful groups or for the well-being of all?" DEM3.		"Do you believe indigenous leaders govern for the well-being of all?" ID22.	
	Few Powerful Groups	For Well-Being of All	Yes (For the Well-Being of All)	Not (Few Powerful Groups)
Has No Plumbing	79	218	145	143
	26.6	73.4	50.4	49.6
Oil Debated or Drilled	76	271	150	189
	21.9	78.1	43.2	54.5
Mining Debated or Underway	61	235	127	118
	20.6	79.4	51.8	48.2
Self-Identified as Indigenous	151	516	372	275
	22.6	77.4	57.5	42.5
Andean Indigenous*	92	228	175	136
	28.7	71.3	56.2	43.7
Amazon Indigenous**	59	288	175	136
	17	83	56.3	43.7
Identifies with Pachakutik	24	102	85	34
	19.1	80.9	71.4	28.6
Agrees With Blocking Freeways***	88	197	135	124
	30.9	69.1	52.1	47.9
Agrees With Blocking Mines****	247	683	391	433
	26.6	73.4	47.5	52.5
Overall National Sample	453	1200	647	839
	27.4	72.6	43.5	56.5

Note: Based on responses to the statement: "For the following questions, please tell me if you are in agreement or disagreement with . . ." *N* shown in parentheses. Percentages do not add up to 100 because some respondents did not reply, or responded "Do not know."
* Self-identify as indigenous and as Andean Kichwa (Saraguros, Salasacas, Chibuelos, Cachas, Coltas, Otavalos, and Kichwa from the Andes).
** Self-identify as indigenous and as Achuar, Shuar, Waorani, and Kichwa from the Amazon.
Based on responses to the statement: "For the following questions, please tell me if you agree or disagree with the following:"
*** "That people participate in blocking roads as a form of protest."
**** "That people organize to prevent the entry of mining or oil companies in their community."

ability to provide corporatist largesse in the 1980s economic crisis and the Zapatista uprising of 1994 brought fear of a more widespread indigenous uprising.

The assertion of multicultural indigenous identity in Latin America since the 1990s has been largely a function of political movements of the last twenty years in Ecuador, Mexico, and Bolivia. A normatively better means of empowering citizens in these nations, and in others, might be for each to universalize the prior consultation mechanism among their entire populations, thereby recognizing the rights of all citizens to use legal mechanisms to guarantee their rights. Indigenous groups could still mobilize to guarantee constitutionally enshrined rights to territory and autonomy, but non-indigenous citizens might also use the mechanism as a focal point for mobilization. Such a move would put the Andean nations squarely within the movement toward participatory democracy in Latin America identified by Fung (2011), Pateman (2012), and Eisenstadt, LeVan, and Maboudi (2017) and illustrated, via Brazil's participatory budgeting, by Avritzer (2009), Spada and Allegretti (2013), Wampler (2012), and others.

In the case of Bolivia, legal tools in the 2009 Constitution provided to protect indigenous organizations have counterbalanced the increasing power of the executive and the Movimiento al Socialismo (MAS). Some minority lowlands indigenous groups have faced obstacles to forcing the Bolivian government to respect their territorial rights even when they are legally protected by International Labor Organization (ILO) 169, the Bolivian constitution, and sectoral prior consultation (PC) legislation. As these communities grow increasingly disenchanted with the Morales government, they seek to express their discontent through new participatory governance institutions, like prior consultation "referenda." Such functions may not have been the intent of the creators of these participatory institutions, but they do bolster the autonomy, strength, and popularity of the institutions.

In Ecuador, individual and group rights were granted to indigenous citizens but never really implemented. No legal representatives for Pachamama (Mother Nature) were empowered, no prior consultations required, and interest groups were molded to the desires of the national government to make sure that oil drilling was permitted. In this environment, polycentric pluralism may offer better opportunities for these communities to articulate more unified interests than they can otherwise. Defined in chapter 1 as an approach where "multiple benefits are created by diverse actions at multiple scales" (Ostrom 2014, 121) in the environmental issue area, we argued that this is, in part, a representation of Dahl's pluralism, where all societal interests may voice their views in the marketplace of ideas rather than being limited by corporatist boundaries on representation. Polycentric pluralism may more readily allow for real participatory governance, rather than just the symbolic participation that seems to have been accorded to indigenous communities under the regime of multicultural rights recognition.

Wampler (2012) may have said it best with regard to the relationship among participatory governance institutions, the state, and petitioners for participatory governance: "Depending on how PG [participatory governance] institutions are grafted onto existing state institutions and representative democracy, there is likely to be significant differences in who participates, who can represent their fellow citizens, how citizens are represented, and the extent to which social justice can be advanced" (682). Still, as Pateman (2012, 12) explains using the example of the most studied deliberative democracy, Brazil's Porto Alegre experiment in participatory budgeting, that process did integrate the poor and redistributed to their benefit. Instructive to the false starts by the Andean states in establishing prior consultation, bounded pluralism, and in efforts to end extraction-related social conflicts, "when citizens see a connection between participation and outcomes they are more likely to take part" (Pateman 2012, 12).

The commitment of indigenous communities and other rural citizens to prior consultation, through their ability to see their input affecting the shape extractive projects take, would no doubt improve relations between mobilized social movements and the state on issues "that are far more important to the lives of voters than the typical election of the next set of government officials" (McGee 2009, 574). In the case of Bolivia, the nearly fifty successful cases of prior consultation involving indigenous communities were possible because prior consultation was perceived as a useful mechanism to enable indigenous access to some of the returns on extractivism. Indigenous and governmental responsiveness to prior consultation filled the vacuum left by corporatist regimes and provided communities with a legal discourse ("we have the right to be consulted") to mobilize the population. We argue that this was an improvement in participatory governance institutions over traditional representative institutions such as the universal vote. However, the bigger quandary facing even progressive governments as they seek to implement prior consultation is the role of international corporations. Just as state-society relations are finding new arenas of polycentric pluralist democratic contention through the creation of new interest groups to represent community livelihoods and lands, international mining conglomerates, with seemingly infinite resources, are pre-negotiating concessions with states (as in the Peruvian case), and then, only when they must, submitting these foregone conclusions to perfunctory plebiscites.

Prior consultation, and polycentric pluralism more broadly, is often viewed as a mere procedural requirement—in most of the literature to date—rather than as an exercise critical to participatory democracy. However, new analyses indicate—surprisingly—that failing to cooperate with indigenous communities and the rest of residents located proximate to oil drilling would also be detrimental to the bottom lines of mining companies. Worldwide, some 250 large-cap extractive companies were found to be exposed to indigenous rights-related risks, according to Experts in Responsible Investment Solutions (Stefani 2009). First Peoples Worldwide (2013) reported that among the 370 extraction sites of its 52 US-based Russell 1000 extractive companies, some 92 percent posed medium or high risks to shareholders due to violations of indigenous peoples' rights. A few of the highest-location risk sites—all but one of which were on indigenous peoples' lands—were in the Andean regions mentioned here, but others were in Argentina, Canada, Indonesia, Ghana, Nigeria, and New Guinea (First Peoples Worldwide 2013, 19–21).

Only one of 52 companies analyzed by First Peoples Worldwide had an explicit policy of abiding by the United Nations–advocated policy of free, prior, and informed consent (FPIC), and "all but four of the companies we analyzed were operating on or near Indigenous land and (. . .) have no agreements with Indigenous Peoples . . . [these] are likely to be facing nonviolent and violent protests, and most likely do not have an Indigenous Peoples policy informing them how to engage" (First Peoples Worldwide 2013, 4). Which land qualifies as indigenous according to national land tenure regimes is not difficult to ascertain. However, given the difficulty of discerning who is indigenous and the dispute over this definition, and given the contention within indigenous groups and between indigenous communities and adjoining communities, we would argue that geographic location would be a more socially inclusive (rather than divisive) means of negotiating consent to drill or mine.

This raises another central issue: the non-binding nature of prior consultation as it has been implemented to date. Companies seem to be following the examples of governments, which have no policy requiring that prior consultations be taken seriously. Extraction-reliant governments in Bolivia, Ecuador, and Peru have sought to have it both ways: to win constituent support for seeking approval for high-impact extractivist projects and others (like the Territorio Indígena y Parque Nacional Isiboro-Sécure, TIPNIS, highway), and at the same time execute these projects, which generate government operating revenue, without forcing hard choices about cutting budgets or raising taxes. Making prior consultation binding may appear democratic in that it would give authority to some of the region's underdog political actors, but on the other hand, putting individual and collective rights into the hands of a small group—if the full range of locally affected actors is not present—could also result in the repression of minority views or positions. As in other forms of pluralism, preference is given to those with the resources to express their interests more boisterously. Furthermore, the structural inequality still pervasive in countries like Peru is reflected in the quality of public services. People's living conditions are among the poorest in the rural areas where the extraction occurs, generating human rights violations and contamination. Royalties from extractive industries should pay for the improvement of services on front line–rural Peruvian towns as well as in the slums of Lima—and across the country—where these royalties are also desperately needed to pay for services.

Given the shortcomings of both pluralism and corporatism, and the even less representative nature of continuing the status quo of dismantling corporatist structures without replacing them with new means for rural groups to express their interests, indigenous leaders in Latin America are going to have to look beyond multicultural autonomy, which granted communities a decisive say in the conduct of local administration at the expense of individual rights and any state presence. In Bolivia, prior consultations have sometimes succeeded, albeit in an atmosphere of heightened expectations by mobilized citizens and politicization. The intercultural justice model in Peru, exemplified by the partnership between Rondas Campesinas (vigilante groups who insure the safety of rural villages from outside threats) and government justice systems, may be a better way to embrace indigenous autonomy and customary norms from a bounded pluralistic standpoint. Negotiations between indigenous communities and the state over the political rules to be applied within indigenous lands is defining domains of bounded pluralism. Inflexible models to protect cultural enclaves are promoted by multicultural *usos y constumbres* (UC) systems, which as we elaborate in chapter 1, often compromise individual rights.

Picking winners from negotiations of terms of extraction might be sidestepped if the consent-seeking process is implemented broadly and over a range of issues. The legal figure of prior consultation might be extended to the holding of public impact hearings across a range of participatory governance areas, such as water rights, mining contamination, and how to best mitigate the effects of climate change. Given the inability—or unwillingness—of some Latin American congresses to subpoena witnesses critical of executive branch programs, prior consultations could help bring transparency and accountability to government administration. And given the urgency of representation of the needs of increasingly isolated rural citizens, the practice of bounded pluralism may offer citizens the chance to express their opinions, rather than just receiving clientelist goods in exchange for supporting the government and ruling political party, as under antiquated corporatist systems. Indeed, even if the consent-seeking process is weak, non-binding, exclusionary, and susceptible to co-optation by wealthy mining companies, the mere existence of this process and the debate it has fostered create demand for a new form of participation and enable citizens in new democracies to imagine idealized processes of representation and deliberation, for perhaps the first time ever. That is no small achievement, and one worthy of much further consideration.

POLYCENTRIC PLURALISM, ENVIRONMENTAL VULNERABILITY, AND EXTRACTIVE POPULISM IN ECUADOR

This book makes the case that environmental attitudes and movements can be better expressed by individuals aggregating their interests into polycentric pluralism than as mere individuals. Our analysis shows that vulnerability to environmental adversity or oil drilling, based on differing individual perceptions, is best addressed by aggregating the interests of individuals not only within indigenous communities but in all communities near the area of project impact to achieve greater environmental protection, rather than creating state-society relations based on traditional multicultural rights recognition. We show that indigenous peoples should indeed be the ones who speak most enthusiastically for nature, but as individuals with a cosmovision prioritizing the active participation of humans within the natural order, rather than as essentialist "museum exhibit" curiosities with static views "frozen in time." Among the indigenous people best equipped to speak for nature, we have tried, in the course of this book, to describe the tech-savvy carbon trading millennials of the COICA and the globe-trotting Sarayaku environmentalists. We have also considered the oil spill–divided Waorani peoples, whose future has been upended as they did succumb to meager offerings from the state and oil companies—as did other "extinct" linguistic groups in the northern Amazon—rather than holding out for stronger environmental protection and more-sustainable development strategies.

Indeed, the wisest among our interviewees, such as former Sarayaku President Hilda Santi, framed the issue of sustainable development of her community also as one of climate change, requiring engagement of the entire world:

> Clearly our fight is against climate change because now we are feeling it in the world; on the planet itself we are witnessing the change. The rain, the sun, everything is undergoing major changes, so we have to unite to be able to save it. . . . we have called at the national and international levels of others to join our struggle and our resistance because this fight is not only for our people; it is a fight to save humanity. (Santi interview)

Hilda Santi also acknowledged (interview) that it was also a fight for the people of Sarayaku, seeking "respect from the oil, mining, and logging companies." But in adopting a more universal frame to her grievance—that of climate change—she helped supersede the provincial interests of corporatism, pluralism, and other forms of interest articulation. She tried to make the issue larger than that, and must be lauded for her efforts.

We have sought to ascribe agency to Santi's indigenous—and trans-indigenous—environmental stewardship as also depicted elsewhere in this book, by dismissing structural explanations for environmental activism which were found repeatedly not to be statistically significant, such as post-materialism, ascriptive ethnic identity, and socioeconomic indicators. Instead we championed agency-driven arguments about how individual perceptions of vulnerability, measured both as whether and how their environments put their lives and/or livelihoods at risk, and whether their immediate environments have been degraded by underregulated extractive processes, such as the notorious Chevron oil spills. Vulnerability is particularly relevant to the study of environmentalism in developing areas because for many poor populations, access to clean water, biodiverse forests, and uncontaminated land are not merely issues related to their quality of life. Such issues are a measure of life itself.

We argue in chapter 2 that motivation for environmentalism among the poor stems not principally from post-materialist concerns for the "rights of other species" or moral concerns for future generations of humans, but rather from "a material interest in the environment as a source and a requirement for livelihood" (Martínez-Alier 2002, 11). However, in chapter 5 we argue that a more holistic cosmovision view of nature does lead to stronger attitudes about climate change than those associated with traditional Western religions. The net finding then, as we interpret it, is that while concrete and individual vulnerability matters, so does a person's individualized view of the relationship between humans and nature. While a range of individual views shapes attitudes about the environment, ranging from the concrete to the abstract, the key to projecting the resulting group views in state-society relations is to aggregate individual views rather than assuming that structurally similar individuals (with the same ethnic identities, for example) also possess similar environmental attitudes.

Overall, our analysis of individual-level survey data does not convey any pastoral post-materialist consensus. However, it does illustrate the dissonance of a fierce debate between citizens seeking to use the environment as a stepping-stone out of poverty and environmentalists seeking to preserve nature. We found that the survey identified key problems in prior interpretations of interest in environmental issues—namely, the debate between economic development and environmental protection. Field research showed that these attitudes are outward manifestations of values formed in relation to political debates in many parts of Ecuador (and in the Andean region of Latin America more broadly), relating to the role of the state in using extraction as a development tool as it simultaneously tries to protect the nation's people living in or near its fragile and unique ecosystems. Meanwhile, the state propels economic growth by staking the nation's public spending on oil royalties and those that can be derived from extracting other resources like hydroelectric power and gold and copper mining. There are some contradictions in government policy which are often reflected in indigenous community reactions to extraction.

The oil frontier in Ecuador moves south and east from the heavily damaged area contaminated in the past by egregious oil spills from wells run by Texaco/Chevron and the Ecuadorian state, into virgin rainforests and unaltered jungle canopies. This oil frontier polarizes citizen attitudes strongly as it extends, giving even greater credence to the vulnerability and political economic explanations for their positions. Importantly, such vulnerability tends to hinge on not only perceptions about how much people are subject to nature's forces, but also on political positions and the belief that extraction has benefits. This debate also materialized quite directly in apparent expectations that support for the government might yield some of the material benefits (in the form of clientelism or even outright bribes) sometimes received by extraction-impacted localities. Peoples' dismissal of concern for the environment in areas where their environment has already been degraded was summed up in polemical but regionally differentiated terms by Shuar leader Romulo Akachu, the former vice president of Confederación de Nacionalidades Indígenas del Ecuador (CONAIE) (interview):

> In the northern Amazon, the people believed that oil is life and a source of work, but they have learned that it is misery and poverty because the land no longer gives them any protection, because they have destroyed it. . . . In the central Amazon, people have realized that petroleum brings contamination, death, poverty and the end of culture. When the environment is destroyed, our identity is terminated, as is the relationship between nature and the community. This means *mestizaje* [mixing of races and cultures] and migration. The Shuar Nation Assembly decided in Morona Santiago [in the southern Amazon] to not permit oil drilling until the end of our days.

Akachu, of the NACSHE group, was contradicted by leaders of the Organization Shuar of Ecuador (OSHE) group, who do want oil drilling, and he seemed mostly to be referring to the oil spills left by Texaco/Chevron and the fate of the Waorani. Environmental consultants such as Thurber point to great improvements in oil industry post-drilling "cleanups," especially with state involvement and international cleanup standards such as those proposed by the EO100 group.[1] However, Akachu's narration points clearly to a principal finding of this book: that after environmental degradation occurs, people stop thinking about the environment and instead reframe their concern as relating to migration, cultural degradation, economic well-being, and public health. When the holistic environment dissolves, people stop conceiving of it as a concept and instead consider means of resolving resulting concrete problems.

BALANCING HUMAN NEEDS, LOCAL ECOLOGICAL DEMANDS, AND INTERNATIONAL IMPERATIVES

In a fascinating study of indigenous collective action successes in Alaska and failures in Ecuador when confronting the same multinational oil company in the 1990s, ARCO, Haley (2004) noted that an Inupiat Eskimo community of 490 residents managed to get community benefits (including rents and royalties in cash) worth $5 billion per year for production of some 100,000 barrels per day as of 2000, whereas the Kichwa communities near Villano (in Pastaza) with 2,000 residents only got about $500,000 per year, all for community assistance projects, for the production starting in 1999 of 30,000 barrels per day. How did the Eskimo communities do so much better than the Kichwas? The answer, in part, is that an institutional infrastructure existed in federalist Alaska to address issues effectively raised, whereas in centralist Ecuador, the infrastructure was based on social movements. Parting from Ostrom (1990), Haley points out that while the Eskimo community had a shareholder group, all of whom received equal benefits. In Villano, the problem among the fourteen communities comprising the oil drilling area was one of dividing the spoils:

> Which communities should directly share in the allocation of community assistance benefits and benefit directly from the sustainable development program? All of Pastaza? All communities within 30 kilometers of the well site and pipeline in Block 10? What about the communities that were local to the exploration activities but not to the current operations? What about the (road-accessible)

---

1. EO100 is a new "self-policing" standard elaborated by a nonprofit group in conjunction with oil companies seeking to improve the industry's international image.

communities local to the central processing facility and sales oil pipeline outside
of Block 10? Are communities the only units of membership, or do regional organizations have standing, too? In the end, ARCO made the unilateral decision
to patronize only communities within 30 kilometers of the well site and pipeline. (Haley 2004, 206)

Furthermore, the Eskimo communities were organized into a corporation, which was able to take transparent decisions on behalf of the collective and resolve disputes via a clear hierarchy that tied the communities
directly to the resource owners and "vested them" as shareholders. These
shareholders were bound by federal courts, and a regulatory review process
ensured conciliation of different proposals set forth by the stakeholders,
the city, and the tribe. While the Alaska state constitution vested all powers
not explicitly held by the federation in the state [including jurisdiction over
oil claims], Ecuador's constitution relegated all powers to the central authority. In Villano, Ecuadorian "institutions of local government were weak
to nonexistent" (Haley 2004, 208).

Amazon indigenous dwellers have complained that the Ecuadorian government has been too explicit about linking social spending to oil extraction. "The strategy of the government is to say that without oil there is
no social spending," complained Achuar leader Diego Callera (interview).
"But the government should use other strategies [to raise funds for social spending]." To address the question raised by Haley (2004) about who
is to benefit from the oil, the Ecuadorian government created Ecuador
Estratégico. But this "squeaky wheel approach" has been controversial.
Critics argue that Ecuador Estratégico offers projects without coordination
with subnational governments (Arruti interview), fails to follow through
(Arruti interview), offers populist "Santa Claus" gifts without coordinating
with local governments to make service provision cost-effective and rational (Laurini interview), and does not offer culturally sensitive projects
(Mendua interview). Projects the parastatal entity sponsors do not seem
to offer a true pathway to development (Santi interview) and focus instead
on just breaking ground on projects in order to placate publics and keep
them from protesting oil extraction. To its credit, Ecuador Estratégico does
target projects geographically rather than directly to ethnic audiences,
as the public goods it provides, like transportation infrastructure, public
housing, and schools, are non-excludable. If the recipients of the projects
also organized geographically, they might be able to influence spending and
programs, rather than often expending much of their effort arguing about
"who will benefit."

In general, relying on social movements to achieve political results
is a dubious proposition. However, at the very least, knowledge-based

movements can build cumulatively on past legal, technical, and scientific expertise and experience, whereas power- and identity-based movements start from scratch every time the movement must be launched anew. Winning litigation in international courts based on scientific evidence is more concrete than getting protest coverage in the newspaper (although governments have sometimes succeeded in ignoring court verdicts too). However, in Ecuador's Amazon region, the other important issues, besides the type of movement in place, include the location of the aggrieved. As succinctly stated by a Sápara leader: "Those in the polluted area are in favor [of extraction], as they already live that reality. Those who are against it are those who are not in polluted areas, and especially [if they live] where there are no roads" (Ushigua interview). However, as Shuar and Achuar leaders—and even unguarded Kichwas from Sarayaku—made clear, their opposition to extractivism was not final. Rather, as they indicated through statements made and those left unstated, their opposition may have been more of a starting position in negotiations they feel may be inevitable, but which may bring dignity, environmental standards, and development to their people, as the Sarayaku lawsuit seems to have partly achieved, or environmental degradation and social disintegration, as suffered by the Waorani as they ceded to unregulated oil drilling.

Ecuador's Amazon region has offered demonstrations of successful knowledge-based movements yielding important lawsuits using scientific measurements of oil spills and cancer rates to draw attention and provoke justice. However, even as he argues for the importance of documenting empirical evidence and the scientific method, the former president of the Confederation of Indigenous Nationalities of Ecuador (Confederación de Nacionalidades Indígenas de Ecuador, CONFENAIE), Franco Viteri (interview), also vindicates the Kichwa cosmovision: "Both cases [Sarayaku and Chevron] have created important judicial precedents and played an important role in gaining natural rights for the constitution of Ecuador. . . . These ideas of the rights of nature were put into effect there. . . . There [in the Amazon] the theory of the rights of nature united with the right to live in peace and care for nature and the mountains. We have to consider nature as a living being, Mother Earth, producer of life."

CALL FOR FURTHER METHODOLOGICAL PRECISION IN STUDYING LATIN AMERICA'S ANTI-EXTRACTIVE MOVEMENTS

Our work has made important contributions to our understanding of extractive conflicts in Ecuador, and the nature of such conflicts more generally. But our study was not fully designed to address several important questions. First, while case studies of resource conflicts generally focus on the estimated 21 percent of campaigns against extraction that succeed (Özkaynak et al. 2015, 53) and mining and drilling permits are withdrawn, such as the Sarayaku case and Íntag, cases are not sufficiently documented where mobilizations do not achieve the reversal of drilling concessions, or where communities bargain for spoils in exchange for accepting extraction on their lands in the true spirit of extractive populism. We have established what causes individuals to adopt strong attitudes toward the environment, but not what makes these attitudes strong enough to manifest in anti-extractive mobilization. For that we need to more systematically select a survey sample at sites of anti-extractive protest and measure what turns some respondents into protestors, some into free riders, some into bystanders, and some into movement opponents. We laud studies by authors like Moseley (2015) and Boulding (2014), which have aggregated individual-level survey data to study country-level characteristics associated with mobilization, but no one has targeted areas where mining directly impacts cultural and economic livelihoods and survival.

We also made important inroads into understanding how individuals' attitudes are shaped by environments where they experience vulnerability. Perhaps our most important finding was that those living where extraction had already occurred had the strongest pro-environment attitudes when comparing the environment to development. Future research might take this finding one step further, better pinpointing the role of individual agency and in the context of group negotiations. This could be achieved by learning who participated in anti-extractive movements (and who did not), and, through the increasingly sophisticated extractive conflict databases in Ecuador (LaTorre 2015) and beyond (Özkaynak et al. 2015), to compare individual responses to group baselines.

Overall, this book has yielded some important conclusions. Our analysis of individual-level survey data discounts the relevance of post-materialism as a source of prioritizing the environment in developing countries like Ecuador. Furthermore, it illustrates the importance of the fierce conflict between development and environmentalism missing from developed country debates. That conflict in Ecuador—as well as in other Andean nations mentioned—is between citizens seeking to use the environment as a stepping-stone out of poverty, and environmentalists seeking to preserve nature. The survey identified key problems in prior interpretations of interest in environmental issues—namely, the tension between economic development (represented by the expectation of benefits) and self-interested motivations for environmental protection (measured by objective vulnerability and proximity to extraction). Ultimately, we find that individuals in Ecuador prioritize the environment when they are objectively vulnerable to environmental damage but prioritize development when they live in areas where mining and oil extraction have already occurred.

Field research showed that these attitudes are outward manifestations of values formed in relation to political debates surrounding the role of the state in using extraction as a development tool. This debate occurs not only in many parts of Ecuador, but across the Andean region of Latin America more broadly, and Correa's "populist extractivism"—continued by Moreno seemingly because he has no choice—is not dissimilar to that of Morales in Bolivia, or models adopted in Colombia, Peru, and Venezuela. Populists like Correa sought to implement new social programs funded directly by the very extraction that is creating the damage. The state propels economic growth by staking the nation's public spending on oil royalties. The oil frontier in Ecuador, moving south and east from the heavily damaged area contaminated by the infamous Texaco (now Chevron) oil spills and then into virgin rainforests, polarizes citizen attitudes as it extends, giving even greater credence to the concern that people feel, particularly when they live in the areas of extraction.

WHO SPEAKS FOR NATURE? FACTORING INEQUALITIES CAUSED BY VULNERABILITY

Much of Ecuador's extractivism debate seems to be driven by who speaks for nature; that is, the diverse interpretations of *sumak kawsay/buen vivir* as a development approach. Though President Correa claimed to desire a developmental approach in harmony with ecological cycles and which promoted solidarity and dignity among living things, he instead prioritized extraction, perpetuating the dichotomy between development and the environment, "a false dilemma posed by Western ideals" (Kauffman 2017, chapter 8, 5). For example, the Ecuadorian state in December 2015 amended the constitution to remove the ability of local communities to regulate extraction, doubling down on the populist "extractive development" side. In interviews, many indigenous leaders openly expressed consternation over Correa's abuse of the *sumak kawsay* concept (Tibán interview 2014) and even went so far as to create alternative Spanish terminology (*vivir bien* instead of Correa's *buen vivir*) to present a more mainstream version of the indigenous belief of development in harmony with nature (Cueva interview 2014).

Survey respondents often had personal needs to address vulnerability to environmental changes—which could worsen poverty—with efforts to insert their communities into regional, national, and global debates about resource extraction and climate change and the equities related to these. Indeed, reconciling these partial contradictions in attitudes may be the attitude-defining debate of the next decade in resource-rich developing nations in the Andes and beyond. Even the poorest and most remote Ecuadorians have positions on these issues, and their perceptions of the urgency of these matters may offer even further evidence of the need to bring vulnerability theory into political science.

Indeed, observation of the United Nations Framework Convention on Climate Change 2014 meeting in Peru revealed that the developing world is a macrocosm of the Ecuadorian people, as their positions regarding climate change policy are dictated in large part on how vulnerable they are to environmental changes exogenous to their national spheres of influence, where they are located on the carbon emissions "frontier," and what domestic actors have to gain or lose from engaging in the international debate.[2] Carbon emissions are not tangible, to be sure, but international efforts like REDD convert the abstract need to reduce emissions into concrete manifestations, like rainforest preserves, which directly affect resident livelihoods. Changes in the political importance of environmental issues are not just changes in esoteric values, but stem from peoples' rational dependence on the environment for day-to-day survival and the extent to which they feel that environmental change may be outside their direct control. And the Paris United Nations climate meeting of 2015, less-well-attended by the Andean indigenous peoples who made their presence strongly felt at the 2014 Lima meeting, did not in any way resolve these inequalities; it merely bracketed them.

The North-South debate, so prominent in the Cold War in provoking geopolitical proclivities toward capitalism or communism, has re-emerged, but with an environmentalist frame. As stated by Najam: "Developing countries have consistently contextualized environmental issues as part of the larger complex of North-South concerns, particularly concerns about an iniquitous international order and their desire to bring about structure change in that order. This has become more poignant in recent years as environmental negotiations on issues such as climate change have become increasingly focused on trade and economic aspects" (Najam, in Axelrod and VanDeveer 2014, 220–21). Our findings show that the struggle between economic development and environmental protection has emerged

---

2. Eisenstadt observed the Lima, Peru, meeting from December 8 through 13, 2014.

as perhaps the single defining issue in Ecuador, elsewhere in Latin America (see, for example, Arce 2014; Hochstetler and Keck 2007; and Perreault 2006), and in many developing countries and regional powers (see, e.g., Chaturvedi 2015 on India; Gilley 2012 on China; and Tynkknen 2010 on Russia).

We conclude from our findings that where extraction has degraded the environment, citizens are less affirmative about the environment, and hence that environmental degradation discourages citizen activism rather than encouraging it. This is bad news for environmental activism precisely where it is needed the most. More research is needed to discern more precisely the scope conditions for applying these representations of development and environmental protection. But we do know that views of extraction are conditioned by political attitudes—parting, but perhaps not limited to, expectations of redistribution—and this may be good news for those seeking to promote strong environmental attitudes.

While often possessing very localized roots, as we have shown, the chasm between development and environmental protection has also possibly been the leading cause of international negotiation failures to reach a United Nations agreement regarding carbon dioxide emissions during the decade prior to the 2015 Paris meeting (for a recent policy review, see Klinsky and Winkler 2014). The bigger question raised by this study is that if this tension is so pronounced within nations, based on polarization and based in part on economic and climatological vulnerability, then how can disparate nations with even more divergent perspectives hope to reach meaningful and lasting agreements without the help of Inglehart's harmonizing values? The good news may be that rather than having to change political culture (a proposition taking decades), reformers might be able to try to materially reduce citizen vulnerability and devise less-contentious extractive policies which do offer some compensation to environmental losers to harmonize norms within countries—if not at the international level—to more convincingly address environmental concerns. This pending international debate, over "loss and damage" in the global climate change adaptation parlance, may have effects which trickle down to the most local of levels. Long ignored at the international level, who speaks for nature will likely be at the center of this discussion.

APPENDIX A

DESCRIPTION OF VARIABLES USED IN ANALYSIS

Table A1 DESCRIPTION OF VARIABLES USED IN ANALYSIS

Variable	Survey Label	Coding	Question Wording
Age	AGE1	Continuous 16–85	*¿Cuantos años tiene Ud.?*
Apocalypse	REL5	1 if agree; 0 otherwise	*Muchos de los problemas en el mundo actual se deben a que estamos entrando en el "apocalipsis" (fin de los días/día de juicio) previsto en la Biblia.*
Catholic	REL10	1 if Catholic; 0 otherwise	*¿Cuál es su religión, si es que practica alguna? [No leer las opciones.]*
Climate Change	CLIMA3	0 if no or maybe; 1 if yes	*¿Cree usted que el cambio climático existe?*
Climate Change Concern	DISASTER1	1 not worried; 2 slightly worried; 3 somewhat worried; 4 very worried	*¿Qué tanto le preocupan los eventos relacionados con cambios dramáticos de clima, tales como sequías o inundaciones que puedan afectarlo a Ud. y a su familia en los próximos seis meses?*
Democracy vs. Development	DEM5	1 if democracy; 0 otherwise	*Cual es para usted más importante: ¿La democracia o el desarrollo?*

(continued)

Table A1 CONTINUED

Variable	Survey Label	Coding	Question Wording
Disagree That Climate Change Is a Problem Only for Rich Countries	CLIMA12	1 if disagree; 0 otherwise	*Para las siguientes preguntas, favor de indicar si esta de acuerdo o en desacuerdo con: "El cambio climático es un problema por el que sólo la gente en los países ricos puede darse el lujo de preocuparse."*
Disagree with Drilling in Yasuní	ENVIRO13	1 if disagree; 0 otherwise	*¿Está Ud. de acuerdo o en desacuerdo en la explotación del parque nacional Yasuní?*
Eco Donation	ENVIRO15	1 if yes; 0 otherwise	*¿Ha donado dinero a una organización ecológica?*
Ecotourism	ENVIRO18	1 if yes; 0 otherwise	*¿Beneficia Ud. directamente del ecoturismo en esta comunidad/ barrio?*
Education	EDUC2	1 if none; 2 incomplete primary; 3 primary; 4 incomplete secondary; 5 secondary; 6 incomplete university; 7 complete university; 8 postgraduate	*¿Cuál fue el máximo nivel de estudios que usted alcanzó?*
Energy Scarcity	ENER2	1 if never, less than 3 hours per day, or between 3 and 12 hours per day; 0 if majority of the day or all the time	*Y en los últimos 6 meses, la energía eléctrica en su hogar estuvo disponible . . .* *1. Nunca, no ha funcionado la energía eléctrica en los últimos 6 meses* *2. Menos de 3 horas por día* *3. Entre 3 y 12 horas por día* *4. La mayor parte del día* *5. Todo el tiempo*
Environmental Concern	PREOC9	0 none; 1 less than many of the problems; 2 more than some of the problems; 3 more than the majority of the problems; 4 more than any other problem	*Tomando en cuenta lo anterior, ¿Qué tanto la preocupa a Ud. el medio ambiente?*
Evangelical	REL10	1 if Evangélica y Pentecostal (Evangélica, pentecostal, la Iglesia de Dios, Asambleas de Dios, Iglesia Universal del Reino de Dios, Iglesia Internacional del Evangelio Cuadrangular, Iglesia Pentecostal de Cristo, Congregación Cristiana, menonita, La Hermandad, Iglesia Cristiana Reformada,	*¿Cuál es su religión, si es que practica alguna? [No leer las opciones.]*

Table A1 CONTINUED

Variable	Survey Label	Coding	Question Wording
		Luz del Mundo, Carismática no católica, Bautista, Nazarena, Ejército de Salvación, Adventista, Adventista del Séptimo Día, Movimiento Sanar Nuestra Tierra); 0 otherwise	
Extraction Benefits Ecuador	ENVIRO8	0 is disagree; 1 is maybe/depends; 2 is agree	*Algunos dicen que permitir a las empresas el acceso a la tierra para extraer recursos es beneficioso para el Ecuador. ¿Está de acuerdo?*
Food Security	FS1	1 if yes; 0 otherwise	*Durante los últimos tres meses, ¿hubo algún día en el que usted o cualquier otro miembro de su hogar no haya comido durante todo un día porque no había suficiente comida? 1. Sí; 2. No*
Heard of Prior Consultation	CP1	1 if yes; 0 otherwise	*¿Ha oído Ud. de la consulta previa?*
Human Rights	PROB1	1 if human rights one of top six problems in Ecuador; 0 otherwise	*En su opinión ¿Cuáles son los 6 problemas más graves que está enfrentando el PAÍS?*
Income	Q1	0 is no income; 5 is $301 to $500; 10 is $2,001 or more	*¿En cuál de los siguientes rangos se encuentran los ingresos familiares mensuales de este hogar, incluyendo las remesas del exterior y el ingreso de todos los adultos e hijos que trabajan?*
Indigenous Closer to Nature	REL7	1 if agree; 0 otherwise	*Los pueblos indígenas están más conectados con la naturaleza y la Madre Tierra, que los "no indígenas."*
Indigenous ID	ETHNIC1	1 if indigenous; 0 otherwise	*¿Usted se considera una persona blanca, mestiza, indígena, negra mulata, u otra?*
Indigenous Leader	ID19	1 if in disagreement; 0 otherwise	*Algunos dicen que los indígenas no son buenos líderes políticos. ¿Está usted de acuerdo o en desacuerdo?*
International Networks	SOCAP20 SOCAP21	Calculated first component of the two variables using principle component analysis	*SOCAP20. ¿Alguién que Ud. conoce se ha reunido con representantes de fundaciones internacionales?SOCAP21. ¿Alguien de Ud. conoce se ha reunido con científicos, técnicos, o universitarios internacionales?*

(continued)

Table A1 CONTINUED

Variable	Survey Label	Coding	Question Wording
Knowledge Index	AI1 AI2 AI3 AI4 AI5 AI6 AI7 AI8 AI9 AI10 AI11 AI12 AI13 AI14	Calculated first component of the fourteen variables using principle component analysis	*En relación con lo que uno oye o comenta, podría decirme si ha oído hablar de . . .* *AI1. ALBA (agrupación de gobiernos latinoamericanos)* *AI2. La movilización de las comunidades indigenas en Bolivia* *AI3. Compañías de envío/recibo de dinero como Western Union* *AI4.El Parque Nacional Yasuní* *AI5. Los Grupos No Contactados* *AI6. Biodiversidad* *AI7. El Convenio 169 de la Organización Internacional de Trabajo (OIT)* *AI8. La Capa de Ozono* *AI9. La Organización de Estados Americanos (OEA)* *AI10. La CONAIE* *AI11. La Universidad Yachay* *AI12. Los Pesticidas* *AI13. El Programa Socio Bosque* *AI13. La corriente del Niño*
Left Ideology	INST26	1 the state can't solve any problems; 2 only a few problems; 3 enough problems; 4 the majority of problems; 5 all problems	*INST26. Se dice que el gobierno nacional puede resolver los problemas de nuestra sociedad porque tiene los medios para hacerlo. ¿Diría usted que el Estado puede resolver . . . ?*
Media Access	MEDIA1	1 never; 2 rarely; 3 few times a month; 4 few times a week; 5 daily	*¿Con qué frecuencia sigue las noticias, ya sea en la televisión, la radio, los periódicos, o el Internet?*
Mother Earth and Scarcity	ST11	1 if agree; 0 otherwise	*La Madre Tierra (La Pacha Mama) se ocupa de los problemas como escasez de agua y comida. (1) De Acuerdo; (0) En desacuerdo/Tal Vez*
Mother Earth Has Rights	ENVIRO12	1 if agree; 0 otherwise	*¿Qué tan de acuerdo está Ud. con la idea que la Madre Tierra tenga derechos?*
Pachakutik Affiliate	POLITICS2	1 if yes; 0 otherwise	*¿Se identifica con algún partido político o movimiento? ¿Con cuál partido político o movimiento?*
PAIS Affiliate	POLITICS2	1 if yes; 0 otherwise	*Se identifica con algún partido político o movimiento? Con cuál partido político o movimiento?*

Table A1 CONTINUED

Variable	Survey Label	Coding	Question Wording
Prior Consultation	CP6	0 do not have to obey it; 1 depends on how informed the people are and depends on how difficult the conditions of the people are; 2 yes, without conditions	*¿El gobierno debería obedecer la consulta previa, diga lo que diga? [Sólo una respuesta—leer alternativas.]* *1. Sí, sin condiciones* *2. Depende de qué tan informada está la gente* *3. Depende de qué tan difícil están las condiciones de la gente* *4. No hay que obedecerla*
Professional	OCUP2	1 if professional, intellectual, scientist, technician or mid-level professional; 0 otherwise	*¿Cuál es la ocupación o tipo de trabajo que realiza?*
Promote Modernity	AC2	1 if promoting modernity and development is most important; 0 otherwise	*¿Cuál de las siguientes características es más importante en un buen gobierno local?* *1. Que defienda las costumbres y tradiciones del pueblo* *2. Que promueva la modernidad y el desarrollo del pueblo*
Protest by Invading Private Land	PROT5	1 if approve; 0 otherwise	*Usted aprueba o desaprueba de lo siguiente: Que las personas invadan propiedades o terrenos privados como forma de protesta*
Protest through Legal Demonstrations	PROT1	1 if approve; 0 otherwise	*Usted aprueba o desaprueba de lo siguiente: Que las personas participen en manifestaciones legales*
Rain/River Water	WATER1	1 if water from rain or river; 0 otherwise	*¿De dónde proviene el agua que se consume en esta casa?*
Religiosity	REL9	1 not important at all; 2 not very important; 3 somewhat important; 4 very important	*Por favor, podría decirme ¿Qué tan importante es la religión en su vida?*
Science vs. Faith	ST4	1 if agree; 0 otherwise	*Dependemos demasiado de la ciencia y no lo suficiente de la Fe.*
Social Media	MEDIA2	1 if yes have used in past week; 0 otherwise	*En la última semana, ¿ha utilizado alguna red social del Internet como Twitter o Facebook?*
Trust in Indigenous Movement	INST2	0 is none; 1 is little; 2 is some; 3 is a lot	*Cuánta confianza tiene en cada uno de los grupos e instituciones? La CONAIE.*

(*continued*)

Table A1 CONTINUED

Variable	Survey Label	Coding	Question Wording
Water Scarcity	WATER3	1 if never, few times a month or few times a week; 0 otherwise	*Aquí en su casa tienen agua disponible para usar . . .* *(1) Nunca* *(2) Algunas veces al mes* *(3) Algunas veces a la semana* *(4) Casi siempre* *(5) Todo el tiempo y todos los días*
Western Science Index	ST1; ST2; ST3; ST9; ST10	1 if never, few times a month or few times a week; 0 otherwise	*Ahora, me gustaría leerle algunas afirmaciones y preguntarle si está de acuerdo o no con cada una de ellas.ST1. La ciencia y la tecnología están haciendo nuestras vidas más saludables. ST2. La ciencia y la tecnología están haciendo nuestras vidas más cómodas. ST3. A causa de la ciencia y la tecnología, la próxima generación tendrá más oportunidades. ST9. Las técnicas de cultivo que enseñan los científicos son mejores que las tradicionales. ST10. Los pueblos indígenas deberían trabajar con científicos nacionales y/o extranjeros para resolver los problemas locales.*

Table A2 DESCRIPTIVE STATISTICS FOR VARIABLES

Variable Name	N	Mean	SD	Minimum	Maximum
Age	1781	37.56	15.45	16 (2.81%)	85 (0.06%)
Apocalypse	1595	1.63	0.67	1 (47.71%)	3 (10.47%)
Catholic	1781	0.76	0.43	0 (24.26%)	1 (75.74%)
Climate Change	1737	1.09	0.37	1 (94.13%)	3 (2.76%)
Climate Change Concern	1757	3.15	0.80	0 (3.36%)	4 (37.56%)
Democracy vs. Development	1781	0.31	0.31	0 (68.67%)	1 (31.33%)
Disagree: Climate for Rich	1781	0.63	0.48	0 (36.55%)	1 (63.45%)
Disagree: Drill in Yasuní	1682	0.56	0.50	0 (44.35%)	1 (55.65%)
Eco Donation	1781	0.04	0.19	0 (96.41%)	1 (3.59%)
Ecotourism	1781	0.14	0.34	0 (86.41%)	1 (13.59%)
Education	1779	4.21	1.41	1 (2.47%)	8 (0.90%)
Environmental Concern	1724	1.93	0.97	0 (2.67%)	4 (7.77%)
Evangelical	1781	0.15	0.35	0 (85.23%)	1 (14.77%)
Extraction Benefits Ecuador	1673	0.86	0.91	0 (49.43%)	2 (35.74%)
Food Security	1766	0.08	0.27	0 (91.79%)	1 (8.21%)
Heard of Prior Consultation	1781	0.34	0.48	0 (65.64%)	1 (34.36%)
Human Rights	1781	0.05	0.22	0 (95.06%)	1 (4.94%)
Income	1688	4.68	1.75	0 (1.30%)	10 (0.71%)
Indigenous Closer to Nature	1730	0.73	0.44	0 (26.88%)	1 (73.12%)
Indigenous ID	1777	0.40	0.49	0 (59.76%)	1 (40.24%)
Indigenous Leader	1781	0.52	0.52	0 (47.89%)	1 (52.11%)
International Networks	1781	0	1.29	−0.44 (88.43%)	4.53 (6.23%)
Knowledge Index	1772	0.01	2.09	−4.34 (3.05%)	3.80 (2.82)
Media Access	1780	4.28	0.99	1 (1.74%)	5 (54.49%)
Mother Earth and Scarcity	1655	0.62	0.49	0 (38.49%)	1 (61.51%)
Mother Earth Has Rights	1781	0.80	0.40	0 (19.82%)	1 (80.18%)
Pachakutik Affiliate	1777	0.07	0.26	0 (92.74%)	1 (7.26%)
PAIS Affiliate	1777	0.10	0.29	0 (90.38%)	1 (9.62%)
Prior Consultation	1677	1.62	0.51	0 (1.25%)	2 (63.57%)
Professional	1781	0.04	0.20	0 (95.79%)	1 (4.21%)
Promote Modernity	1781	0.48	0.50	0 (51.82%)	1 (48.18%)
Protest: Legal Demonstration	1781	0.75	0.44	0 (25.77%)	1 (74.23%)
Protest: Private Land	1781	0.06	0.23	0 (94.16%)	1 (5.84%)
Rain/River Water	1781	0.18	0.39	0 (81.86%)	1 (18.14%)
Religion	1767	3.50	0.72	1 (2.09%)	4 (60.55%)
Science vs. Faith	1709	0.66	0.47	0 (34.17%)	1 (65.83%)
Social Media	1781	0.38	0.49	0 (61.88%)	1 (38.12%)
Trust in Indigenous Mvmnt	1781	0.27	0.45	0 (72.71%)	1 (27.29%)
Water Scarcity	1775	0.11	0.31	0 (89.18%)	1 (10.82%)
Western Science Index	1612	0	1.56	−2.61 (8.13%)	1.86 (21.84%)

APPENDIX B

Survey Sample Design

The nationwide survey was conducted in Ecuador between March and June 2014 after several focus groups and trial questionnaires were administered throughout different parts of the country in January 2014. The sampling method, designed by the Ecuadorian survey company CEDATOS, which also administered the survey, consisted of a three-stage procedure. The three strata were organized based on three criteria. The first criterion dictated the selection of cases in the following national geographic areas: 1. Sierra, 2. Costa, 3. Oriente. The second criterion designated cases between urban and rural areas, and the third criterion designated cases in the following fields: 1. Quito, 2. Guayaquil, 3. Cities with more than 100,000 inhabitants, 4. Cities with 25,000 to 100,000 inhabitants, 5. Cities with fewer than 25,000 inhabitants, and 6. Rural parishes. Probability sampling was used at all stages: stratified, multistage, by cluster, with the random selection of the units in each stage, including the final selection of the adult to be interviewed in the household sample selected.

Sampling was stratified by region (Coast, Highlands, and East) and areas (urban and rural) and was multistage because of the selection of the Primary Sampling Units (PSU, cantons); followed by secondary units in each PSU formed by census sectors (using 2010 National Population and Housing Census data as processed by CEDATOS); then Third Stage Units (blocks or segments) and Final Sampling Units (FSU) formed into clusters sizes of 6 to 8 in urban areas and 10 to 12 in rural areas and dispersed populations. In each of these clusters' housing units, a single household unit was selected as the unit of observation and then, as a Final Unit of Study; one and only one adult of voting age was selected by a random process (Córdova). At the final stage, a quota system was used to probabilistically select the adult in each household, in a manner that considered gender categories and three age groups. The probabilistic selection rule did not support the substitution or replacement of the selected units.

The national probability sample design was of voting-age population (over sixteen years old), with a total size (N) of 1,781 persons. Data were collected via face-to-face interviews conducted in Spanish as well as in other languages, as the study included a booster sample of 640 indigenous people, representing the following groups: Kichwa (Sierra), Shuar, Achuar, Andoa, Chibuleos, Salasacas, Cachas/Coltas, and Otavalos. CEDATOS included on its interviewer team monolingual as well as bilingual and trilingual speakers (Spanish and other indigenous languages). The confidence level expected for the entire national sample is 95 percent (Z .95 = 1.965) with a margin of error of ±2.33 percent, assuming a 50/50 ratio (P = 0.50, Q = 1 – P); for the dichotomous variables, in the worst of cases.

The sample design considered stratification, clustering, and weighting procedures. The sample is composed of six strata representing the three main geographical regions: coast, highlands, and the Amazon, as well a sub-stratification by urban and rural areas. Since the Amazon region has a small population, a larger sample of respondents from this region is drawn, and sample weights were incorporated to reflect the actual known distribution of the population between the three regions. The sample was weighted to produce representative national results.

The sample consisted of 285 primary sampling units (PSUs), with a stratification according to their condition of urban and rural areas (PSU: 114 urban and 109 rural), and 12 identified strata. This sample was selected in twenty-three provinces that represent the country in total. The insular province of Galápagos is not included in the survey. A total of 685 respondents were surveyed in urban areas and 445 in rural areas. A booster sample of indigenous population of size of 640 was drawn to have deep information regarding this particular population. The total sample size of the study is 1,781, which draw an estimated margin of error for the survey of ±2.3 percent. Indeed, the confidence level expected for the entire national sample is 95 percent (Z .95 = 1.965) with a margin of error of ±2.33 percent, assuming a 50/50 ratio (P = 0.50, Q = 1 – P); for the dichotomous variables, in the worst of cases. It assumes a DEF of 1.022 by the system of cluster sampling for the highlands and coast, and a DEF of 1.011 for the East, which had been internally stratification by north and south.

To ensure the efficiency, adequacy and accuracy of the sample, an "Adjust for non-coverage" sample system was adopted, ensuring the implementation of the sample sizes as minimum estimates within the confidence levels and maximum allowable error. Additionally, the system ensures the elimination of bias resulting from the substitution or replacement of units that are unable to be survey subjects. While this system presented a significant cost for CEDATOS, it ensured the quality of the information. The method is possible by the knowledge that CEDATOS has regarding "No Coverage" observed in similar studies in national, urban, and rural areas. The non-response rate was 26 percent, and non-responses were substituted by other cases after the third interviewer visit to a given household.

BIBLIOGRAPHY

Acción Ecológica. 2012. *Sumak Kawsay o Plan Nacional del Buen Vivir: ¿Qué está detrás del discurso?* Quito, Ecuador: Acción Ecológica.

Acosta, Alberto. 2012. *Buen vivir sumac kawsay: Una oportunidad para imaginar otros mundos.* Quito, Ecuador: Abya Yala.

Acosta, Alberto and Esperanza Martínez (eds.). 2009. *El buen vivir: Una vía para el desarrollo.* Quito, Ecuador: Abya Yala.

Adger, W. Neil. 2006. "Vulnerability." *Global Environmental Change* 16 (2006): 268–81.

Aguilar, Daniela. 2017. "Conflict Erupts between Chinese Mining Company, Government, and Indigenous Communities in Ecuador." *Mongabay*, 26 January 2017. Retrieved from: https://news.mongabay.com/2017/01/conflict-erupts-between-chinese-mining-company-govt-and-indigenous-communities-in-ecuador. Accessed on March 29, 2017.

Aguilar, Ricardo. 2013. "Los Datos sobre identidad indígena no socavan el carácter plurinacional." *La Razón*, August 25, 2013. Retrieved from: http://www.la-razon.com/suplementos/animal_politico/identidad-indigena-socavan-caracter-plurinacional_0_1894010662.html. Accessed on December 27, 2013.

Aguilar Camin, Hector, Lorenzo Meyer, and Luis Alberto Fierro. 1993. *In the Shadow of the Mexican Revolution: Contemporary Mexican History, 1910–1989.* Austin: University of Texas Press.

Aklin, Michaël and Johannes Urpelainen. 2013. "Political Competition, Path Dependence, and the Strategy of Sustainable Energy Transitions." *American Journal of Political Science* 57(3): 643–658.

Alberti, Carla. 2013. "Indigenous Governance and Associational Life: Explaining Subnational Regimes in Rural Bolivia." Paper presented at the 2013 Meeting of the Latin American Studies Association, May 26–29 (Washington DC).

Amazon Watch. 2010. "Challenging Emerging Threats in Ecuador: Amazon Oil Expansion in Ecuador's Southern Rainforests." Retrieved from: http://amazonwatch.org/work/challenging-emerging-threats-in-ecuador. Accessed on August 6, 2016.

Andolina, Robert James. 1999. *Colonial Legacies and Plurinational Imaginaries: Indigenous Movement Politics in Ecuador and Bolivia.* PhD Thesis. University of Minnesota.

Andrade, Susana. 1999. "Adaptive Strategies and Indigenous Resistance to Protestantism in Ecuador." *Diogenes* 47(3): 38–50.

Andresen, Steinar and Shardul Agrawala. 2002. "Leaders, Pushers, and Laggards in the Making of the Climate Regime." *Global Environmental Change* 12: 41–51.

Ansolabehere, Stephen and David M. Konisky. 2014. *Cheap and Clean: How Americans Think about Energy in the Age of Global Warming.* Cambridge, MA: MIT Press.

Arbuckle, Matthew and David M. Konisky. n.d. "The Role of Religion in Environmental Attitudes." Typescript.

Arce, Moisés. 2014. *Resource Extraction and Protest in Peru.* Pittsburgh: University of Pittsburgh Press.

ARCOM. 2012. "Ecuador." Retrieved from: http://www.arcom.gob.ec/index.php/mapas-tematicos.html?start=5. Accessed on November 23, 2014.

Arellano Yanguas, Javier. 2010. *Local Politics, Conflict, and Development in Peruvian Mining Regions.* PhD Thesis. Universidad de Sussex.

Ascher, William. 1984. *Scheming for the Poor: The Politics of Redistribution in Latin America.* Cambridge, MA: Harvard University Press.

Audiencia Temática: Derecho a la Asociación de los Pueblos Indígenas en el Ecuador. 2016. "Pontificia Universidad Católica Human Rights Institute." Typescript.

Avritzer, Leonardo. 2009. *Participatory Institutions in Democratic Brazil.* Baltimore: The Johns Hopkins University Press.

Baird, Vanessa. 2008. "Endgame in the Amazon." *New Internationalist.* July 2008.

Barrera Guarderas, Augusto. 2001. *Acción colectiva y crisis política: El movimiento indígena ecuatoriano en la década de los noventa.* Quito: Abya Yala.

Bascopé, Iván. 2012. "Consulta previa: Reto de democracia comunitaria." In Boaventura de Sousa Santos and Jose Luis Exeni (eds.). *Justicia indígena, plurinacionalidad e Bounded Pluralism en Bolivia,* 381–406. Quito: Abya Yala-Fundación Rosa Luxemburg.

Becker, Mark. 2012. "Ecuador: The New Upsurge—Marching for Life, Water, and Dignity." *Against the Current* July: 9–10.

Becker, Mark. 2013a. "The Stormy Relations between Rafael Correa and Social Movements in Ecuador." *Latin American Perspectives* 40(3): 43–62.

Becker, Mark. 2013b. "Resource Extraction and the Yasuní National Park." *Z Magazine.* November 24.

Birnir, Johanna Kristin. 2004. "Stabilizing Party Systems and Excluding Segments of Society?: The Effects of Formation Costs on New Party Foundation in Latin America." *Studies in Comparative International Development* 39(3): 3–27.

Boanada Fuchs, Vanessa. 2014. "When Emerging Expressions of Citizenship Meet Neoextractivism in Latin America: Prior, Free, and Informed Consultation in a Deadlock." Paper presented at the International Studies Association Annual Conference, Toronto, March 26–29.

Boelens, Rutgerd, Jaime Hoogesteger, and Michiel Baud. 2015. "Water Reform Governmentality in Ecuador: Neoliberalism, Centralization, and the Restraining of Polycentric Authority and Community Rule-Making." *Geoforum* 64: 281–91.

Bolpress. 2006. "Quechuas del Ecuador en apronte por la nacionalización del petróleo." Retrieved from: http://www.bolpress.com/art.php?Cod=2006022203. Accessed on August 17, 2016.

Bolsen, Toby, James N. Druckman, and Fay Lomax Cook. 2015. "Citizens', Scientists', and Policy Advisors' Beliefs about Global Warming." *The ANNALS of the American Academy of Political and Social Science* 658(1), 271–295.

Boulding, Carew. 2014. *NGOs, Political Protest, and Civil Society.* New York: Cambridge University Press.

Brechin, Steven R. 1999. "Objective Problems, Subjective Values, and Global Environmentalism: Evaluating the Postmaterialist Argument and Challenging a New Explanation." *Social Science Quarterly* 80(4): 793–809.

Brechin, Steven R. 2010. "Public Opinion: A Cross-national View." In Constance Lever-Tracy (ed.). *Routledge Handbook of Climate Change and Society*, 179–209. New York: Routledge.

Brown, Marilyn A. and Benjamin K. Sovacool. 2011. *Climate Change and Global Energy Security: Technology and Policy Options*. Cambridge, MA: MIT Press.

Brulle, Robert J., Jason Carmichael, and J. Craig Jenkins. 2012. "Shifting Public Opinion on Climate Change: An Empirical Assessment of Factors Influencing Concern over Climate Change in the US, 2002–2010." *Climatic Change*. doi: 10.1007/s10584-012-0403-y.

Brysk, Alison. 2000. *From Tribal Village to Global Village: Indian Rights and International Relations in Latin America*. Stanford, CA: Stanford University Press.

Burguete Cal y Mayor, Araceli. 2013. "Constitutional Multiculturalism in Chiapas: Hollow Reforms That Nullify Autonomy Rights." In Todd A. Eisenstadt, Michael S. Danielson, Jaime Bailón Córres, and Carlos Sorroza (eds.). *Latin America's Multicultural Movements and the Struggle between Communitarianism, Autonomy, and Human Rights*, 40–66. New York: Oxford University Press.

Business Human Rights. 2016. "Bolívar Wasump." Retrieved from: https://www.business-humanrights.org/en/bol%C3%ADvar-wasump. Accessed on May 7, 2018.

Carlin, Ryan E., Gregory J. Love, and Elizabeth J. Zechmeister. 2014. "Trust Shaken: Earthquake Damage, State Capacity, and Interpersonal Trust in Comparative Perspective." *Comparative Politics* 46 (4): 419–53.

Carlin, Ryan E., Matthew M. Singer, and Elizabeth J. Zechmeister. 2015. *The Latin American Voter: Pursuing Representation and Accountability in Challenging Contexts*. Ann Arbor: University of Michigan Press.

Cederman, Lars-Erik et al. 2013. *Inequality, Grievances, and Civil War*. New York: Cambridge University Press.

Chalmers, Douglas A. 1977. "The Politicized State in Latin America." In Malloy, James (ed.). *Authoritarianism and Corporatism in Latin America*, 23–46. Pittsburgh: University of Pittsburgh Press.

Chandra, Kanchan (ed). 2012. *Constructivist Theories of Ethnic Politics*. New York: Oxford University Press.

Chaturvedi, Vaibhav. 2015. "The Costs of Climate Change Impacts for India—Working Paper 2015/11." New Delhi: Council on Energy, Environment, and Water. Typescript.

Chicaiza, Gloria. 2014. *Mineras chinas en Ecuador: Nueva dependencia*. Quito: Acción Ecológica.

"CIDOB, APG, y CONAMAQ asestan un duro golpe al proyecto de ley de Consulta gubernamental." In *Bolpress*, last modified on March 22, 2013. Retrieved from: http://www.bolpress.com/art.php?Cod=2013032206. Accessed on May 13, 2013.

CNE (*Consejo Nacional Electoral*). 2018. "Referéndum y Consulta Popular 2018." Retrieved from: http://cne.gob.ec/es/?option=com_content&view=article&layout=edit&id=4230. Accessed on May 7, 2018.

"COICA: Two Agendas on Amazon Development." In Conca, Ken and Geoffrey D. Dabelko (eds.). 2014. *Green Planet Blues: Critical Perspectives on Global Environmental Politics*, 80–86. 5th ed. Boulder, CO: Westview Press.

Colchester, Marcus and Fergus MacKay. 2004. "In Search of Middle Ground Indigenous Peoples, Collective Representation and the Right to Free, Prior and Informed Consent." Paper presented to the 10th Conference of the International

Association for the Study of Common Property Oaxaca, August 2004. Retrieved from: http://www.forestpeoples.org/sites/fpp/files/publication/2010/08/fpicipsaug04eng.pdf. Accessed in May 2013.

Conaghan, Catherine. 2011. "Ecuador: Rafael Correa and the Citizens' Revolution." In Steven Levitsky and Kenneth M. Roberts (eds.). *The Resurgence of the Latin American Left*, 260–82. Baltimore: The Johns Hopkins University Press.

Conaghan, Catherine M. 2015. "Surveil and Sanction: The Return of the State and Societal Regulation in Ecuador." *European Review of Latin American and Caribbean Studies* 98 (April): 7–27.

CONAIE (Confederación de Nacionalidades Indígenas del Ecuador). 1989. *Las nacionalidades indígenas en el Ecuador: Nuestro proceso organizativo*. Quito, Ecuador: CONAIE.

CONAIE. 2011. "Letter to Secretary-General of the United Nations." *Consorcio para el Derecho Socio-Ambiental*. July 4, 2011.

CONAIE 2012. "2012 Reunión Rigoberta Menchu y Humberto Cholango Presidente de la CONAIE." January 14, 2012. Retrieved from: http://ecuarunari.org/portal/noticias/Reuni%C3%B3n-Rigoberta-Menchu-y-Humberto-Cholango-Presidente-de-la-CONAIE. Accessed on August 17, 2016.

Constitution of Bolivia. 2009. English translation (Georgetown University). Retrieved from: http://pdba.georgetown.edu/Constitutions/Bolivia/bolivia09.html. Accessed on August 1, 2016.

Constitution of Ecuador. 2008. English translation (Georgetown University). Retrieved from: http://pdba.georgetown.edu/Constitutions/Ecuador/english08.html. Accessed on August 1, 2016.

Dahl, Robert A. 1961. *Who Governs?: Democracy and Power in an American City*. New Haven: Yale University Press.

Dahl, Robert A. 1979. *Polyarchy*. New Haven: Yale University Press.

Danielson, Michael S. 2013. "Community Strength and Customary Law: Explaining Migrant Participation in Indigenous Oaxaca." In Todd A. Eisenstadt, Michael S. Danielson, Jaime Bailón Córres, and Carlos Sorroza (eds.). *Latin America's Multicultural Movements and the Struggle between Communitarianism, Autonomy, and Human Rights*, 192–215. New York: Oxford University Press.

de la Torre, Carlos. 2010. *Populist Seduction in Latin America*. Athens: Ohio University Press.

de la Torre, Carlos. 2018. "La perestroika de Lenín Moreno en Ecuador." Retrieved from: http://www.letraslibres.com/espana-mexico/politica/la-perestroika-lenin-moreno-en-ecuador. Accessed on May 7, 2018.

de la Torre, Carlos and Andrés Ortiz Lemos. 2016. "Populist Polarization and the Slow Death of Democracy in Ecuador." *Democratization* 23(2): 221–41.

De Echave, José, Alejandro Diez, Ludwig Huber, Bruno Revesz, Xavier Ricard Lanata, and Martín Tanaka. 2009. *Minería y conflicto social*. Lima: Instituto de Estudios Peruanos.

Deloria Jr., Vine. 2003. *God Is Red: A Native View of Religion*. Golden, CO: Fulcrum Publishing.

Doherty, Daniel, Alan S. Gerber, and Donald P. Green. 2006. "Personal Income and Attitudes toward Redistribution: A Study of Lottery Winners." *Political Psychology* 27(3): 441–58.

Dunlap, Riley E. and Richard York. 2012. "The Globalization of Environmental Concern." In Paul F. Steinberg and Stacy D. VanDeveer (eds.). *Comparative Environmental Politics: Theory, Practice, and Prospects*, 89–112. Cambridge, MA: MIT Press.

Eckberg, D. L. and J. Blocker. 1996. "Christianity, Environmentalism, and the Theoretical Problem of Fundamentalism." *Journal for the Scientific Study of Religion* 35(4): 343–55.

Eisenstadt, Todd A. 2004. *Courting Democracy in Mexico: Party Strategies and Electoral Institutions.* New York: Cambridge University Press.

Eisenstadt, Todd A. 2006. "Indigenous Attitudes and Ethnic Identity Construction in Mexico." *Estudios Mexicanos/Mexican Studies* 22(1): 107–29.

Eisenstadt, Todd A. 2009. "Agrarian Tenure Institution Conflict Frames, and Communitarian Identities: The Case of Indigenous Southern Mexico." *Comparative Political Studies* 42(1): 82–113.

Eisenstadt, Todd A. 2011. *Politics, Identity, and Mexico's Indigenous Rights Movement.* New York: Cambridge University Press.

Eisenstadt, Todd A., Michael S. Danielson, Jaime Bailón Córres, and Carlos Sorroza (eds.). 2013. *Latin America's Multicultural Movements and the Struggle between Communitarianism, Autonomy, and Human Rights.* New York: Oxford University Press.

Eisenstadt, Todd A., Daniel Fiorino, and Daniela Stevens León. 2018. "National Environmental Policies as Shelter from the Storm: Specifying the Relationship between Extreme Weather Vulnerability and National Environmental Performance." *Journal of Environmental Studies and Science* (October). doi: 10.1007/s13412-018-0523-4.

Eisenstadt, Todd A., Carl LeVan, and Tofigh Maboudi. 2017 *Constituents before Assembly: Participation, Deliberation, and Representation in the Crafting of New Constitutions.* New York: Cambridge University Press.

Eisenstadt, Todd A. and Viridiana Ríos. 2014. "Multicultural Institutions, Distributional Politics, and Postelectoral Mobilization." *Latin American Politics and Society* 56(2): 70–92.

Eisenstadt, Todd A. and Karleen Jones West. 2017. "Environmentalism in a Climate-Vulnerable State: Rainforests, Oil, and Political Attitudes along Ecuador's Extractive Frontier." *Journal of Comparative Politics* 49(1): 231–51.

Eisenstadt, Todd A. and Marcela Torres Wong. 2016. "Interest Articulation in Indigenous Rural Latin America: From Corporatism to Bounded Pluralist 'Interculturalismo' and Prior Consultations." Typescript.

El Tiempo. July 19, 2011. "ONG: 189 indígenas están acusados de terrorismo y sabotaje." Retrieved from: http://www.eltiempo.com.ec/noticias/ecuador/4/264672/ong-189-indigenas-estan-acusados-de-terrorismo-y-sabotaje. Accessed on April 3, 2017.

El Tiempo. November 16, 2015. "Gabriela Rivadeneira apoya posibilidad reelección de Correa." Retrieved from: http://www.eltiempo.com.ec/noticias/ecuador/4/362784/gabriela-rivadeneira-apoya-posibilidad-reeleccion-de-correa. Accessed on April 1, 2017.

El Universo. February 19, 2006. "Pachakutik pide nacionalización total de petróleo." Retrieved from: http://www.eluniverso.com/2006/02/19/0001/9/730BC38DD F874924B8CF8D617C6490F3.html. Accessed on August 17, 2016.

El Universo. May 23, 2017. "Secretaría del Buen Vivir no consta en cronograma de nuevo gabinete de Lenín Moreno." Retrieved from: https://www.eluniverso.com/noticias/2017/05/23/nota/6196906/novedades-gabinete-presidencial-lenin-moreno. Accessed on May 7, 2018.

Engle, Karen. 2010. *The Elusive Promise of Indigenous Development: Rights, Culture, Strategy.* Durham, NC: Duke University Press.

Environmental Justice Atlas. 2014. "Ecuador's Prior Consultation in the Oil Blocks 20 and 29." Retrieved from: https://ejatlas.org/conflict/ecuadors-prior-consult-in-the-oil-blocks-20-and-29-ecuador. Accessed on August 3, 2016.

Environmental Justice Atlas. 2016. "Exploración de petroleo en Bloque 7 y 21, Ecuador." Retrieved from: https://ejatlas.org/conflict/bloques-7-y-21. Accessed on August 3, 2016.

Equitable Origin. 2018. "EO100™ Standard for Responsible Energy." Retrieved from: https://www.equitableorigin.org/eo100-for-responsible-energy/over-view/. Accessed on: 12 Nov 2018.

Escobar, Arturo. 2010. "Latin America at a Crossroads: Alternative Modernizations, Post-Liberalism, or Post-Development." *Cultural Studies* 24(1): 1–65.

Eugen, Fernando. 2006. "Agrarian Policy, Institutional Change, and New Actors in Peruvian Agriculture." In John Crabtree (ed.). *Making Institutions Work in Peru: Democracy, Development, and Inequality since 1980*. Institute for the Study of the Americas. London: University of London.

Evans, John H. and Justin Feng. 2013. "Conservative Protestantism and Skepticism of Scientists Studying Climate Change." *Climatic Change* 121(4): 595–608.

Fabricant, Nicole. 2013. "Good Living for Whom? Bolivia's Climate Justice Movement and the Limitations of Indigenous Cosmovisions." *Latin American and Caribbean Ethnic Studies* 8(2): 159–78.

Falleti Tulia G. and Thea Riofrancos. 2013. "Endogenous Participation: Prior Consultation in Extractive Economies." Paper presented at the 2013 Meeting of the Latin American Studies Association, Washington, DC.

Falleti, Tulia, and Thea Riofrancos. 2014. "Participatory Democracy in Latin America: The Collective Right to Prior Consultation in Ecuador and Bolivia." Paper presented at Lasa Conference. Chicago, May 27–30.

Fernández, Blanca S., Liliana Pardo, and Katerine Salamanca. 2014. "El buen vivir en Ecuador: ¿marketing político o proyecto en disputa?" *Iconos* 48 (January 2014): 101–17.

Fernández, Marcelo. 2010. *Pluriversidad. Colonialidad de los usos y costumbres. Naciones y pueblos indígena originario campesinos de tierras altas*. La Paz-Oruro: Órgano Electoral Plurinacional.

First Peoples Worldwide. 2013. First Peoples Worldwide's Indigenous Rights Risk Report for the Extractive Industry (U.S.). Retrieved from: http://www.firstpeoples.org/images/uploads/R1KReport2.pdf. Accessed on January 18, 2014.

Fox, Jonathan. 1994. "The Difficult Transition from Clientelism to Citizenship: Lessons from Mexico." *World Politics* 46(2): 151–84.

Fung, Archon. 2011. "Reinventing Democracy in Latin America." *Perspectives on Politics* 9(4): 857–71.

García, Alan. 2007 "El síndrome del perro del hortelano." *El Comercio*, October 28, 2007. Retrieved from: https://www.scribd.com/document/26539211/Alan-Garcia-Perez-y-el-perro-del-hortelano. Accessed on April 6, 2017.

Gauchat, Gordon. 2012. "Politization of Science in the Public Sphere: A Study of Public Trust in the United States, 1974–2010." *American Sociological Review* 77(2): 167–87.

Gerlach, Allen. 2003. *Indians, Oil, and Politics: A Recent History of Ecuador*. Lanham, MD: Rowman & Littlefield.

Gibson E. 2005. "Boundary Control. Subnational Authoritarianism in Democratic Countries." *World Politics* 58: 101–32.

Giddens, Anthony. 2011. *The Politics of Climate Change*. Cambridge, UK: Polity Press.

Gilley, Bruce. 2012. "Authoritarian Environmentalism and China's Response to Climate Change." *Environmental Politics* 21(2): 287–307.

Giraudy, Agustina. 2015. *Democrats and Autocrats: Pathways of Subnational Undemocratic Regime Continuity within Democratic Countries*. Oxford: Oxford University Press.

Goodman, Gary L. and Hiskey, Jonathan T. 2008. "Exit without Leaving: Political Disengagement in High Migration Municipalities in Mexico." *Comparative Politics* 40(2): 169–88.

Gourevitch, Peter. 1978. "The Second Image Reversed: The International Sources of Domestic Politics." *International Organization* 32(4): 881–912.

Guamán, Jorge. 2007. "Breve informe del Comité Ejecutivo Nacional." CONAIE Website. http://www.conaie.org/IIIconaie/pachakutik.html. Accessed on January 24, 2008 .

Gudynas, Eduardo. 2009. "La ecología política del giro biocéntrico en la nueva Constitución de Ecuador." *Revista de Estudios Sociales* 32 (January–April): 34–46.

Guerrero, Andrés. 1991. *De la economía a las mentalidades: Cambio social y conflicto agrario en el Ecuador*. Quito: El Conejo.

Guha, Ramachandra and Joan Martínez Alier. 1997. *Varieties of Environmentalism: Essays North and South*. New York: Routledge Publishers.

Hale, Charles R. 2002. "Does Multiculturalism Menace?: Governance, Cultural Rights and the Politics of Identity in Guatemala." *Journal of Latin American Studies* 34(3): 485–524.

Haley, Sharman. 2004. "Institutional Assets for Negotiating the Terms of Development: Indigenous Collective Action and Oil in Ecuador and Alaska." *Economic Development and Cultural Change* 53(1): 191–213.

Hall, Anthony. 2012. *Forests and Climate Change: The Social Dimensions of REDD in Latin America*. New York: Edward Elgar Publishing.

Hardin, Russell. 1971. "Collective Action as an Agreeable n-Prisoners' Dilemma." *Behavioral Science* 16 (September): 472–81.

Harrison, Kathryn and Lisa McIntosh Sundstrom (eds.). 2010. *Global Commons, Domestic Decisions: The Comparative Politics of Climate Change*. Cambridge, MA: MIT Press.

Hartley, Thomas and Bruce Russett. 1992. "Public Opinion and the Common Defense: Who Governs Military Spending in the United States?" *American Political Science Review* 86 (December): 905–15.

Hochstetler, Kathryn and Margaret E. Keck. 2007. *Greening Brazil: Environmental Activism in State and Society*. Durham, NC: Duke University Press.

Hochstetler, Kathryn and Ricardo Tranjan. 2016. "Environment and Consultation in the Brazilian Democratic Developmental State." *Comparative Politics* 48(4): 497–516.

Hoffman, Samantha and Johnathan Sullivan. 2015. "Environmental Protests Expose Weakness in China's Leadership." *Forbes Asia*. Retrieved from: https://www.forbes.com/sites/forbesasia/2015/06/22/environmental-protests-expose-weakness-in-chinas-leadership/#203cce933241. Accessed on June 22, 2015.

Holsti, Oli. 1996. *Public Opinion and American Foreign Policy*. Ann Arbor: University of Michigan Press.

Holt, Flora Lu. 2005. "The Catch-22 of Conservation: Indigenous Peoples, Biologists, and Cultural Change." *Human Ecology* 33(2): 199–215.

Holzner, Claudio A. 2010. *The Poverty of Democracy: The Institutional Roots of Political Participation in Mexico*. Pittsburgh: University of Pittsburgh Press.

Horowitz, Donald L. 1985. *Ethnic Groups in Conflict*. Berkeley: University of California Press.

Hurtig, Anna-Karin and Miguel San Sebastián. 2002. *Cancer en la Amazonia del Ecuador (1985–1998)*. Coca, Ecuador: Instituto de Epidemiologia y Salud Comunitaria "Manuel Amunarriz."

IAHRC (Inter-American Human Rights Commission). 2012. "Case of the Kichwa Indigenous People v. Ecuador: Judgment of June 27, 2012." Typescript.

Inclán, María. 2009. "Sliding Doors of Opportunity: Zapatistas and Their Cycle of Protest." *Mobilization: An International Journal* 14(1): 85–106.

"Indígenas bolivianos llegan triunfantes a La Paz pidiendo anular proyecto de carretera." *Noticias 24*, October 19, 2011. Retrieved from: http://www.noticias24.com/actualidad/noticia/336223/indigenas-bolivianos-llegan-triunfantes-a-la-paz-pidiendo-anular-proyecto-de-carretera-fotos. Accessed on April 8, 2012.

Inglehart, Ronald. 1990. *Culture Shift in Advanced Industrial Society*. Princeton: Princeton University Press.

Inglehart, Ronald. 1995. "Public Support for Environmental Protection: Objective Problems and Subjective Values in 43 Societies." *PS: Political Science and Politics* 28(1): 57–72.

Inglehart, Ronald. 1997. *Modernization and Postmodernization: Cultural, Economic, and Political Change in 43 Societies*. Princeton: Princeton University Press.

Inglehart, Ronald and Scott C. Flanagan. 1987. "Value Change in Industrial Societies." *American Political Science Review* 81(4): 1289–1319.

Instituto Nacional de Estadística y Censos (INEC)—Secretaría Nacional de Planificación y Desarrollo (SENPLADES). Ecuador—VII Censo de Población y VI de Vivienda 2010. Retrieved from: http://anda.inec.gob.ec/anda/index.php/catalog/270. Accessed on June 3, 2018.

Inter-American Development Bank. 2004. "Evaluación del Programa de PAIS: Ecuador 1990–2002." Office of Evaluation and Supervision. Washington, DC.

International Work Group for Indigenous Affairs. 2009. *The Indigenous World*. Retrieved from: http://www.iwgia.org/publications/search-pubs?publication_id=212. Accessed on January 21, 2014.

IPSOS MORI. 2014. "Global Trends 2014." Retrieved from: http://www.ipsosglobaltrends.com/environment.html. Accessed on April 6, 2017.

Jacobs, Lawrence R. and Benjamin I. Page. 2005. "Who Influences US Foreign Policy?" *American Political Science Review* 99(1): 107–23.

Jensen, Christian B. and Jae-Jae Spoon. 2011. "Testing the 'Party Matters' Thesis: Explaining Progress towards Kyoto Protocol Targets." *Political Studies* 59(1): 99–115.

Jinnah, Sikina. 2014. *Post-Treaty Politics: Secretariat Influence in Global Environmental Governance*. Cambridge, MA: MIT Press.

Jones (West), Karleen Alice. 2008. *Ethnic Party Success in Latin America: A Study of Campaigns and Elections in Ecuador*. Ph.D. dissertation. University of Iowa, Department of Political Science.

Kahan, Dan M. et al. 2012. "The Polarizing Impact of Scientific Literacy and Numeracy on Perceived Climate Change Risks." *Nature Climate Change* 2(10): 732–35.

Kamieniecki, Shannon (ed). 1993. *Environmental Politics in the International Arena: Movements, Parties, Organizations, and Policy*. New York: SUNY Press.

Kane, Joe. 1995. *Savages*. New York: Alfred A. Knopf.

Katzenstein, Peter J. 1985. *Small States in World Markets: Industrial Policy in Europe*. Ithaca, NY: Cornell University Press.

Kauffman, Craig M. 2017. *Grassroots Global Governance: Local Watershed Management Experiments and the Evolution of Sustainable Development.* New York: Oxford University Press.

Kauffman, Craig M. and Pamela L. Martin. 2014. "Scaling Up Buen Vivir: Globalizing Local Environmental Governance from Ecuador." *Global Environmental Politics* 14(1): 40–58.

Kauffman, Craig M. and Pamela L. Martin. 2017. "Can Rights of Nature Make Development More Sustainable? Why Some Ecuadorian Lawsuits Succeed and Others Fail." *World Development* 92: 130–42.

Keck, Margaret and Kathryn Sikkink. 1998. *Activists beyond Borders: Advocacy Networks in International Politics.* Ithaca, NY: Cornell University Press.

Kilburn, H. Whitt. 2014. "Religion and Foundations of American Public Opinion towards Global Climate Change." *Environmental Politics* 23(3): 473–89.

Kim, So Young and Yael Wolinsky-Nahmias. 2014. "Cross-National Public Opinion on Climate Change: The Effects of Affluence and Vulnerability." *Global Environmental Politics* 14(1): 79–106.

Kimerling, Judith. 2013. "Oil, Contact, and Conservation in the Amazon: Indigenous Huaorani, Chevron, and Yasuní." *Colorado Journal of International Environmental Law and Policy* 24(1): 44–115.

Klinsky, Sonja and Harold Winkler. 2014. "Equity, Sustainable Development, and Climate Policy." *Climate Policy* 14(1): 1–7.

Koenig, Kevin. 2017. "Community Consent: Business Lessons from the Amazon." Typescript. Retrieved from: https://business-humanrights.org/sites/default/files/documents/Community%20Consent-%20Business%20lessons%20from%20the%20Amazon.pdf. Accessed on March 29, 2017.

Konisky, David M., Jeffrey Milyo, and Lilliard E. Richardson. 2008. "Environmental Policy Attitudes: Issues, Geographical Scale, and Political Trust." *Social Science Quarterly* 89(5): 1066–85.

Kurtz, Marcus J. 2004. *Free Market Democracy and the Chilean and Mexican Countryside.* New York: Cambridge University Press.

Kvaloy, Berit, Henning Finseraas, and Ola Listhaug. 2012. "The Publics' Concern for Global Warming: A Cross-National Study of 47 countries." *Journal of Peace Research* 49(1): 11–22.

La Hora. 2018. "Consideran que explotación minera en Íntag es un pésimo negocio para el Estado." Retrieved from: https://lahora.com.ec/imbabura/noticia/1102138220/consideran-que-explotacion-minera-en-Íntag-es-un-pesimo-negocio-para-el-estado. Accessed on May 7, 2018.

Lalander, Rickard. 2014. "The Ecuadorian Resource Dilemma: Sumak Kawsay or Development?" *Critical Sociology* 42(4): 1–21.

Laplante, Lisa J. and Suzanne A. Spears. 2008. "Out of the Conflict Zone: The Case for Community Consent Processes in the Extractive Sector." *Yale Human Rights and Development Law Journal* 11: 69–116.

LaTorre, Sara, et al. 2015. "The Commodification of Nature and Socio-environmental Resistance in Ecuador: An Inventory of Accumulation by Dispossession Cases, 1980–2013." *Ecological Economics* 116: 58–69.

Lewis, Tammy L. 2016. *Ecuador's Environmental Revolutions: Ecoimperialists, Ecodependents, and Ecoresisters.* Cambridge, MA: MIT Press.

Llori, Guadalupe. 2010. "Elected in Ecuador, Imprisoned for Dissent." *Oslo Freedom Forum.* https://oslofreedomforum.com/talks/elected-in-ecuador-imprisoned-for-dissent. Accessed November 27, 2018.

Lucero, José Antonio. 2008. *Struggles of Voice: The Politics of Indigenous Representation in the Andes*. Pittsburgh: University of Pittsburgh Press.

Lucero, José Antonio. 2013. "Ambivalent Multiculturalisms: Perversity, Futility, and Jeopardy in Latin America." In Todd A. Eisenstadt, Michael S. Danielson, Jaime Bailón Córres, and Carlos Sorroza (eds.). *Latin America's Multicultural Movements and the Struggle between Communitarianism, Autonomy, and Human Rights*, 18–39. New York: Oxford University Press.

Macas, Luis. "Foreword." In Selverston-Scher, Melina. 2001. *Ethnopolitics in Ecuador: Indigenous Rights and the Strengthening of Democracy*, xi–xix. Miami: North-South Center Press.

Madrid, Raúl L. 2012. *The Rise of Ethnic Politics in Latin America*. New York: Cambridge University Press.

Mahdavi, Paasha. 2017. "No Taxation, No Representation? Oil-to-Cash Transfers and the Dynamics of Government Responsiveness." Typescript.

Mähler, Annegret and Jan H. Pierskalla. 2015. "Indigenous Identity, Natural Resources, and Contentious Politics in Bolivia: A Disaggregated Conflict Analysis, 2000–2011." *Comparative Political Studies* 48(3): 301–32.

Marapi, Ricardo. 2013. "Perú: Crece el debate sobre aplicación de Ley de Consulta Previa a Pueblos Indígenas." *Amarc*, May 10, 2013. Retrieved from: http://www.agenciapulsar.org/dd-hh/pueblos-originarios/peru-crece-el-debate-sobre-aplicacion-de-ley-de-consulta-previa-pueblos-indigenas. Accessed on December 27, 2013.

Margheritis, Ana and Anthony W. Pereira. 2007. "The Neoliberal Turn in Latin America: The Cycle of Ideas and the Search for an Alternative." *Latin American Perspectives* 34(3): 25–48.

Márquez, Cristina. 2015. "La división achuar complica a la Confeniae." *El Comercio*, October 3. Retrieved from: http://www.elcomercio.com/actualidad/division-achuar-confeniae-conaie-politica.html. Accessed on August 3, 2016.

Martin, Pamela L. 2011. *Oil in the Soil: The Politics of Paying to Preserve the Amazon*. Lanham, MD: Rowman & Littlefield.

Martínez, Esperanza. 1995. "Rechazo a la Séptima Ronda de Licitaciones Petroleras." In *Marea negra en la Amazonia: Conflictos socioambientales vinculados a la actividad petrolera en el Ecuador*, 181–218. Quito: Editorial Abya Yala.

Martínez, Juan and Víctor Leonel 2013. "What We Need Are New Cusotms: Multiculturality, Autonomy, and Citizenship in Mexico and the Lessons from Oaxaca." In Todd A. Eisenstadt, Michael S. Danielson, Jaime Bailón Córres, and Carlos Sorroza (eds.). *Latin America's Multicultural Movements and the Struggle between Communitarianism, Autonomy, and Human Rights*, 111–34. New York: Oxford University Press.

Martínez-Alier, Juan. 2002. *The Environmentalism of the Poor: A Study of Ecological Conflicts and Valuation*. Cheltenham: Edward Elgar Publishing.

Martínez Dalmau, Rubén. 2016. "Democratic Constitutionalism and Constitutional Innovation in Ecuador: The 2008 Constitution." *Latin American Perspectives* 206: 158–64.

Martínez Novo, Carmen. 2013. "The Backlash against Indigenous Rights in Ecuador's Citizen's Revolution." In Todd A. Eisenstadt, Michael S. Danielson, Jaime Bailón Córres, and Carlos Sorroza (eds.). *Latin America's Multicultural Movements and the Struggle between Communitarianism, Autonomy, and Human Rights*, 111–34. New York: Oxford University Press.

Martinez Novo, Carmen. 2017. "La minería amenaza a los indígenas shuar en Ecuador." *New York Times*, March 27, 2017. Retrieved from: https://www.nytimes.com/es/2017/03/27/la-mineria-amenaza-a-los-indigenas-shuar-en-ecuador. Accessed on March 29, 2017.

Mattiace, Shannan. 2003. *To See with Two Eyes: Peasant Activism and Indian Autonomy in Chiapas, Mexico*. Albuquerque: University of New Mexico Press.

Mattiace, Shannan. 2013. "The Multiculturalism That Wasn't: Legislative Reforms for Mexico's 'Tranquil' Indians in Yucatán." In Todd A. Eisenstadt, Michael S. Danielson, Jaime Bailón Córres, and Carlos Sorroza (eds.). *Latin America's Multicultural Movements and the Struggle between Communitarianism, Autonomy, and Human Rights*, 217–45. New York: Oxford University Press.

Mazzuca, Sebastian L. 2013. "The Rise of Rentier Populism." *Journal of Democracy* 24(2): 108–22.

McCright, Aaron M. and Riley E. Dunlap. 2011a. "The Politicization of Climate Change and Polarization in the American Public's Views of Global Warming 2001–2010." *The Sociological Quarterly* 52(2): 155–94.

McCright, Aaron M. and Riley E. Dunlap. 2011b. "Cool Dudes: The Denial of Climate Change among Conservative White Males in the United States." *Global Environmental Change* 21(4): 1163–72.

McGee, Brant. 2009. "The Community Referendum: Participatory Democracy and the Right to Free, Prior, and Informed Consent to Development." *Berkeley Journal of International Law* 27(2): 570–635.

McNeish, John-Andrew. 2017. "A Vote to Derail Extraction: Popular Consultation and Resource Sovereignty in Tolima, Colombia." *Third World Quarterly* 38(5): 1128–45. doi: 10.1080/01436597.2017.1283980.

Mendes, Chico (with Tony Gross). 1992. *The Fight for the Forest: Chico Mendes in His Own Words*. London: Latin America Bureau.

Molyneux, Maxine. 2008. "The 'Neoliberal Turn' and the New Social Policy in Latin America: How Neoliberal, How New?" *Development and Change* 39(5): 775–797.

Moreno, Daniel E. 2011. "La Identidad de los bolivianos y el próximo censo nacional." *Nueva Crónica*, May 2011. Retrieved from: http://ciudadaniabolivia.org/tl_files/Publicaciones/moreno85.pdf. Accessed on December 27, 2013.

Moseley, Mason. 2015. "Contentious Engagement: Understanding Protest Participation in Latin American Democracies." *Journal of Politics in Latin America* 7(3): 3–48.

Najam, Adil, 2014. "The View from the South: Developing Countries in Global Environmental Politics." In Regina Axelrod and Stacy VanDeveer (eds.). *The Global Environment: Institutions, Law, and Policy*, 224–243. Los Angeles: CQ Press.

Narváez Q., Iván. 2009. *Yasuní en el vórtice de la violencia legítima y las caras ocultas del poder*. Quito: Cevallos Librería Jurídica.

Neil, Peter. 2014. "Law of Mother Earth: A Vision from Bolivia." *Huffington Post*, November 18, 2014. Retrieved from: http://www.huffingtonpost.com/peter-neill/law-of-mother-earth-a-vis_b_6180446.html. Accessed on December 27, 2016.

Nincic, Miroslav. 1990. "US Soviet Policy and the Electoral Connection." *World Politics* 42: 370–96.

O'Donnell, Guillermo. 1973. *Modernization and Bureaucratic-Authoritarianism*. Studies in South American Politics 9. Berkeley: University of California.

O'Donnell, Guillermo. 2007. *Dissonances: Democratic Critiques of Democracy*. South Bend, IN: University of Notre Dame Press.

Olmos, José. December 9, 2007. "Detenida la prefecta Llori por terrorismo." *El Universo*. Retrieved from: http://www.eluniverso.com/2007/12/09/0001/9/DA58C77D8 88842E1A9C2F934C507ABDF.html. Accessed on April 3, 2017.

Olson, Mancur. 1965. *Logic of Collective Action; Public Goods and the Theory of Groups*. Cambridge, MA: Harvard University Press.

Organization of American States. 2009. *Indigenous and Tribal Peoples' Rights over Their Ancestral Lands and Natural Resources: Norms and Jurisprudence of the Inter-American Human Rights System*. Washington, DC: Organization of American States. Retrieved from: http://cidh.org/countryrep/Indigenous-Lands09/TOC.htm. Accessed on April 7, 2017.

Ostrom, Elinor. 1990. *Governing the Commons: The Evolution of Institutions for Collective Action*. Cambridge, UK: Cambridge University Press.

Ostrom, Elinor. 2010. "Polycentric Systems for Coping with Collective Action and Global Environmental Change." *Global Environmental Change* 20(4): 550–57.

Ostrom, Elinor. 2014. "Collective Action and the Evolution of Social Norms." *Journal of Natural Resources Policy Research* 6(4): 235–52.

Otero, Gerardo. 2007. "Review Article: Class or Identity Politics? A False Dichotomy." *International Journal of Comparative Sociology* 48(1): 73–80.

Özkaynak, Begüm, Beatriz Rodriguez-Labajos, Cem Iskender Aydın, I. Yanez, and C. Garibay. 2015. "Towards Environmental Justice Success in Mining Conflicts: An Empirical Investigation." *EJOLT Report* 14: 96.

Pachamama Alliance. 2016. "Reflecting on 20 Years and Where We're Headed." Retrieved from: *Pachamama.org*. Accessed on April 25, 2016.

Pallares, Amalia. 2002. *From Peasant Struggles to Indian Resistance: The Ecuadorian Andes in the Late Twentieth Century*. Norman: University of Oklahoma Press.

Pateman, Carole. 2012. "Participatory Democracy Revisited." *Perspectives on Politics* 10(1): 7–19.

Perreault, Thomas. 2006. "From the *Guerra del Agua* to the *Guerra del Gas*: Resource Governance, Neoliberalism, and Popular Protest in Bolivia." *Antipode* 38(1): 150–72.

Ponce, Aldo F., and Cynthia McClintock. 2014. "The Explosive Combination of Inefficient Local Bureaucracies and Mining Production: Evidence from Localized Societal Protests in Peru." *Latin American Politics and Society* 56(3): 118–40.

Purdon, Mark. 2015. "Advancing Comparative Climate Change Politics: Theory and Method." *Global Environmental Politics* 15(3): 1–26.

Putnam, Robert D. 1988. "Diplomacy and Domestic Politics: The Logic of Two-Level Games." *International Organization* 42(3): 427–60.

Ray, Rebecca and Adam Chimienti. 2015. "A Line in the Equatorial Forests: Chinese Investment and the Environmental and Social Impacts of Extractive Industries in Ecuador." Workng paper of the Global Economic Governance Initiative of Boston University.

Recasens, Andreu Viola. 2014. "Discursos 'pachamamistas' versus políticas desarrollistas: el debate sobre el sumac kawsay en los Andes." *Iconos* 48 (January): 55–72.

Red Amazónica Jurídica. 2013. *Sentencias Caso Texaco/Chevron*. Quito: Red Amazónica Jurídica.

REDD-Monitor in Conca, Ken and Geoffrey D. Dabelko, eds. 2015. *Green Planet Blues: Critical Perspectives on Global Environmental Politics*, 364–68. 5th ed. Boulder, CO: Westview Press.

Reyna, J. L. and Weinert, R. S. 1977. "Authoritarianism in Mexico." *Anthropology News* 18: 23.

Roberts, Kenneth. 1995. "Neoliberalism and the Transformation of Populism in Latin America: The Peruvian Case." *World Politics* 48(1): 82–116.

Roberts, Kenneth M. 2006. "Populism, Political Conflict, and Grass-roots Organization in Latin America." *Comparative Politics* 38(2): 127–48.

Rodríguez-Garavito, Cesar. 2011. "Ethnicity.gov: Global Governance, Indigenous Peoples, and the Right to Prior Consultation in Social Minefields." *Indiana Journal of Global Legal Studies* 18(1): 263–305.

Rosenau, James. 1969. "Toward the Study of National-International Linkages." In James Rosenau (ed.). *Linkage Politics: Essays on the Convergence of National and International Systems*, 44–66. New York: Free Press.

Rosenau, James. 1973. "Theorizing across Systems: Linkage Politics Revisited." In Jonathan Wilkenfeld (ed.). *Conflict Behavior and Linkage Politics*, 25–56. New York: David McKay.

Rus, Jan. 1994. "The 'Comunidad Revolucionaria Institucional': The Subversion of Native Government in Highland Chiapas, 1936–1968." In Gilbert M. Joseph and Daniel Nugent (eds.). *Everyday Forms of State Formation: Revolution and the Negotiation of Rule in Modern Mexico*, 265–300. Durham, NC: Duke University Press.

Russett, Bruce. 1990. *Controlling the Sword: The Democratic Governance of National Security*. Cambridge, MA: Harvard University Press.

Saavedra, Luis Ángel. 2011. "Ecuador: Consultation or Prior Consent?" Lima: Latin America Press.

Sabin, Paul. 1998. "Searching for Middle Ground: Native Communities and Oil Extraction in the Northern and Central Ecuadorian Amazon, 1967–1993." *Environmental History* 3(2): 144–68.

Sánchez Botero, Ester. 2010. *Justicia y pueblos indígenas de Colombia*. 3rd ed. Bogotá: Universidad Nacional de Colombia.

San Sebastián, Miguel, Ben Armstrong, and Carolyn Stephens. 2002. "Outcomes of Pregnancy among Women Living in the Proximity of Oil Fields in the Amazon Basin of Ecuador." *International Journal of Occupational Environmental Health* 8: 312–19.

San Sebastián, Miguel and Anna-Karin Hurtig. 2004. "Oil Exploitation in the Amazon Basin of Ecuador: A Public Health Emergency." *Panameircan Journal of Public Health* 15(3): 205–12.

San Sebastián, Miguel, B. Armstrong, J. A. Cordoba, and C. Stephens. 2001. "Exposures and cancer incidence near oil fields in the Amazon basin of Ecuador." *Occupational, Environmental and Medical Journal* 58(8): 517–22.

Schilling-Vacaflor, Almut. 2013. "Prior Consultation in Plurinational Bolivia: Democracy, Rights, and Real Life Experiences." *Latin American and Caribbean Ethnic Studies* 8(2): 202–20.

Schilling-Vacaflor, Almut. 2014. "Rethinking the Consultation-Conflict Link: Lessons from Bolivia's Gas Sector." *Canadian Journal of Development Studies* 35(4): 503–21.

Schmitter, Philippe. 1974. "Still the Century of Corporatism?" *The Review of Politics* 36(1): 85–131. doi: 10.1017/S0034670500022178.

Secretaría de Hidrocarburos de Ecuador (SHE). n.d. Retrieved from: http://www.hidrocarburos.gob.ec/mapa-de-bloques-petroleros. Accessed on November 23, 2014.

Seiwald, Markus. 2012. *REDD and Indigenous Peoples: The Socio Bosque Programme in Ecuador.* Saarbrücken, Germany: Akademikerverlag.

Selverston-Scher, Melina. 2001. *Ethnopolitics in Ecuador: Indigenous Rights and the Strengthening of Democracy.* Miami: North-South Center Press.

Servindi, 2015. "Nativos sobre Lote 192: No permitiremos que se repita la misma historia de impunidad y muerte." Retrieved from: https://www.servindi.org/node/56727. Accessed on April 25, 2016.

Shankland, Alex and Leonardo Hasenclever. 2011. "Indigenous Peoples and the Regulation of REDD+ in Brazil: Beyond the War of the Worlds?" *IDS Bulletin* 42(3): 80–88.

Sheahan, John. 1987. *Patterns of Development in Latin America.* Princeton: Princeton University Press.

Shue, Henry. 2014. *Climate Justice: Vulnerability and Protection.* New York: Oxford University Press.

Silva, Eduardo. 2009. *Challenging Neoliberalism in Latin America.* New York: Cambridge University Press.

Smith, N. and Leiserowitz, A. 2013. "American Evangelicals and Global Warming." *Global Environmental Change* 23(5): 1009–17.

Sobel, Richard (ed.). 1993. *Public Opinion in US Foreign Policy: The Controversy over Contra Aid.* Lanham, MD: Rowman & Littlefield.

Sobel, Richard. 2001. *The Impact of Public Opinion on US Foreign Policy since Vietnam.* New York: Oxford University Press.

Sonnleitner, Willibald and Todd A. Eisenstadt. 2013. "Conclusion: Balancing Tensions between Communitarian and Individual Rights and the Challenges These Present for Multicultural States." In Todd A. Eisenstadt, Michael S. Danielson, Jaime Bailón Córres, and Carlos Sorroza (eds.). *Latin America's Multicultural Movements and the Struggle between Communitarianism, Autonomy, and Human Rights.* New York: Oxford University Press.

Sorroza Polo, Carlos and Michael S. Danielson. 2013. "Political Subsystems in Oaxaca's Usos y Costumbres Municipalities: A Typology Based on the Civil-Religious Service Background of Mayors." In Todd A. Eisenstadt, Michael S. Danielson, Jaime Bailón Córres, and Carlos Sorroza (eds.). *Latin America's Multicultural Movements and the Struggle between Communitarianism, Autonomy, and Human Rights.* New York: Oxford University Press.

Spada, Paolo and Giovanni Allegretti. 2013. "The Role of Redundancy and Diversification in Multi-Channel Democratic Innovations." Paper prepared for the 2013 Annual Meeting of the American Political Science Association, August 29–September 1.

Spronk, S. and Webber, J. 2007. "Struggles against Accumulation by Dispossession in Bolivia: The Political Economy of Natural Resource Contention." *Latin American Perspectives* 34(2): 31–47.

Staiger, Robert W. and Guido Tabellini. 1999. "Do GATT Rules Help Governments Make Domestic Commitments?" *Economics and Politics* 11(2): 109–44.

Stefani, Sheila. 2009. "Indigenous rights: risks and opportunities for investors." Experts in Responsible Investment Solutions. Retrieved from: http://www.eiris.org/files/research%20publications/indigenousrightsjun09.pdf. Accessed on January 18, 2014.

Steinberg, Paul F. and Stacy D. VanDeveer. 2012. *Comparative Environmental Politics: Theory, Practice, and Prospects.* Cambridge, MA: MIT Press.

Tarrow, Sidney. 1998. *Power in Movement: Social Movements and Contentious Politics.* Cambridge, UK: Cambridge University Press.

Teele, Dawn Langan (ed.). 2014. *Field Experiments and Their Critics: Essays on the Uses and Abuses of Experimentation in the Social Sciences.* New Haven: Yale University Press.

Tegel, Simon. 2018. "A Referendum in Ecuador Is Another Defeat for South America's Left-Wing Populists." *Washington Post*, February 5, 2018. Retrieved from: https://www.washingtonpost.com/news/worldviews/wp/2018/02/05/a-referendum-in-ecuador-is-another-defeat-for-south-americas-left-wing-populists/?utm_term=.ae6a8ea87cdf. Accessed on May 7, 2018.

"Tierras en manos indígenas llegan a 37 millones de ha." *Cambio*, February 15, 2013. Retrieved from: http://www.cambio.bo/economia/20130215/tierras_en_manos_indigenas_llegan_a_37_millones_de_ha_88794.htm. Accessed on May 24, 2013.

Tilly, Charles and Sidney Tarrow. 2006. *Contentious Politics.* Boulder, CO: Paradigm Publishers.

Torres Wong, Marcela. 2016. "Prior Consultation and Resource Extraction in Latin America." PhD Thesis. Department of Government, American University. Typescript.

Trejo, Guillermo. 2012. *Popular Movements in Autocracies: Religion, Repression, and Indigenous Collective Action in Mexico.* Cambridge: Cambridge University Press.

Trejo, Guillermo, and Sandra Ley. 2018. "Why Did Drug Cartels Go to War in Mexico? Subnational Party Alternation, the Breakdown of Criminal Protection, and the Onset of Large-Scale Violence." *Comparative Political Studies* 51(7): 900–937.

Tribunal Supremo Electoral. 2006. *Resultados electorales 2006.* Quito: República del Ecuador.

Tribunal Supremo Electoral. 2007. *Resultados electorales al Asamblea Constituyente 2007.* Quito: República del Ecuador.

Tynkknen, Nina. 2010. "A Great Ecological Power in Global Climate Policy? Framing Climate Change as a Policy Problem in Russian's Public Discussion." *Environmental Politics* 19(2): 179–95.

Van Cott, Donna Lee. 2003. "Institutional Change and Ethnic Parties in South America." *Latin American Politics and Society* 45(2): 1–39.

Van Cott, Donna Lee. 2005. *From Movements to Parties in Latin America: The Evolution of Ethnic Politics.* New York: Cambridge University Press.

Van Cott, Donna Lee. 2008. *Radical Democracy in the Andes.* Cambridge, UK: Cambridge University Press.

Varas, Eduardo, Marcela Ribadeneira, and Jonathan Watts. "Ecuador Election: Rafael Correa Set to Win despite Fossil Fuel Fears." *The Guardian*, February 14, 2013. Retrieved from: https://www.theguardian.com/world/2013/feb/14/ecuador-election-president-rafael-correa. Accessed on April 3, 2017.

Vasquez, Patricia. 2014. *Oil Sparks in the Amazon: Local Conflicts, Indigenous Populations, and Natural Resources.* Athens: University of Georgia Press.

Vidal, John. 2014. "Ecuador Rejects Petition to Stop Oil Drilling in Yasuní National Park." *The Guardian*, May 8, 2014. Retrieved from: https://www.theguardian.com/environment/2014/may/08/ecuador-rejects-petition-oil-drilling-yasuni. Accessed on March 28, 2017.

Waltz, Kenneth. 1979. *Theory of International Politics.* Reading, MA: Addison-Wesley.

Wampler, Brian. 2012. "Participation, Representation, and Social Justice: Using Participatory Governance to Transform Representative Democracy." *Polity* 44(4): 666–82.

Weyland, Kurt. 1998. "Swallowing the Bitter Pill: Sources of Popular Support for Neoliberal Reform in Latin America." *Comparative Political Studies* 31(5) (October): 539–68.

Wittkopf, E. 1990. *Faces of Internationalism: Public Opinion and American Foreign Policy.* Durham, NC: Duke University Press.

Yanza, Luis. 2014. *UDAPT vs. Chevron-Texaco: Las Voces de las Victimas.* Nueva Loja, Ecuador: Union de Afectados y Afectadas por las Operaciones Petroleras de Texaco (UDAPT) y Fundacion Regional de Asesoria en Derechos Humanos (INREDH).

Yashar, Deborah. 2005. *Contesting Citizenship in Latin America: The Rise of Indigenous Movements and the Postliberal Challenge.* New York: Cambridge University Press.

Zamosc, Leon. 2007. "The Indian Movement and Political Democracy in Ecuador." *Latin American Politics and Society* 49: 1–34. doi: 10.1111/j.1548-2456.2007. tb00381.x.

INTERVIEWS CITED

Akachu, Rómulo, vice president of the CONAIE and leader of the Shuar (NACSHE group). Interview June 16, 2016, in Quito, Ecuador.

Ampush Juan, member of the Council of Nationalities of the provincial government of Orellana. Interview June 19, 2014, in Coca, Ecuador.

Aragón, Wilfrido, Kichwa de Pastaza, and head of Department of Nationalities and Sustainable Local Development, City of Puyo. Interview June 13, 2014, in Puyo, Ecuador.

Arpi, Abel, coordinator in San Isabel of the Assembly of Peoples of the South. Interview June 5, 2014, in San Isabel, Ecuador.

Arruti, Jon, adviser to the Mayor of Coca on public health issues. Interview June 20, 2014, in Coca, Ecuador.

Ávila, Ramiro, YasUnidos lawyer and professor at Universidad Andina. Interview June 16, 2016, in Quito, Ecuador.

Ayarza, Peter, administrative manager, Walsh Ecuador. Interview June 17, 2016, in Quito, Ecuador.

Bonilla, Omar, representative of YasUnidos, a movement to stop oil drilling in Yasuní National Park. Interview June 2, 2014, in Quito, Ecuador.

Cahauigia, Alicia, vice president of the Waorani Nation, Interview June 14, 2014, in Puyo, Ecuador.

Callera, Diego, leader of the Achuar community of Charapacocha. Interview June 18, 2014, in Charapacocha, Ecuador.

Callera, Pasqual, Achuar Nation of Ecuador (NAE) director of economic development. Interview June 18, 2014, in Charapacocha, Ecuador.

Chimbo, Nelly, president of the Qichwas of Kallary Kausay-Romipampa. Interview June 19, 2014, in Coca, Ecuador.

Chongo, Guido Grefa, president of the Federation of Peasant and Indigenous Organizations of Napo (FOCIN). Interview June 10, 2014, in Tena, Ecuador.

Coka, Denise, provincial governor of Pastaza. Interview June 17, 2014, in Puyo, Ecuador.

Cueva, José, engineer and leader of the Bien Vivir movement. Interview June 6, 2014, in Cotacachi, Ecuador.

de la Torre, Roberto, mayor of Puyo. Interview June 18, 2014, in Puyo, Ecuador.

Dulchea, Luis Felipe, Global Adviser for Indigenous Peoples, World Bank. Interview March 20, 2017, in Washington, DC.

Enomenga, Moi, president of the Waorani Nation. Interview June 14, 2014, in Puyo, Ecuador.

Entza, Hipólito, mayor of Macas. Interview June 9, 2014, in Macas, Ecuador.

Falconi, Esteban, judicial adviser to the Ministry of Environment. Interview July 5, 2017, in Quito, Ecuador.

Flores Castro, Franz, Bolivian political scientist and doctoral student, Latin American Faculty for Social Sciences (FLACSO). Interview August 15, 2013, in Quito, Ecuador.

Granja, Diego, director of the Chontapunta (Napo) Water Council. Interview June 11, 2014, in Chontapunta, Ecuador.

Greene, Natalia, board member of NGOsTerraMater y Global Alliance for the Rights of Nature. Interview June 15, 2016, in Quito, Ecuador.

Grefa, Blanca, president of FICCKAE (Interprovincial Federation of Kichwa Communities of the Ecuadorian Amazon). Interview June 19, 2014, in Coca, Ecuador.

Grefa, Lenin Alfredo, president of the Evangelical Federation of the Kichwa Nationality of Napo (FENAKIN). Interview June 10, 2014, in Tena, Ecuador.

Gualinga, Jose. ex-president of the Sarayaku People and leader of the CONAIE. Interview June 18, 2016, in Quito, Ecuador.

Katan, Tuntiak, technical coordinator of climate change area for COICA (Coordinating Body for the Indigenous Peoples' Organizations of the Amazon Basin). Interview June 28, 2014, in Quito, Ecuador.

Lara, Rommel, anthropologist at the Universidad Salesiana (Department of Applied Anthropology). Interview on June 20, 2016, in Quito, Ecuador.

Larrea, Carlos, former government technical director of the Yasuni Project. Interview June 21, 2016, in Quito, Ecuador.

Lascano, Max, director of Ecuador government's Socio Bosque Program from 2008 to 2015. Interviews June 27, 2014, and July 4, 2017, in Quito, Ecuador.

Laurini, Tania, director of International Cooperation for Morona Santiago. Interview June 9, 2014, in Macas, Ecuador.

Licuy, Marco Aurelio, president of the Federation of the Indigenous Organizations of Napo (FOIN)/Coordinator of the Kichwa Nationality of Napo (CONAKIN). Interview June 9, 2014, in Tena, Ecuador.

López, Victor, civil servant and member of the non-governmental organization EcoCiencia. Interview June 26, 2014, in Quito, Ecuador.

Loza, Guillermo, director of environmental control in the Napo Province. Interview June 10, 2014, in Tena, Ecuador.

Maldonado, Adolfo, director of Clínicas Ambientales para el Sumak Kawsay (Environmental Clinic). Interview July 7, 2017, in Lago Agrio, Ecuador.

Martínez, Esperanza, oil project director of Acción Ecológica. Interview July 7, 2017, in Quito, Ecuador.

Mazabanda, Carlos, researcher at Centro de Derechos Humanos PUC and consultant to the NGO Terra Mater. Interview June 15, 2016, in Quito, Ecuador.

Melo, Mario, director of the human rights commission, Pontificia Universidad Católica de Ecuador. Interviews June 2, 2014, and June 14, 2016, in Quito, Ecuador.

Mendua, Eduardo, president of the COFAN-Dureno community. Interview June 23, 2014, in Dureno, Ecuador.

Moncayo Jimenez, Donald Rafael, subcoordinator of Union of the People Affected by Texaco (UDAPT: Unión de Afectados y Afectadas por las Operaciones Petroleras de Texaco). Interview July 14, 2017, in Lago Agrio, Ecuador.

Montúfar-Galárraga, Rommel, biologist, Pontificia Universidad Católica de Ecuador. Interview August 12, 2013, in Quito, Ecuador.

Nantip, Elvis, president of the Inter-Provincial Federation of Schuar Centers (FISCH). Interview July 14, 2017, in Sucúa, Ecuador.

Omentoque Tega Baihua, Mima, head of the Association of Waorani Women of Orellana. Interview June 19, 2014, in Coca, Ecuador.

Paes, Roberto, vice president of the Achuar Nation (NAE). Interview June 13, 2014, in Puyo, Ecuador.

Pérez, Carlos, president of national ECUARUNARI movement. Interview June 4, 2014, in Cuenca, Ecuador.

Pidru, Efrén, president of the Four Federations (Shuar Organization of Ecuador). Interview June 11, 2014, in Shuar HQ near Macas, Ecuador.

Pinos, Bairon, Azuay director of Ecuador Estratégico. Interview June 6, 2014, in Cuenca, Ecuador.

Portilla, Saul, chair of reforestation and the environment. Interview June 11, 2014, in Chontapunta, Ecuador.

Proaño, Alexandra, president of the Andwa Community. Interview June 14, 2014, in Puyo, Ecuador.

Quimontari Waewa, Tipaa, septegenarian Waorani elder. Interview June 21, 2014, in Yawepare, Ecuador.

Rivadeneyra, Teodoro, president of the Shiripuno Community. Interview June 11, 2014, in Misahuallí, Ecuador.

Sallo, Ángel, director of Strategic Ecuador (Ecuador Estratégico) government agency. Interview June 25, 2014, in Lago Agrio, Ecuador.

Santi, Fernando, president of the Shiwiar Nationality. Interview June 16, 2014, in Puyo, Ecuador.

Santi, Hilda, former president of the Sarayaku People. Interview July 11, 2017, in Puyo, Ecuador.

Santi, Lucy, leader of the Association of Sápara Women. Interview June 18, 2016, in Puyo, Ecuador.

Santi, Mario, coordinator of the municipal presidents. Interview June 16, 2014, in Puyo, Ecuador.

Santi, Marlon, former president of CONAIE and leader of Sarayaku. Interview June 13, 2014, in Sarayaku, Ecuador.

Shiguango, Cristina, president of the Amazonian Federation of Indigenous Organizations of Napo (FAOICIN). Interview June 9, 2014, in Tena, Ecuador.

Tentets, Agustine, president of the Achuar Nation of Ecuador. Interview June 18, 2016, in Quito, Ecuador.

Thurber, Mark, general manager, Walsh Ecuador. Interview June 17, 2016, in Quito, Ecuador.

Tibán, Lourdes, elected Pachakutik representative in the Ecuadorian National Assembly. Interview June 2, 2014, in Quito, Ecuador.

Tibi, Gonzalo, head of external relations for the Shuar Nation. Interview June 10, 2014, in Macas, Ecuador.

Tsakimp, Vicente, president of the Shuar Arutam Peoples in the Province of Morona Santiago. Interview July 14, 2017, in Sucúa, Ecuador.

Tuazas, Luis Alberto, Riobamba area priest for indigenous communities. Interview August 27, 2015, in Quito, Ecuador.

Tumink, Tito, Shuar leader and head of the Ancestral Patrimony Department of the government of Coca. Interview June 19, 2014, in Coca, Ecuador.

Ushigua, Ricardo, Sápara community leader. Interview June 12, 2014, in Coca, Ecuador.

Vallejo, Ivette, professor of anthropology at FLACSO Ecuador. Interview June 27, 2014, in Quito, Ecuador.

Viteri, Franco, president of the CONFENAIE. Interview April 14, 2015, in Washington, DC.

Wachapa Atsau, Augustín, then national president of FISCH (Federación Interprovincial de Centros Shuar). Interview June 10, 2014, in Sucúa, Ecuador.

INDEX